Relationships with Pictures
an Oblique Autobiography

Students of all aspects of material culture need
to pursue historical questions without becoming
bogged down in the usually irrelevant issue of
artistic merit. This is not to say that the concept
of art is insignificant or unworthy of investigation;
on the contrary, there are many reasons to study
why some objects are called art, what particular
artefacts are so designated, and how the social
organizations which surround them function.
In short, art should be studied as a historical
and sociological phenomenon. It is intellectually
irresponsible to continue to unreflectively confer
the honorary degree of art on a small segment of
the artifactual world of the past, blithely ignoring
most of the surviving artefacts because they do
not measure up to an unstated but implicit
canon of acceptability.

Kenneth L. Ames,
Beyond Necessity.
Art in the Folk Tradition, 1977

For Jenifer Coombe-Tennant
(1925–2012)
patron and friend.

Relationships with pictures

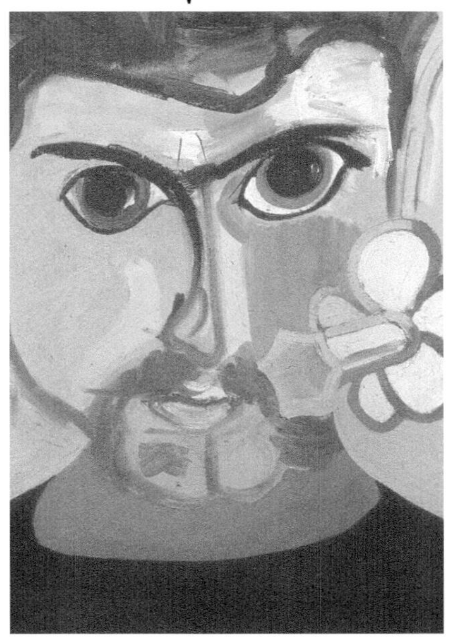

PETER LORD

PARTHIAN

an oblique autobiography

Parthian
The Old Surgery
Napier Street
Cardigan
SA43 1ED

www.parthianbooks.com

First published in 2013
Reprinted 2025
© Peter Lord 2013
All Rights Reserved

ISBN 978-1-917140-69-0

Editor: Jon Gower

Designed by Olwen Fowler

Printed and bound by 4Edge

Cover image: Peter Lord, *Self-portrait*, c.1968
(National Library of Wales)

The publisher acknowledges the
support of the Books Council of Wales

British Library Cataloguing in Publication Data

A cataloguing record for this book
is available from the British Library

Contents

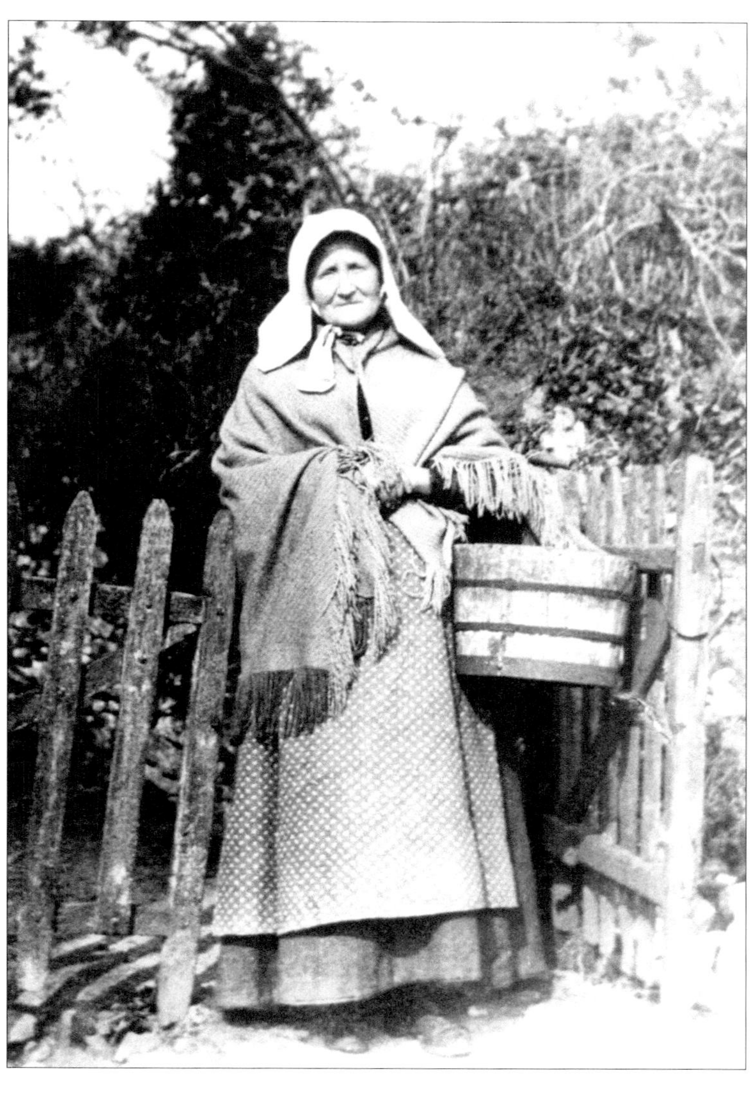

1
Unknown photographer,
A Portrait of Sarah Drewer,
'Grannie Horner', c.1910

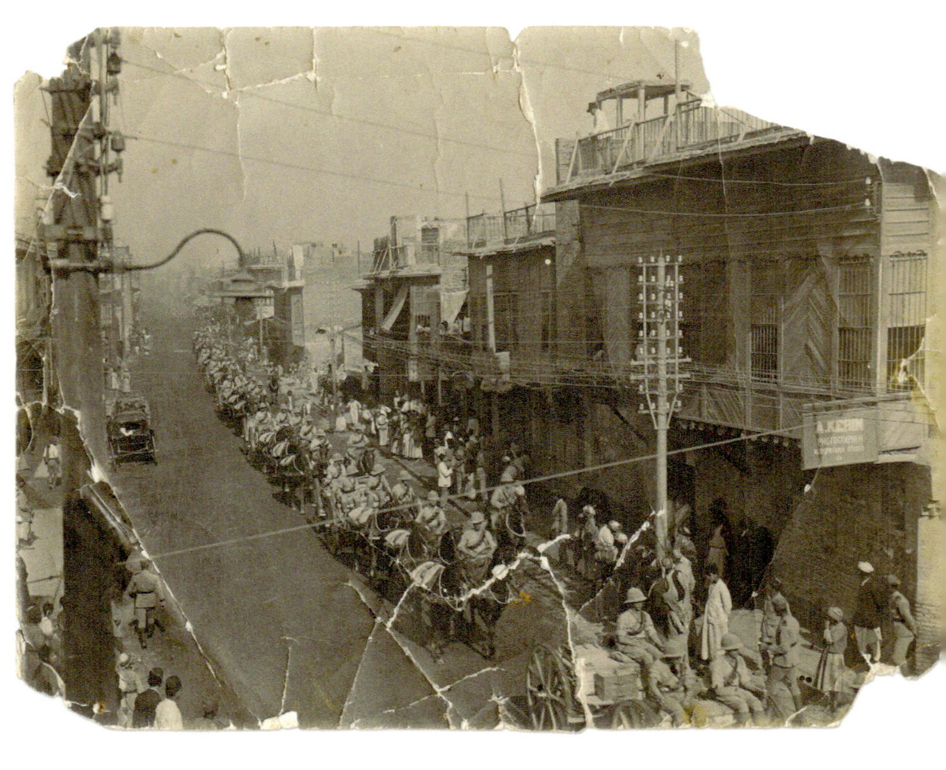

2
A. Kerim, *The Mesopotamia Studio,*
Baghdad, c.1920

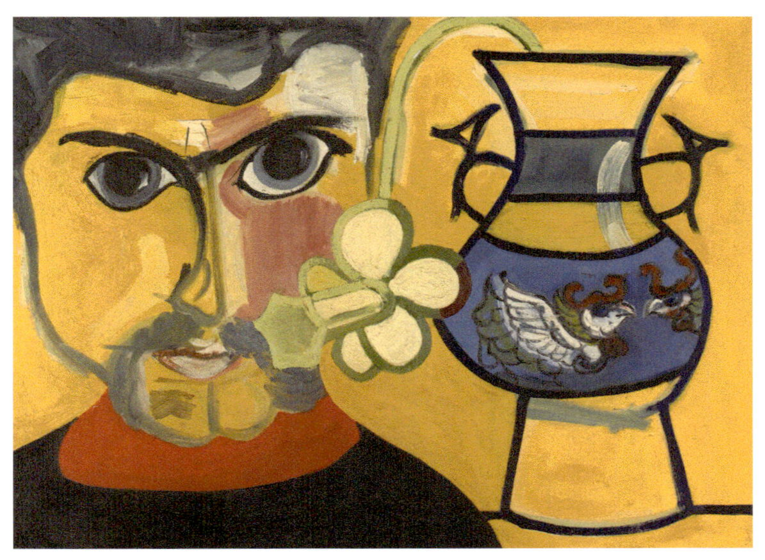

3
Peter Lord, *Self-portrait with an Enamelled Jug, c.1968*
National Library of Wales

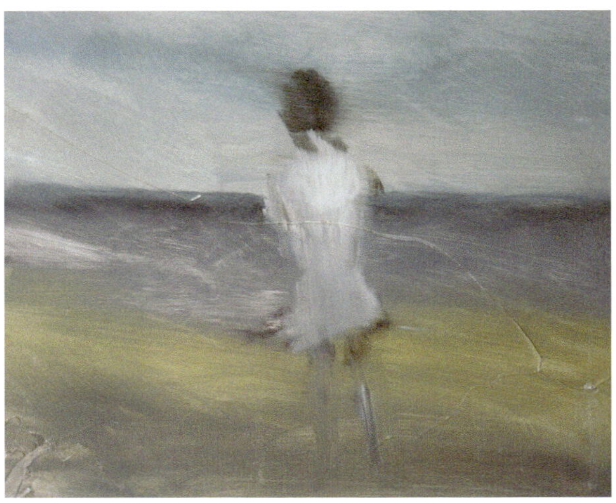

4
Sidney Nolan,
*The Little Girl on the Beach
(Jinx Being Thoughtful), c.1954*

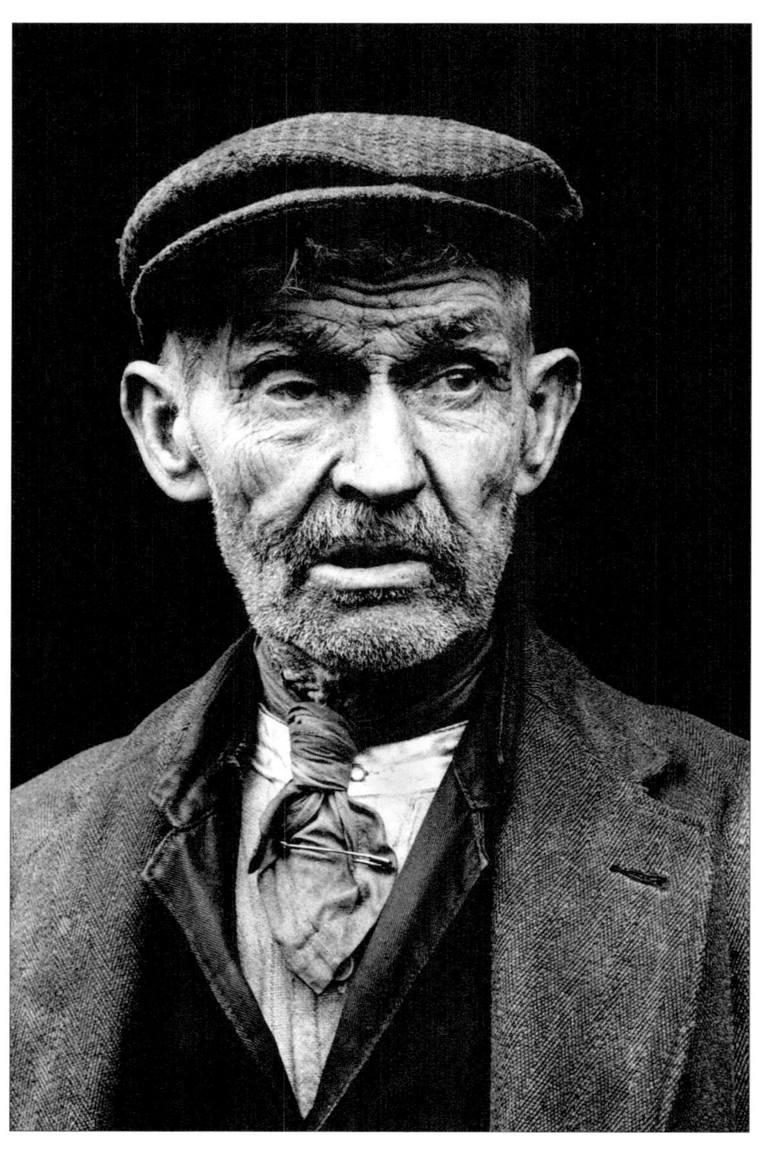

5
Marian Delyth,
Twm Penllwynbedw, c.1976–7
© Marian Delyth

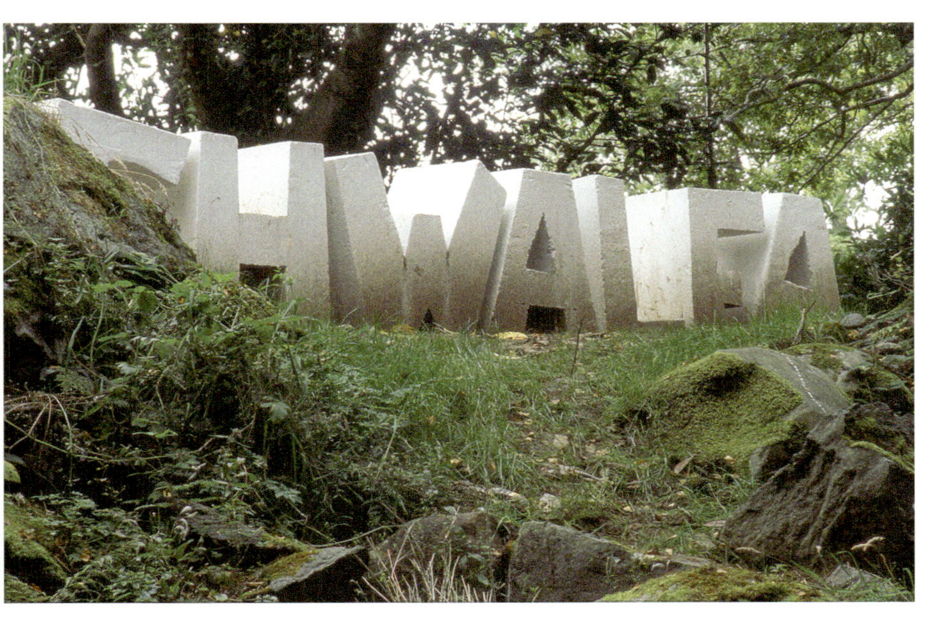

6
Peter Lord,
Chwalfa, 1993

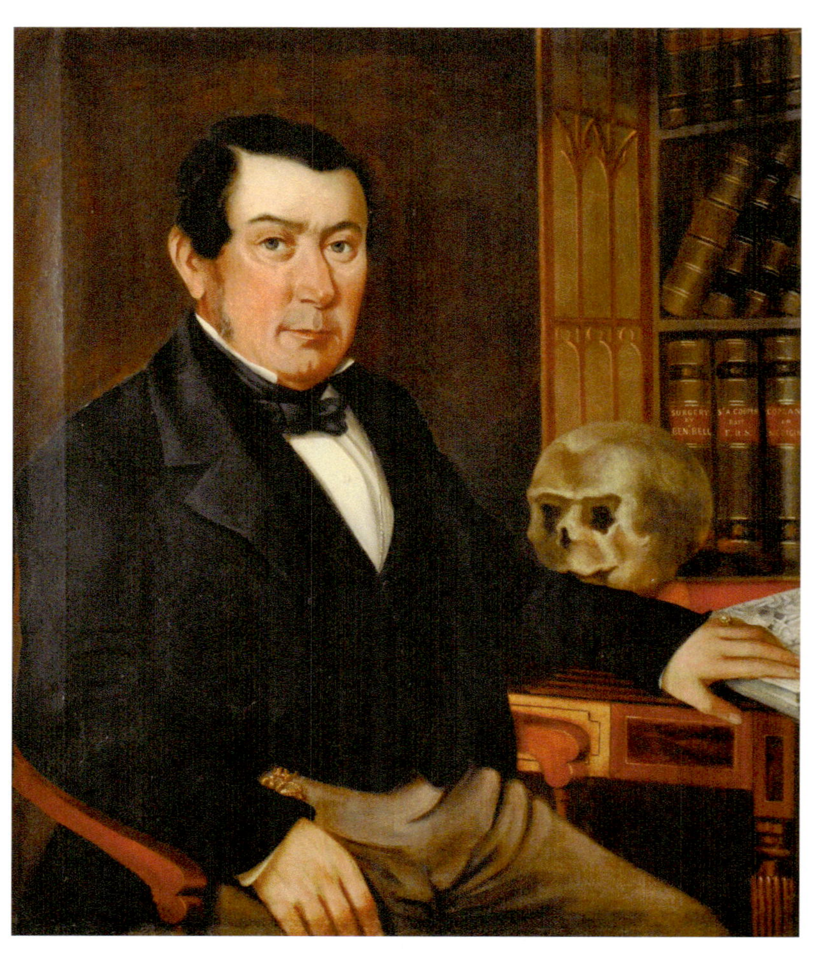

7i
John Roberts,
The Surgeon Apothecary, c.1845

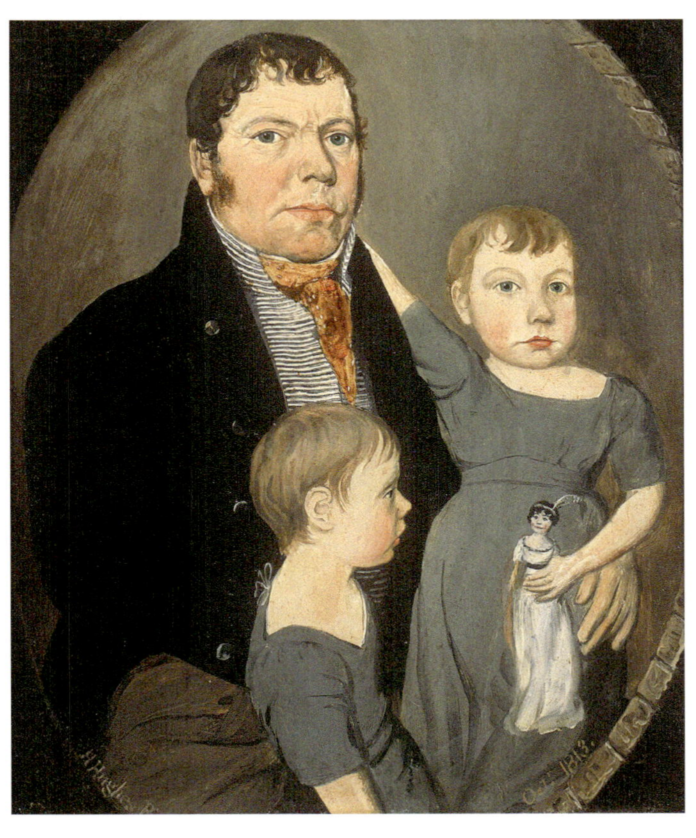

7ii

Hugh Hughes, *Huw Griffith of Bodwrdda with His Children,
Margaret and William*, 1813

Private collection

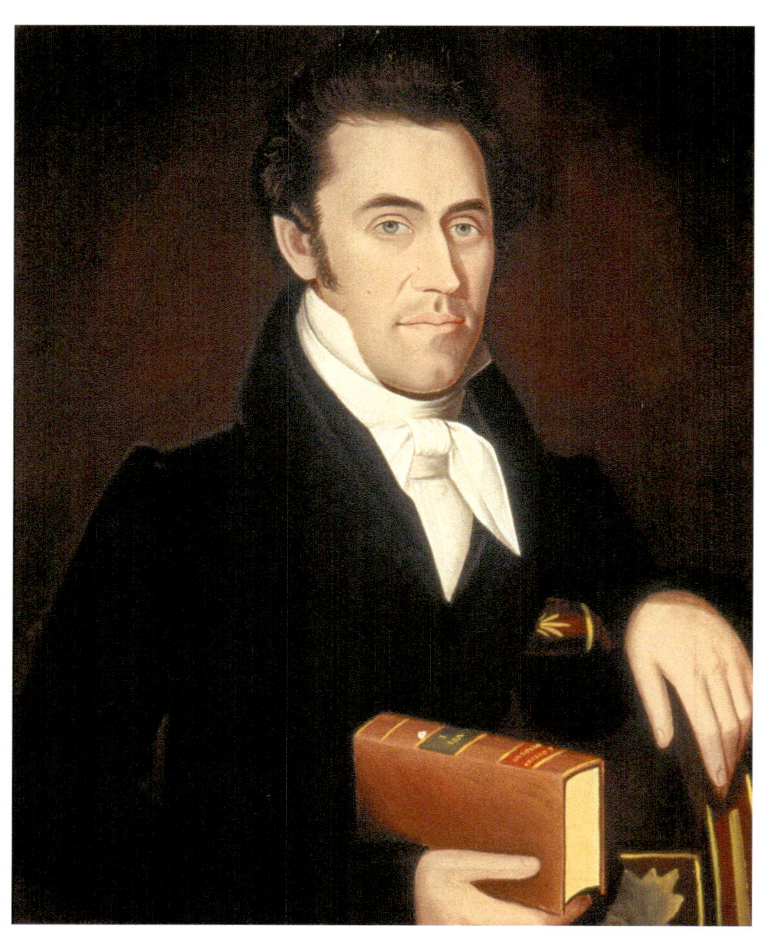

7iii
Ammi Phillips, *The Young Physician*, c.1830
Abby Aldridge Rockefeller Folk Art Center,
Williamsburg

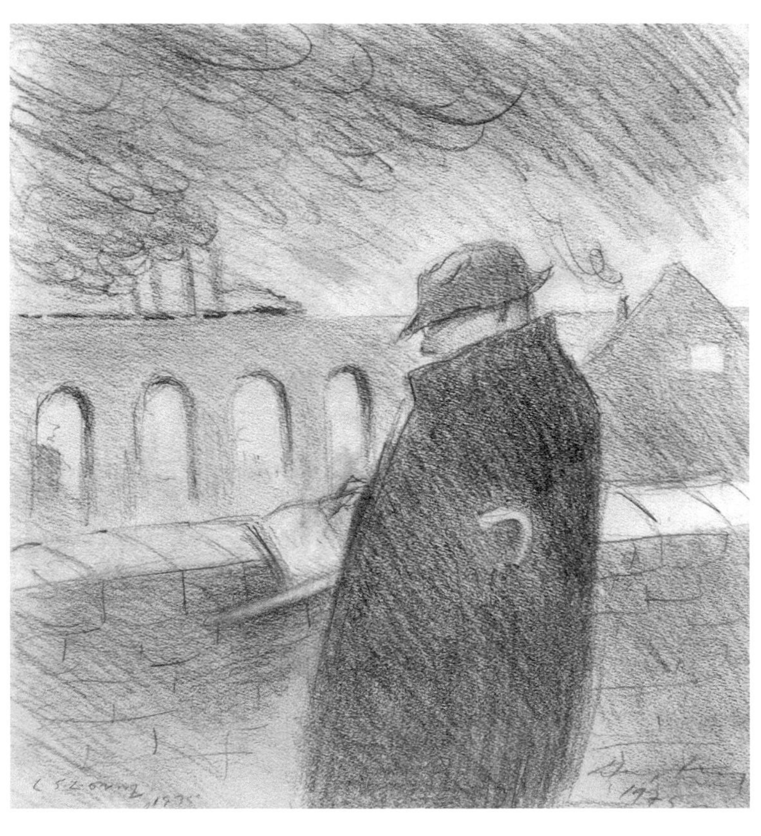

8
Mervyn Levy,
L.S. Lowry drawing the
Stockport Viaduct, 1975

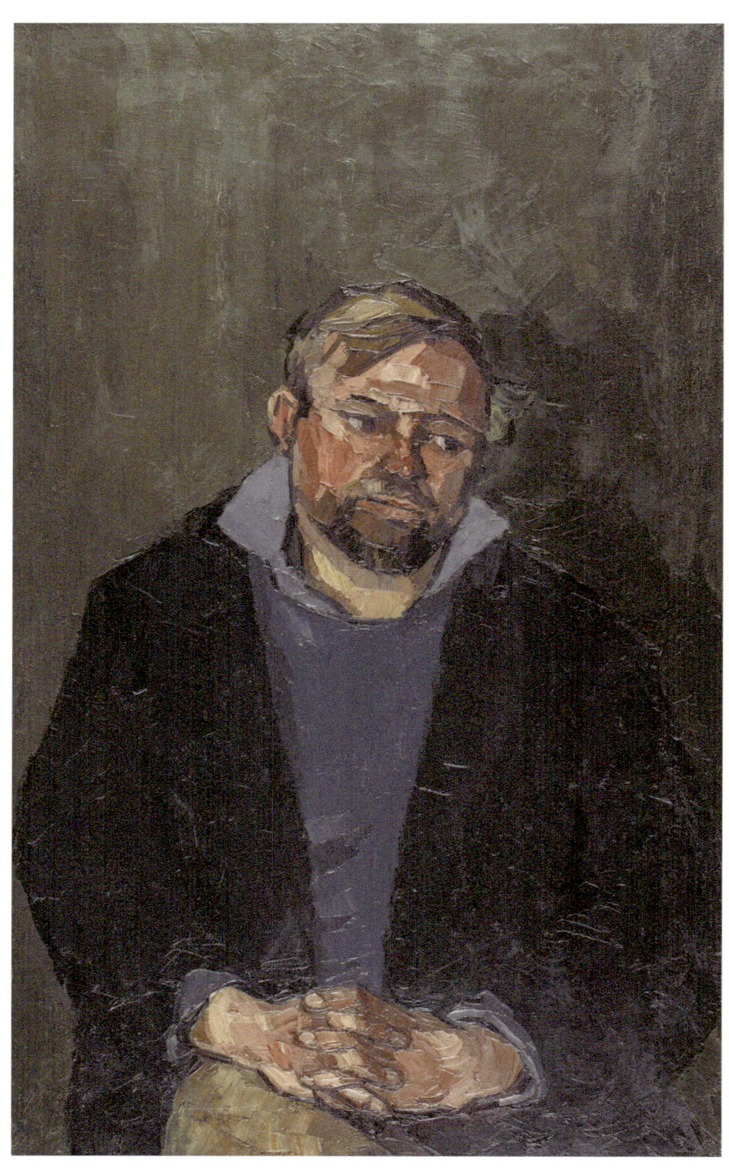

9

Kyffin Williams,
A Portrait of Jack Jones, 1969
National Library of Wales

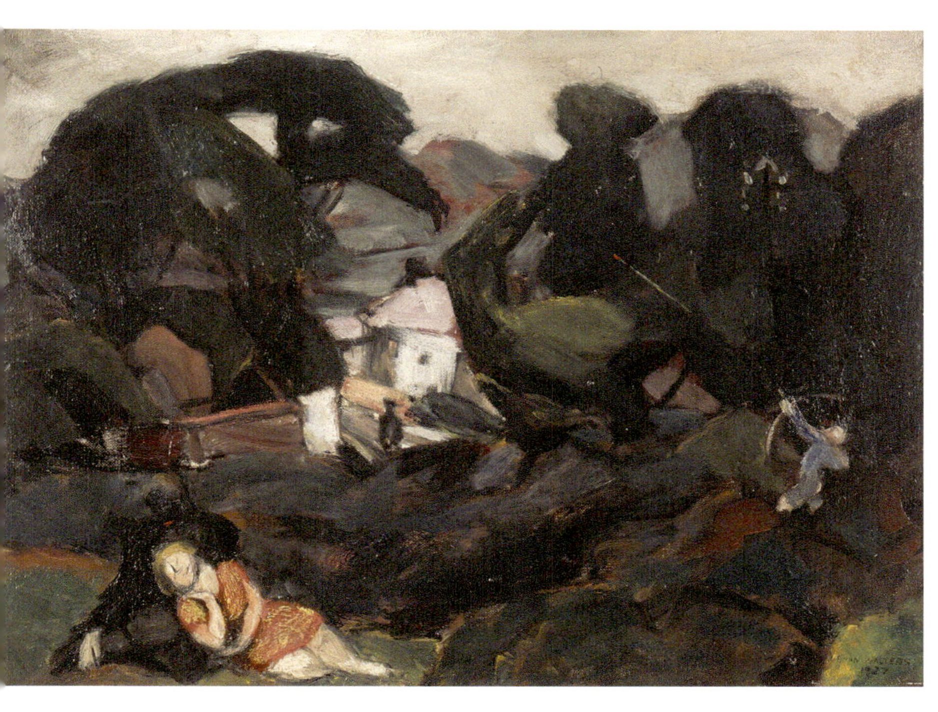

10
Evan Walters,
Courting, c.1927

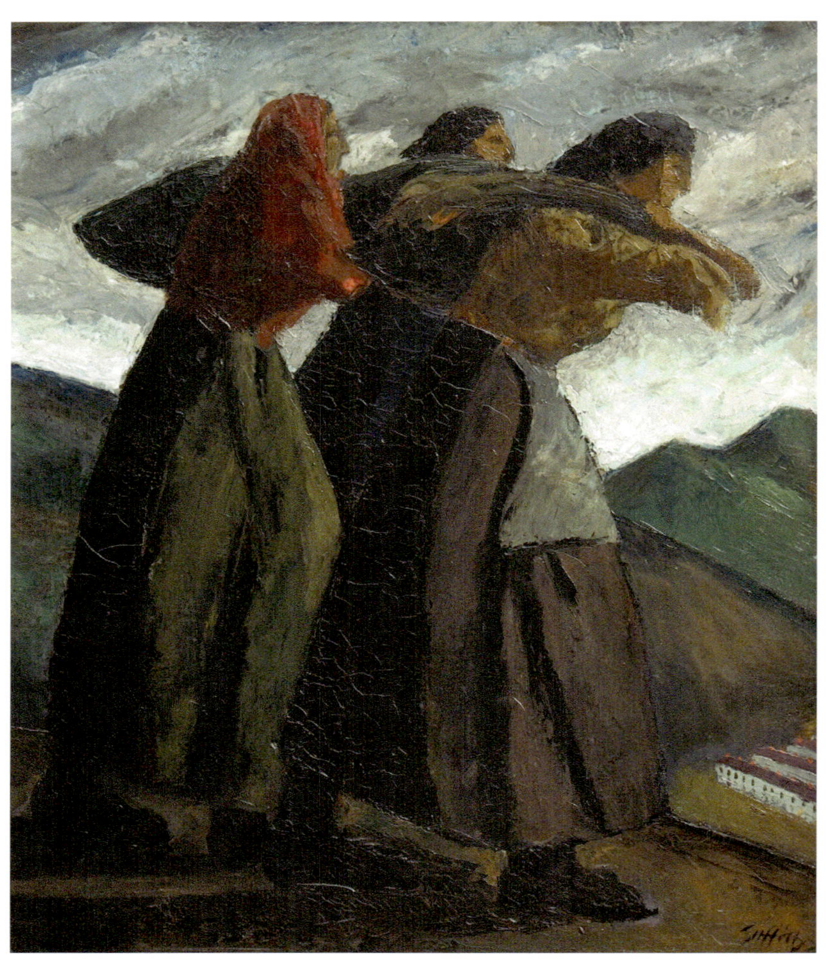

11
Archie Rees Griffiths,
On the Coal Tips, c.1929–31

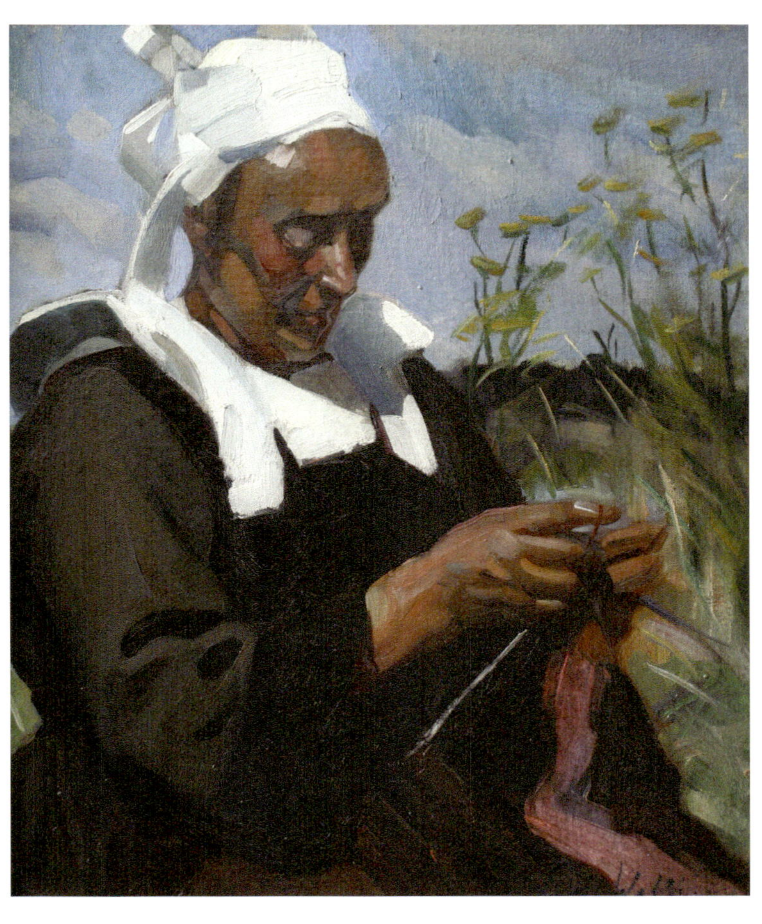

12
John Cyrlas Williams,
Breton Woman, c.1927
Private collection

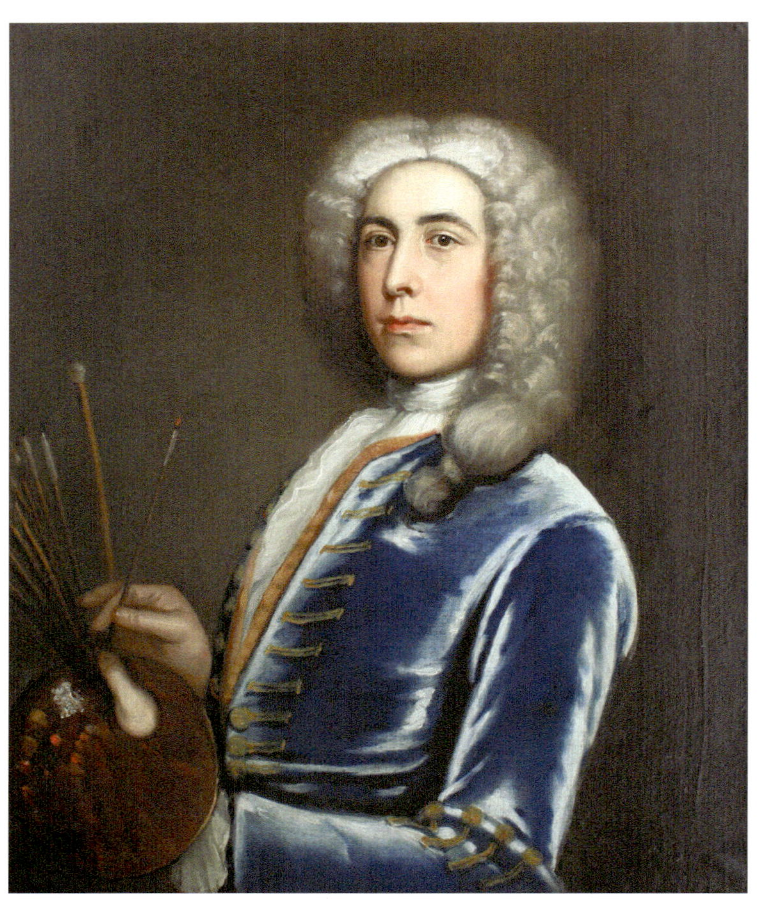

13

Edward Owen of Penrhos,
Self-portrait, 1732

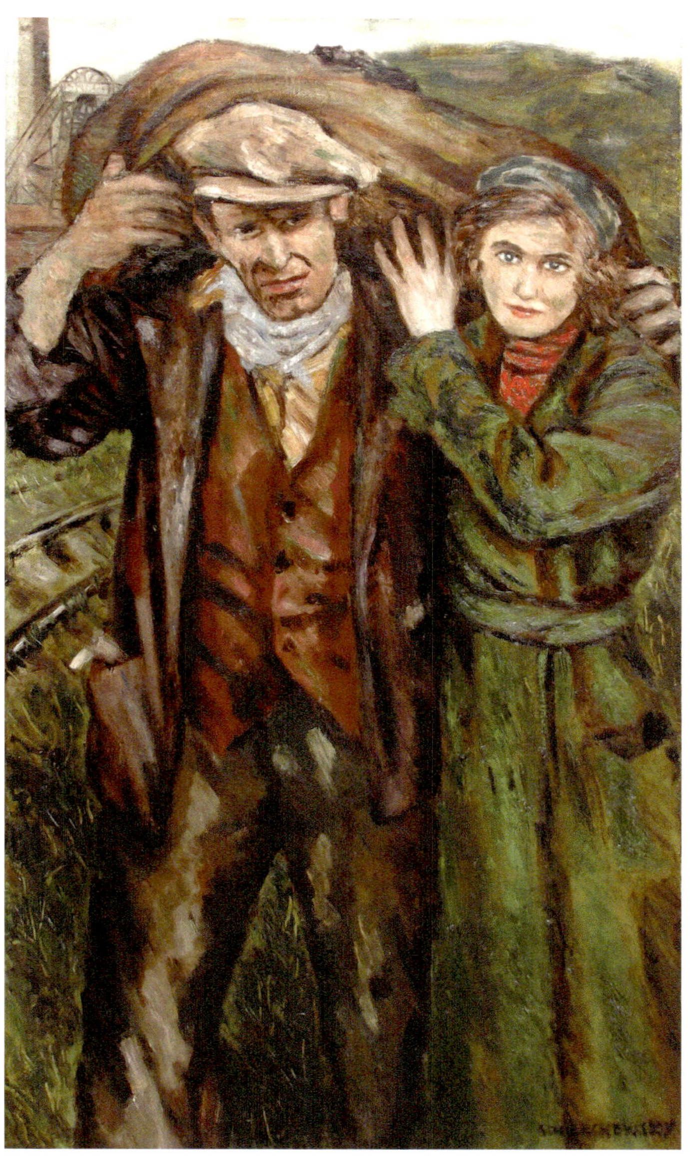

14
Maurice Sochachewsky,
Their Burden, 1937

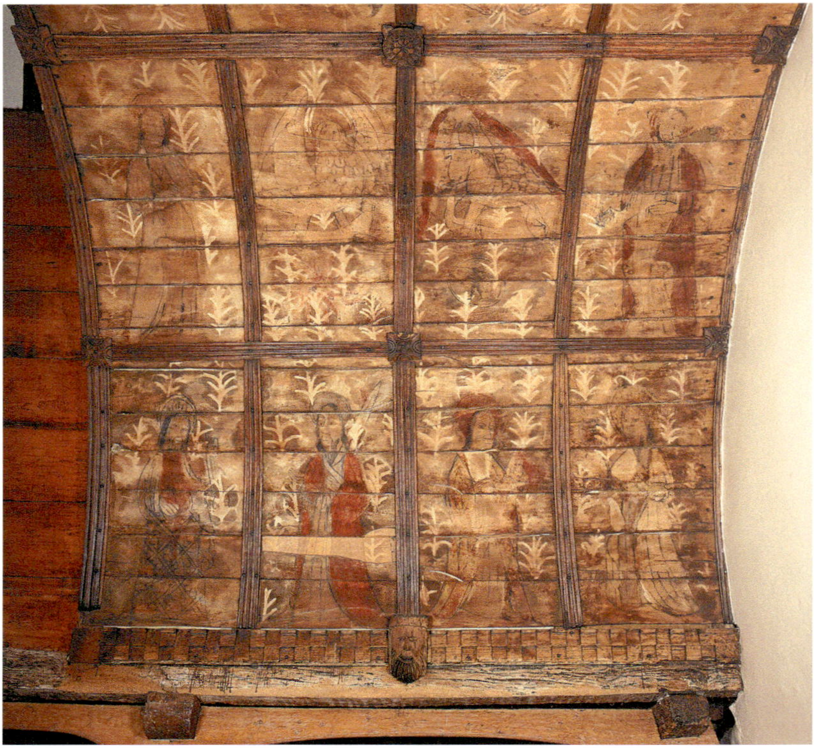

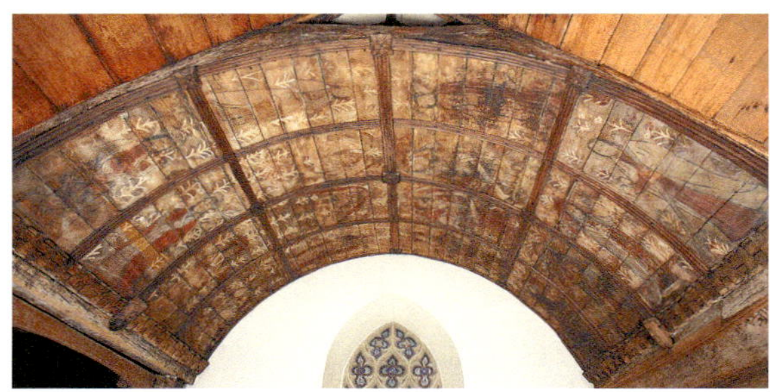

15
Unknown painter, *The Canopy of Honour*
at the Church of St Benedict, Gyffin, 15th century.
Photograph: Charles and Patricia Aithie ©ffotograff

Every picture has a biography, according to Peter Lord. To deny that is to deny its relationship to the times in which it was painted, to the life of the painter, and its history as it passes through the hands of successive owners.

But a picture is also a mirror, and in *Relationships with Pictures* Peter Lord presents the reader with fifteen images that reflect key periods in his life. Mostly these are paintings by artists with whom, in one way or another, he has been closely associated; a few are photographs – of his great-grandmother; of a British Army supply column on a Baghdad street, circa 1920; of Twm Penllwynbedw in Marian Delyth's striking portrait.

The Danish poet Knud Sørensen makes a distinction between one's 'home-ground' – the *bro* of Welsh tradition – and one's 'elected-ground', the place where you take root for a second time. Peter Lord's home-ground, his *bro*, was Exeter and the hinterland of rural Devon where he grew up identifying with the agricultural-labouring background of his father's family, rather than the 'posh' aspirations of his mother's side. His elected-ground of course has been Wales, and specifically Welsh-speaking Wales.

There is a sense, though, in which he has always been an outsider – rejecting at an early age the 'empire loyalist' values and assumptions of his parents' world; feeling disoriented and alone in his years as an art student at Reading University; then plunged into the complexities and tensions of being an Englishman in Welsh-speaking Ceredigion after his move to Trefenter in 1974, tensions that persisted even when he became a fluent Welsh speaker himself.

On his elected-ground, however, he is an outsider with a difference, for he belongs to that distinguished band of incomers who, since the 1970s, have made a considerable contribution to Welsh culture. In Peter Lord's case this has been in the field of visual art, and it is no exaggeration to say that in a series of books and articles over the past thirty years he has invented Welsh art history, refuting forever the canard based on ignorance that there is no such thing because the Welsh have never been a visual nation.

Relationships with Pictures is subtitled *An Oblique Auto-biography*. What Peter Lord means by this becomes clear as the book proceeds, for after the account of his decision to settle in West Wales, there is a shift in focus away from himself, the individual, to the painters and paintings he has, over the years, helped to recover as part of our visual inheritance. One of the pleasures of these chapters is the insights they provide into that process – allowing us to share in his excitement when, after hours of painstaking investigation, he is suddenly rewarded by the discovery of a cache of paintings in an attic or a bundle of revelatory letters.

There is indeed something of the detective in Peter Lord. He is adept at the patient trawl through archives, garnering clues from interviews, seizing on the chance phone call or e-mail that leads to a new find or adds another detail to an artist's biography.

In this way, painters like Archie Rees Griffiths, John Cyrlas Williams and Maurice Sochachewsky – painters who were barely names before he started investigating them – are brought back into the light to live once more in our culture, each adding to and changing our understanding of Wales's visual past.

This is why *Relationships with Pictures* is an 'oblique' auto-biography, because for Peter Lord, in the end, it is the pictures that matter, and the artists who created them. To understand how he came by these pictures, how he pieced together the often buried lives of their creators, is consequently to understand the man himself.

John Barnie

A Portrait
of Sarah Drewer
'Grannie Horner'

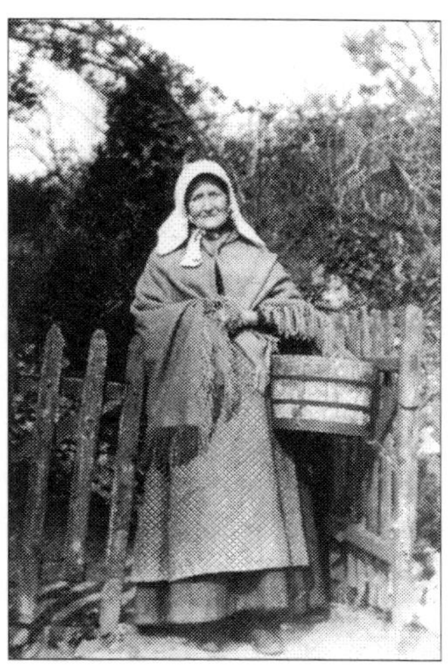

We grow up in belief and we grow old in belief. Somewhere in the middle, sometimes, facts press doubt upon us. But, in the end, only belief is real.

In December 1934 my great-grandmother, Grannie Horner, was looking forward to the return from India of her daughter, Polly, with her husband, Will, and their children. Though I know her only from her photographs, I can almost hear Grannie Horner's voice in her letters. Her dialect would have been stronger in speech. She probably had some schooling, where she would have learned to write a little more formally than she spoke:

My Dearest Polly & Will

Many thank for your welcome letter to day Mon – glad to heare you are all keeping well as it leaves us about the same – yes we are in our last week before Xmas & I expect everybody is killing poultery this week I thought off having the <u>Old</u> Gander for our dinner but Father wont have him til you comes home he have wrot to Ley & ask them to save back a Turkey for him so he thinks you shall have a good feed when you do come home I ask him who was goine to cook it all it will be a fuss for me to do it all the Butcher brout me a bobs worth a Bacon last week so I have a bit to go on with I told I should wants some more soon yes the time is Rolling on I suppose you are leaveing out there on a Sunday & Sailing on the Tuesday the 15. I hope you will send us a wire when you Lands to Southampton it dont seem hardly worth Elsie's trip up to Southampton to meet you unless you are comeing to Exeter with hir it would be alright for May if she is goine to Exeter but I don't think May will want to leave you til you gets there you will get uste to the cold weather before you come home for we have got it cold & wet I washd last Wed – have not dryed yet. I don't know what its comeing too for it rains every day & the mud it stogs you in it …

good luck from your ever loveing

Mam & dad Horner

Grannie Horner was baptised Sarah in 1862 at the church of Buckland St Mary in the east of Devon, where it borders both Dorset and Somerset. Her family name was Drewer, but it was written in the records as Drower – a variation which echoes the pronunciation in

Grannie Horner (left) and
Polly Horner (third from left), c.1910

John Horner
(second from left), c.1910

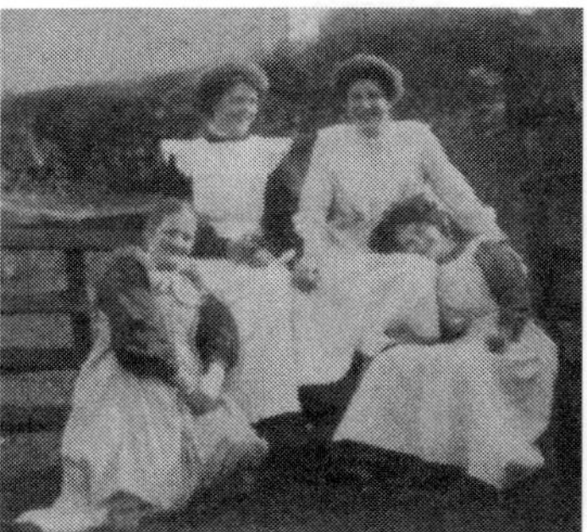 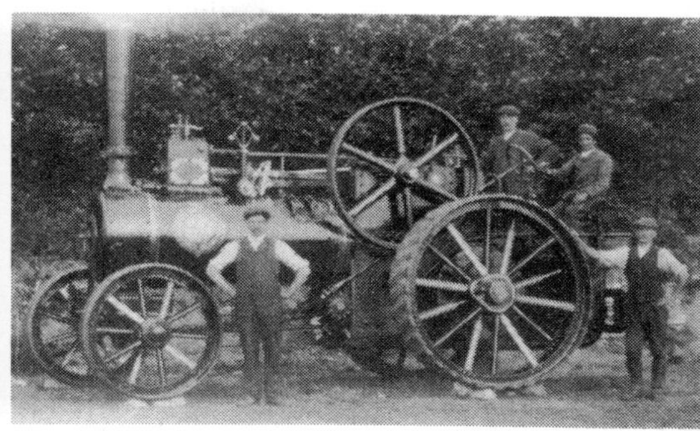

that part of Devon. Sarah's family were shoemakers. Her grandfather was born in the eighteenth century, in the time of John Wesley, who created the people's religion in the south-west of England. Grannie Horner became a midwife and attended Wesleyan chapel, but it hadn't made her a misery. In fact, my father and his sisters remembered her in old age as a jovial person. In other photographs she smiles happily. Before the war, she sits on the ground in an apple orchard at harvest time with her daughter-in-law, a girl friend, and Polly, as yet unmarried. They wear white smocks and offer apples to the unknown photographer – John, perhaps, her son, who drove the traction engine. She is still smiling for the camera in the 1930s, seated at the back door beside her husband, John Thomas Horner. He does not smile. He wears a Farmer George beard, thick corduroy trousers, gaiters, a shirt without a collar and a waistcoat. John Thomas Horner was a ploughman, and given to drink. He would disappear for days on a binge. On one occasion, regaining consciousness, he is reputed to have addressed himself in the mirror with the question 'Be I Thomas Horner?' By the 1920s he was in a bad way. Grannie Horner wrote to Polly that 'he has been in bed 9 weeks and I have had 1 Bottle of Brandy an 2 Bottles of Whiskey and 2 of Port Wine.

Grannie and Grandpa Horner,
c.1920–30

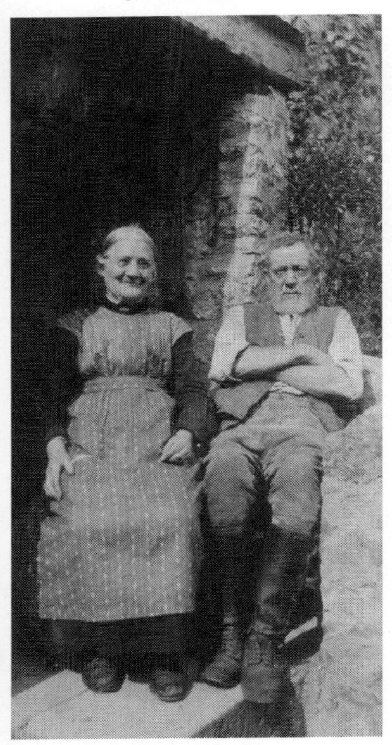

I might be glad of some of your money for another Bottle of Port I give 4s.6d for it I still give him his Scotts Emulsion I have got to have fire in the bedroom but still I would not mind all this if I was looking forward to any betterment but I know there is not ...'

Sarah's photograph was taken in the garden at Primrose Cottage, Shore Bottom, near Yarcombe. It is a country of deep, damp, fertile valleys. At the end of the garden at Primrose Cottage was a gate, and beyond the gate was a stream where, in the picture, she has drawn water for the house. She wears a long skirt and an apron made of material with a pattern of spots or little stars, which I imagine is dark blue. Over her shoulders is a shawl of a very rough weave, like a blanket, and with a tassled edge. She squints into the sunlight, and this must be a working day because on her head she wears the kind of coarse long bonnet that was worn by farm workers in the fields to protect them from the sun, as well as from the rain. It covers her shoulders and her neck. A painting by Sidney Curnow Vosper shows labourers on the land in Brittany just a little earlier wearing these bonnets.[1] In a sense these people lived at the very end of the Middle Ages. Sarah Drewer's ancestors had probably laboured in the same place as far back as there was a farming community there, which is a long time. In 1970, on a farm called Higher Holcombe, which is worked by descendents of Sarah's family, a Celtic mirror was turned up on the site of a late Iron

Age settlement. The Holcombe Mirror probably was hidden, rather than lost or abandoned, perhaps during the Roman conquest, when Vespasian attacked the area in AD44. Roman settlers, or members of the Romanised local ruling class, later built a villa over the site – I have some pieces of its tessellated pavement. The mirror is engraved with what the archaeologist who described it called a 'double lyre pattern', typical of Insular Celtic art.

It is fanciful, of course, to think of Sarah Drewer as being a descendent of those Celtic-speaking people who farmed the land at the same time as Jesus lived in Palestine, though it is possible, and ancestry is all about fancy. We tend to think of it as a matter of facts, but in reality, it is a matter of choices, because there are so many genealogical routes that we can take into the past. Sometimes, in an MA class about Welsh identities that I teach, I choose a student and ask him or her to tell me about their grandfather. In reply, students never ask 'Which one?', or tell me that their mother's father was such and such, and their father's father something else. Invariably, they launch into the story of a single grandfather, almost always identifying him by his work. Very often, he will have been a collier. This is not merely a reflection of the fact that the students mostly come from south and west Wales. Although mining remained the biggest single industry in the area until after the Second World War, when their grandfathers were young, there were still far more grandfathers who were not colliers. However, I have never been told that grandfather was an accountant. The students' characteristic response to my enquiry reflects a choice they make about the construction of their own identities – perhaps ones that reflects only what they feel is the appropriate answer in the context of the course, or perhaps choices they make for life.

In this respect I am no different to my students. In 1945, when my mother told her mother that she was going to marry my father – Sarah Drewer's grandson – there were hysterics in the kitchen, because he lived in a council house. My mother had grown up in a nice bungalow along a private road, with a retired member of the Indian civil service on one side and a maiden lady of independent means on the other. She liked to point out that she was related to the remarkably named Vansittart Bowater family, one of whom had become Lord Mayor of London. Hers was the world of tea on the lawn and beaded doilies on the milk jug – or, at least, it pretended to be. In fact, Grandpa had an affair with the matron at a local hospital, and Uncle Frank went bankrupt and did a bunk to Australia with the family heirlooms. Among her ancestor choices was a successful painter, and in the drawing room – the very existence of which reveals all – hung the evidence, in the form of a pair of large, full-length, watercolour portraits. I remember the gentleman, in particular, for his shiny chisel-toed shoes of about 1840, planted at my child's eye-level on a black and white marble floor. He leaned nonchalantly against a column. The lady carried a golden brown shawl, fashionably low-slung to display her slim figure. Sarah Drewer's shawl protected her from the weather. Early in life, like most of the students I have taught, I chose not to identify as posh. Sarah Drewer was of the common people, and that is why she, and no-one else, is my great-grandmother.

I think that a thorough exploration of the motives underlying this choice would involve an analysis of the sociology and politics of immediate post-war England, in which I grew up. Other people might simply attribute it to an inverted form of the snobbery that, in the past, drove the nouveaux riches (or gentry families who found themselves, for some reason, deprived of images of their illustrious lineage), to purchase ancestor portraits. Here is a nice example: In 1885, a Mr Dowling, who had inherited Llantarnam Abbey in Monmouthshire, ancestral home of the Morgan family, fell upon hard times. There was a sale of the house and its contents, which included an early seventeenth-century portrait of Edward Morgan:

> The portrait of Edward Morgan had been withdrawn from the sale and taken to London by an auctioneer, who offered it for sale by public auction at Robinson and Fisher's sale-rooms in Old Bond Street, on February 10, 1886, when a Mr. M.S. Williams, attending the sale, made a bid of twelve guineas, and so became possessed of this portrait, which he now represents as a portrait of his own ancestor. The portrait thus acquired in a London sale-room has been renamed by its new owner 'a Williams of Aberpergwym,' Aberpergwym, Neath, Glamorganshire, being the residence of Mr. Williams ...[2]

Annoyed by Williams's appropriation of a member of his family, G. Blacker Morgan, compiler of the Morgan family history, challenged the new owner on the matter in 1889, but was rebuffed. Undeterred, Morgan sought the assistance of Hugh Thomas, a carpenter who had worked at Llantarnam back in the days of King William IV. Thomas had helped to reframe the picture of Edward Morgan in 1834, and was willing to testify before a magistrate as to its correct identity, of which he had been informed at the time. Nevertheless, over at Aberpergwm, M.S. Williams chose not to reveal the truth to his heirs, who, naturally, assumed the portrait to be not only a seventeenth-century Williams, but indeed Jenkyn Williams, 'the son of Jenkyn ap William of Blaen Baglan, and the first to settle at Aberpergwm', since his name had been inscribed in gold letters on the face of the picture, soon after its acquisition. In 1962 this fictitious identity was stamped with the authority of the Keeper of Art at the National Museum, John Steegman, who reproduced a photograph of the picture as the frontispiece to the second volume of his *Survey of Portraits in Welsh Houses*.[3]

Unfortunately, this exercise in the appropriation of ancestors would land me in more trouble than it did its perpetrator. Having come across G. Blacker Morgan's documentation, I published the picture with its original identity, but owing to a misunderstanding about who held the right to reproduce the photograph of it, before doing so I failed to consult the owner. Quite understandably, I received an indignant letter from him, irritated by what, as far as he was concerned, was my unjustified transmogrification of his ancestor. He had every reason to feel aggrieved, since the narrative of his identity was being undermined. Portraits matter.

Like that of Edward Morgan, most painted portraits are dominated by the sitter's sense of self, since generally it is he or she who is paying for them – though painters do take liberties with their patrons' self-image on occasions. A part of the attraction of a portrait such as that of Sarah Drewer is that she, though the subject, is not the patron of the photographer. The image is therefore devoid of pretentions on her part. This quality sits well with the narrative of the picture, which expresses my desire to reclaim identification with the common people. Lack of pretention is among the virtues which I like to attribute to them. Some years ago, at a village exhibition in which the picture was shown, it was suggested that Sarah had been photographed in fancy dress – the Devon equivalent of a Welsh lady in a tall black hat. The quality and the mood of the photograph seem to me to make this most unlikely. Nevertheless, if not a family member, the intention of the photographer may have been documentary, since

Unknown photographer,
Albert J. Coles (Jan Stewer), c.1930

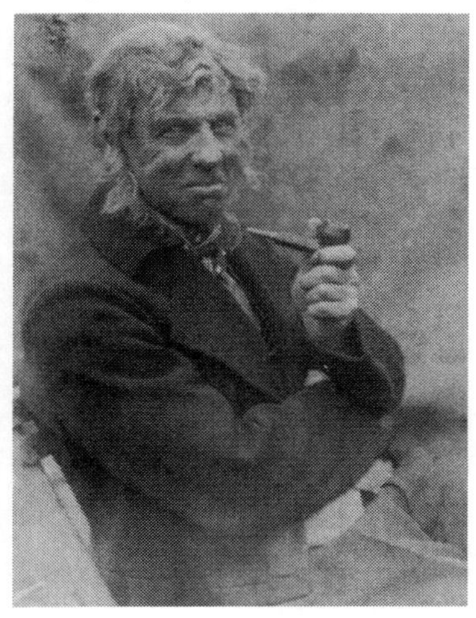

the picture was taken at a period when intellectuals took great interest in folk life in Devon. When Sarah wrote her letters to Polly in India, she would often send also a copy of the local newspaper, the *Western Morning News*. Among its most popular features was a column written by the folklorist Albert J. Coles, under the pseudonym 'Jan Stewer'. My father, growing up with no memory of England, liked to hear Polly read Jan Stewer, when the paper arrived. Here, Coles recreates the kind of conversations that went on in the carrier's cart, which was a thing of the past even in his present because, as he says, ''tis all moters now':

I minds very well the conversation on one journey, which will show 'ee the sort o' rummage that was told up when us was in the mood fer't. 'Twas a winter's mornin' I remember, and mid-dlin yark, and Mrs. Endycott keeped on grum'lin' cus us did'n get along vaster.

"What be grousin' about so much missis?" says Tom Zalter. "I wonder you daun' get out and walk."

"I wude if I was in a hurry," her says.

"Furst time I knowed you when you wad'n in a hurry," says Tom. Lias said, "Mrs. Endycott likes gwain slow when her's ridin' cus her gets more fer her money that way."

"But it means puttin' up with you for longer time," her says, "so that's worse again."

"'Tis no use you pretendin' that missis. You knows very well you'd miss me like anything if I wad'n yer."

"That's right. Same as I shude miss the teeth's ache arter it got better. A very gude miss."

"You'd soon be wishin' you cude zee me back, Mrs. Endycott."

"I wude'n mind seein' yer back. 'Tis yer faace I objec's to."

"Never mind missis. I be gwain to take you to the picshers nex' week, when you pays me that sixpence you owes me fer carr'ing they two gurt baskets o' poultry into the station. 'Twill be dark as a bag in there so you won't be able to see my faace, and us can sit and hold hands all the time instaid."

"My dear zaul, I shuld be sorry to have you hold my hand. If you was to hold yer tongue 'twude be a blessin'. But 'tis too late fer that, I'm 'fraid."[4]

The fascination for my father of listening to his mother read such pieces would, I imagine, have lain in the contrast they made with her everyday speech. Polly had long since lost or, more likely, discarded the dialect that she must have spoken as a child. When she left home, she went into service with a well-to-do family at Redlands in Bristol. She had begun the long move away that continues through me – away from Devon, away from the Middle Ages, and away from the common people. Language is the first signifier of the move away, and there is no going back. Nevertheless, in so far as I have had any control of the direction of my own evolution, then I have been guided by the signifiers of a past to which I am, by descent, connected, and by the narrative I have constructed around them: Grannie Horner's letters and her picture, the sound of her voice in my mind and the stilled image of her lost reality.

2

The Mesopotamia Studio, Baghdad

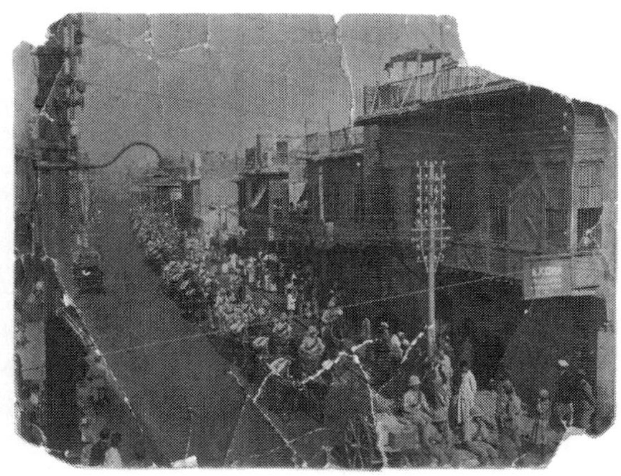

Of the few happy things I inherited from my father, football has been the most important to me. My father loved football, and so do I. Going to the match was the only time I felt close to him, and able to share something with him. His feeling for the game, like mine, was rooted in that combination of beauty and tribalism which seems paradoxical to those who do not experience it. The development of my sense of belonging was focussed on football in the particular time and place in which I watched it – St James' Park, in Exeter – thick foggy days, pressed against the iron railings of the shallow cinder terrace by men in wet gaberdine macs, smoking cheap cigarettes. I thank my father for giving me that. It was not, however, a straightforward gift of loyalty, transferred from one generation to another. Although my father's family, on both sides, belonged to Devon for hundreds of years, his own experience of that bond was at one remove, because of his childhood in India. That country seems to have meant little to him in sensual terms. He remembered bad smells, the red spots of betel juice spat on the ground, fruit bats hanging in the trees, and kite flying on the plain around Jubalpur – 'Jubb' to the soldiers. It had been captured by the East India Company in 1817, and still in my father's time was the main military base of the Central Provinces.

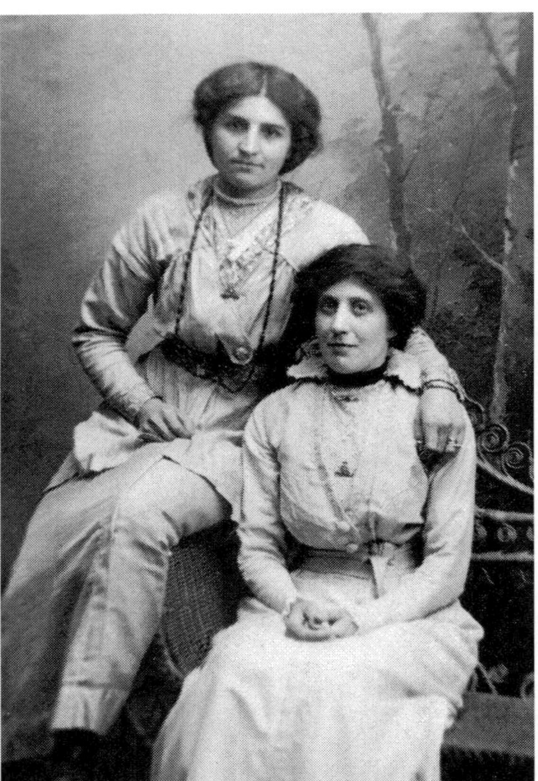

Polly Horner (right) and Cousin Gladys c.1914

He learned a little Hindi – even the children of the common soldiers were cared for by Ayahs. But my father's deeper identity, formed in India, was conceptual rather than sensual. The place that truly framed his sense of self was the British Empire and its army. The dissolution of that place through his lifetime left him angry and homeless – conceptually homeless.

After she went into service and moved to Bristol, Polly Horner, my father's mother, had maintained contact with home. There are letters and postcards: 'It is Yarcombe Club tomorrow your mam is going but I can't go very well I am looking forward to our club I wish you were coming to have a waltz ...' They suggest that the myth of a tranquil rural England – of a peaceful rhythm that was the product of many generations living a settled life – was not entirely without a foundation in the experience of those among the common people who were able to earn a living wage in the place where they had grown up. Cousin Gladys kept Polly in touch with local events: 'We'll have a happy time together when you come home. Try to come home for the flower show August 5 ...', she says – but it was now 1914, and the fifth of August would be the first day of the Great War. I do not know if Polly was able to go, or whether she and Gladys experienced foreboding or excitement, because 1914 was simply a number to them, with no more resonance than the number of the year in which I write in my present.

However, William Lord may have been excited, because he enlisted three weeks later, and it was because of the war that he met Polly, on a railway station. It was probably either Honiton or Exeter, since both were points of intersection on the routes they travelled to and from their homes. Will had been born on the other side of Devon. Like Polly's parents, his mother and father were common

Peter Lord at Foggintor, 2012
Olwen Fowler

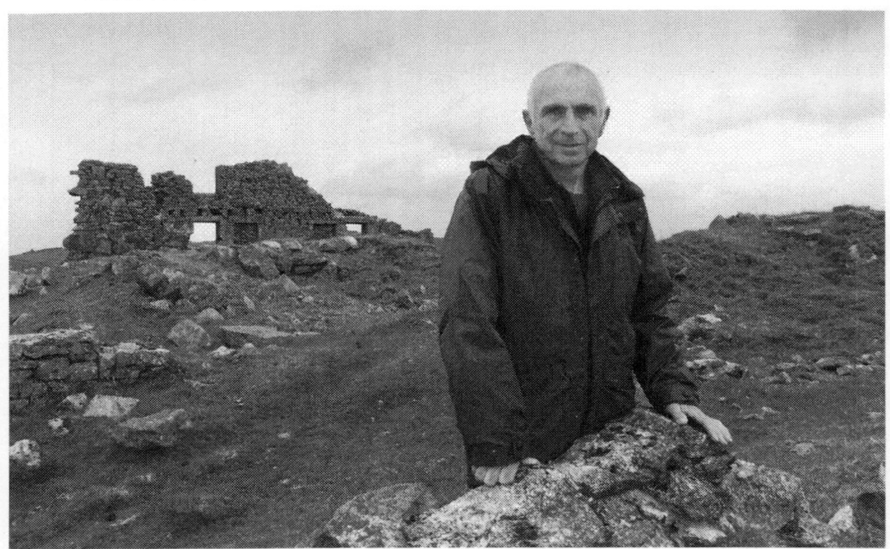

people, though they lived different lives from the farming community in the east. Will was born on Dartmoor, where three generations of his family had laboured in the stone quarries at Foggintor, near Princetown. His great-grandfather, Richard, had moved there from his home in St Cleer, over the border in Cornwall, where his father in turn had been born at a time when a few people still spoke Cornish. Richard probably arrived in Princetown in the early 1820s, shortly after the quarries were opened. By the early 1840s the owner's agent reported extensive buildings, modern machinery, and about 300 people working there – smiths, carpenters and turners in their workshops, and outside, the labourers and masons:

> … in another part I found a number of men engaged in facing up with a stone wall of considerable thickness and strength a heap of Rubbish brought out of the Quarry, on the summit of which

I was told an extensive Shed was to be erected under the Roof
and shelter of which the Stone Masons may work in all weathers.[5]

The heap of rubbish grew into the long tip which still juts out from
the quarry onto the common, with its prehistoric stone rows, sloping
down and away towards Merrivale. The workshop that was about
to be built on top of it was reconstructed later as housing for the
workers. My great aunt Elsie was born in that desolate place, but her
mother, Sarah Jane, was used to the life. She had also grown up on
the moor, a little to the west, at Powdermills. The works, stores and
houses of the mills, where gunpowder was made to fight the wars of
the empire, were made of huge blocks of granite that must have been
quarried at Foggintor. They were jointed as tightly as the walls of
Zimbabwe. Sarah Jane was a cousin to her husband. Two years after
Elsie, she gave birth to Will at a house in Princetown.

The Richard Lord from whom Will was descended had many
children, and at least three of the boys and one of the girls lived their
lives in Princetown. One of them, George, became a stonemason,
rather than a labourer. Like many skilled workers from the peripheries
of England and from Wales, he more than once travelled to North
America to work, probably at quarries in Maine. When he came
back for good he cut an obelisk of pink granite to mark his burial
place in Princetown churchyard, and carry the names of some of
his descendents. In 1864 his wife had given birth to a son, George
Wallace Lord, who would also become a mason. Over a century
later, a strange thing happened concerning this George. A friend of
mine was visiting Hay-on-Wye to buy books. In the first shop she
entered, the first book she took down from the shelf was F.A. Paley's
A Manual of Gothic Mouldings. She found it annotated with many

little drawings in pencil, including some heads of the kings of England. These reminded her of the way that I drew and so she bought the book as a present for me. The next day we sat down together to look at it closely. On the title page we found the signature of G.W. Lord and the date, November 1898.

By that time George was living in Exeter. His cousin Will, my grandfather, would also leave the moor, perhaps because of the hardness of the life, but more likely because there was no longer work there. Will became a porter on the railway until he joined the Royal Artillery in 1914. In May 1915 he crossed to France, and he fought there for over two years. During the Battle of the Somme he won the Military Medal, though I don't know what he did, because only officers' citations were published in the newspapers. Then he went on leave and met Polly on the railway station. They were

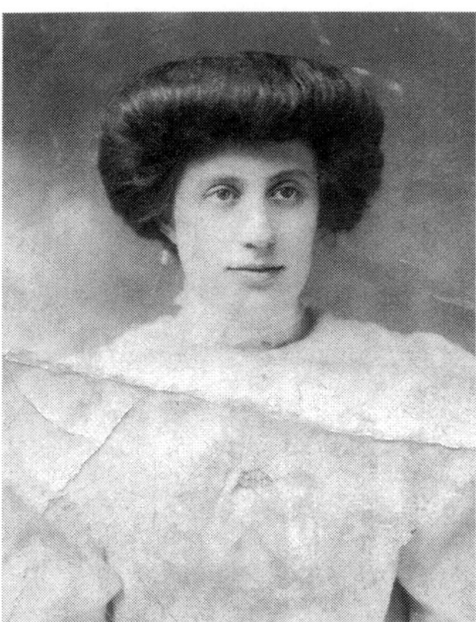

Polly Horner,
c.1910

married in September 1917. Polly returned to service in Bristol when Will was sent back to France. He was gassed and spent a long time recuperating, dressed in his hospital blues. He recovered enough to return to the RA base at Woolwich sometime in 1918, but wasn't sent back to France. He served on after the war until he was demobilised on 17 June 1919. He re-enlisted the next day.

Will stayed in England another six months, and then, just before Christmas 1919, he sailed with his unit for Egypt. He sent Polly postcards from Gibraltar, Malta and Alexandria: 'Cheer up and the time won't be long going by and then we'll be able to settle down somewhere in Blighty, I hope.' At Shore Bottom, Grannie and Grandpa Horner received pictures of the Citadel at Cairo and of a caravan at the caves of the Caliphs: 'Dear Dad, These postcards represent the country and the travelling by camels which is carried on in the desert just about where we are now. It's frightfully hot by day and cold by night. Will.' He was sent to Palestine. He visited Jerusalem, sent more postcards, and bought two picture books as souvenirs – though the city was not at all the untroubled and unchanging place they depicted. The worst violence came later in the period of the British Mandate, but even by 1920 there was fighting between different factions. In August that year Will was again in Alexandria, but writing to Polly to say that he was about to go through the desert to rejoin his unit at Haifa. The soldiers called that journey going 'into the blue'. By this time there was trouble in Iraq, and Will was among the troops sent there. It was the start of the two year revolt against the British Mandate of Mesopotamia.

It must have been at this time that he acquired the photograph. It shows a supply column in Baghdad. The wagons are driven on the left of the street. Apart from an army officer, who hurries away along the pavement, the people observe them quietly, apparently thoughtful. Protest was mostly peaceful in Baghdad. Above the street, from a wooden building, hangs a sign that says 'A. Kerim, Photographer, Mesopotamia Studio'. Some of Kerim's landscape photographs survive, and perhaps many portraits also, unidentified in the albums of soldiers and the local middle class. It was Kerim who recorded the passing column. Is my grandfather there? Why else would he keep the photograph? His job was to ride the lead horse of the team that drew the supply wagons and the gun carriages. I have one of his spurs.

Later, as promised, Polly and Will would live together in England, but only long enough for my grandmother to become pregnant and give birth to my aunt Audrey in Exeter. She was two months old when Will sailed back to Egypt, though this time accompanied by his family. They were soon parted again. European Turkey remained occupied by the British, but from the other side of the Bosphorus the Turks were fighting the Greeks. In September 1922 Turkish troops entered an allied demarcation zone around Gallipoli and threatened Chanak. Reinforcements were sent from Egypt to Chanak and by Christmas 1922 Will was among them. For the troops, it was one of the many arseholes of the empire. He sent a sardonic greetings card to his parents-in-law:

> *San fairy an*, we aint dead yet
> (And don't intend to be, you bet!),
> And one fine day a ship we'll get
> 'Way from Chanak!

Life was no more comfortable for Polly, left in Egypt, than it was for Will in the Dardanelles. In January, his mother wrote to her from home to say that she and the children were always in her mind. She wished 'that Will were with you and the children in the place you are their, you could get on better but am pleased to hear that you have a good Companion in your tent and the Children so good …' Polly's tent was pitched at Moascar Camp, a flat plain of gravel on the edge of the desert. There was little privacy for married couples. Tents were arranged in rows of four, and each was divided into rooms only by canvas curtains. She lived there with Audrey and her elder daughter, May, until Will returned in June 1923. They spent some leave at Cairo and at Sidi Bish, on the Mediterranean, just outside Alexandria. There were fancy-dress parties on the sand, they rode on donkeys, and they swam. Polly became pregnant again, and my father was born in the wooden hospital building back at Moascar Camp. When my aunt would tell me as a child that he was born in a tent under a palm tree, she was exaggerating only a little. Two months later the family entrained in the desert for Port Said or Alexandria, from where they sailed for home. But scratch the surface of almost any family in Britain and a few generations back, somewhere, there will be India. At Southampton, four years later, they boarded HMT Somersetshire for Bombay.

I was born two years after Indian independence. Perhaps my generation is the last to have been shaped by the collapse of the Empire. The physical environment of my childhood was drenched in its mythology. It is now difficult to convey the totality of the psychological corral that it provided, from within which the world was perceived. My friends went to Ladysmith School; there was Pretoria Road and Roberts Road. Auntie Elsie lived down Buller Road. Elsie's husband, Uncle Jack had been named for Buller – John Redvers. The massive equestrian statue of the general, born in Crediton, stood at the top of St David's Hill, his entry point into the city of Exeter. The naming proved to be a doubtful honour, for it was claimed soon after Uncle Jack's christening that the hero had been a bungler, and he was dismissed. The war was a mess and Buller probably a scapegoat, but the Empire was already creaking, even if few people let the fact dampen their appetite for celebrations at the relief of Mafeking and Ladysmith. It was the Second Boer War, of course, but simply *the* war to those at the time, before its dishonourable place was usurped in 1914. By my own time, *the* war had become that of 1939, and it remains so in my mind. Will joined up for the third time. He became batman to an officer at Topsham Barracks, but his work still involved the horses that he had ridden in his previous military incarnation. Now he groomed his officer's mount.

My father joined the home guard and kept a diary. He looked out at night as Exeter burned in the air raids of 1942.[6] Two years later, just turned 20 years old, he was in France, then Belgium, Holland and over the Rhine. Hamburg was a flattened smoking ruin. His work was to find targets for the self-propelled guns of his unit in the Guards Armoured Division. In his Jeep he scouted in advance, surveyed the land, and worked out the co-ordinates for destruction. He was among the first troops to enter Brussels on 3 September 1944. The streets to the west of the town were lined with cheering French-speaking Belgians urging them on at the Germans, retreating in the east – 'Bosch partir, Bosch partir!' From his animated accounts I sensed even as a child that the experience was the high point of his life. His diary confirms it: 'Words cannot describe the scene. We entered about 12.00 midnight (our Div. took it at 9.00). We were mobbed, people kissing us, giving us drinks (champagne etc!) anything – never in my life have I seen anything like it before. Dug a slit trench in the main street with bullets flying up the length of the street – drinking champagne …' Yet although, as a young man, I learned a good deal about what he did, I knew little of what he felt, other than what I could intuit. My father's account of the war did not engage with the essence of it. Only once did he mention death, and reveal some emotion and deeper thought about the meaning of it all. Two weeks after the liberation of Brussels, the Guards Armoured Division was among the forces deployed to relieve the paratroopers who had attempted to take the Rhine bridges at Arnhem and Nijmegen. They were delayed, and the advanced troops were decimated in holding on. By the time my father's group arrived at the Nijmegen bridge and saw the carnage, they were angry. They captured a stranded German soldier. He seemed to my father to be an old man. They took him to the back of a building and shot him. My father told me this in terms of 'they'. I do not know whether he might more accurately have said 'we'.

The defeat of Germany preserved in my father's mind for a few years the illusion of Britain as a great power, and the sense that a vast standing army, to which almost everyone in his world had been connected, was a part of the natural order of things. In 1951 he and my mother took the excursion to the Festival of Britain – the last mirage of optimism on the downhill post-war road. Back home, on the green-streaked lino of the kitchen floor in our prefab, my father and I attempted to play with a little toy train he had bought there. It didn't work. Through the ensuing decade the symbols of the earlier age began to disappear – 'Empire Made' identified fewer and fewer of the things we bought. Yet, unknowingly I continued to absorb the self-deceptions of my parents' generation. I marched with my friends round the playground chanting 'We won the war/In 1954!' We celebrated with fragile desperation the final flickerings of the candle of supremacy. In 1956 the world speed record was again ours, won back by the test pilot Peter Twiss flying a Fairey Delta II, and I do not have to consult Wikipedia to remind me that he reached 1,132 miles per hour. But through the newspapers and the wireless which impressed that number for ever on my memory, also filtered stories that began to erode belief. We burned Colonel Nasser as the guy on Bonfire Night in 1956, but his name, along with that of Archbishop Makarios and Jomo Kenyatta, EOKA and Mau Mau, infiltrated my consciousness, reinforced by my father's intense reactions to the deeper implications they symbolised. I think my father could not help but feel the collapse of the Empire as a personal humiliation. He withdrew into a state of resentment which seemed to find its outward expression in frustration and anger directed largely at me. I lived in fear of him.

I suspect that he had become not only increasingly angry with the world, but also with himself – trapped by a conflict between his creative potential and fulfilment of the social expectations of his time. Grannie Horner's Methodism was manifest in him in the form of a protestant ethic of self-reliance and aversion to risk. I was often kept awake in my bed by the weekly apportioning of the wage packet, down to the last sixpence. Debt was inconceivable, so nothing came into the house until it could be paid for with cash. My father would have nothing acquired on the never-never but neither would he buy second hand. My mother despised the neighbours who bought old cars and tinkered with them on the kerbside on Sunday mornings. Dad went to work on the bus.

Paradoxically, as the world of his childhood identity crumbled, my father rose in a contrary motion of material security. When he left school, soon after coming home from India, he had joined a building firm as an office boy. After the war, he returned to work for the same

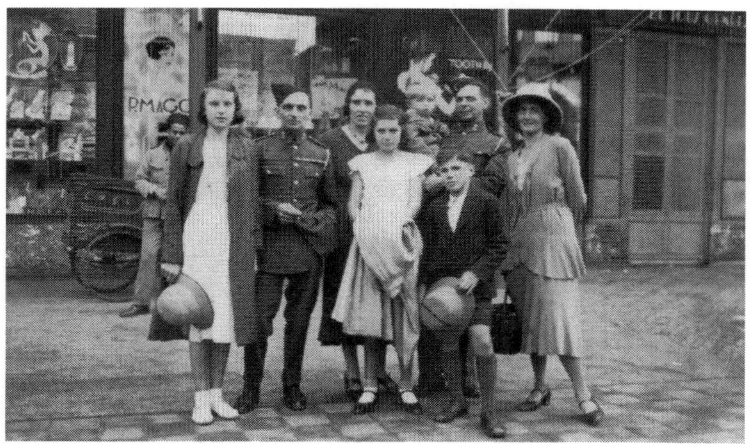

Family group, Port Said, Egypt, 1935
(front row, from left, May, Will, Audrey, Charlie and Polly Lord)

firm, and stayed with them for most of his life. From the council prefab in which I grew up, we moved when I was thirteen to a new red and yellow brick semi-detached house on a barren private estate. After thirty years he became a junior director of the building firm. He changed his name. He had always been Charlie, but on joining the board he became Charles. Next, he built his own detached house in a picturesque village. I hope he took some pleasure in the improvement that his hard work, ability and loyalty had brought him, but I know it did not transform him fundamentally into a happy man. Indeed, I suspect that he felt further imprisoned by it.

In Kerim's photograph, the world that formed my father is already collapsing. The war in Mesopotamia was a fiasco. It was the bumbling fag end of the Empire, though the momentum of its history was far from exhausted. The political class had still not escaped its compulsive drive in 2003, when Blair sent the remnant army back to the same country. My father never saw that war. He died in Exeter in 2001. The last year of his life was a particular ordeal for him. He had become ill with a kidney infection which had not been diagnosed, and subsequently was not treated promptly. By the time a huge abscess was drained, the strain on his body was resulting in strokes that debilitated him mentally. He was transferred to a cottage hospital where the carelessness of the nurses caused him to become dehydrated. In transfer back to the general hospital he suffered a major stroke. He was revived after several days of coma. The staff who inflicted this cruelty on him were delighted with their work. He was transferred to a geriatric hospital, where maintaining human dignity was not a priority. My father was a proud man, and the daily humiliations to which he was subjected there, in the company of dementia patients, drove him further inwards. He could not bear his dependence on others. He seldom opened his eyes and would not speak to my mother. We found him a place in an old people's home. It had once been my doctor's surgery, where I remember being taken as a child. My father would not leave his room. It was a five-hour drive to Exeter, but I visited as often as I was able. The last time, I arrived home in Wales very late to find there had been a phone call to say that his condition had deteriorated after I left. I drove back through the night. When I arrived his eyes were open but blind. His breath came in gasps at erratic and lengthening intervals. After an hour the gasps ceased, and I witnessed for the first time that subtle transformation of death which turns the live body into an alabaster image of itself. It was six o'clock. My mother kissed his forehead and we began immediately to deal with the formalities. Later that morning the registrar wrote his name in the book. There was no funeral – my mother's family do not indulge in death rituals.

3

Self-portrait
with Enamelled Jug

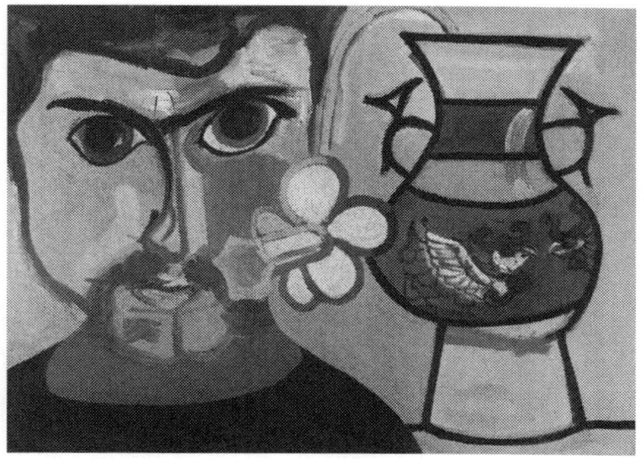

I was working on one of the big tables at the back of the art room. My teacher appeared and put a small brown pamphlet on the table in front of me. 'That's where you're going', he announced. It was a prospectus for the Fine Art Department at the University of Reading. I had no idea where Reading was – just that it was up north, like everywhere else if you come from Devon or Cornwall. I took the train and arrived for interview at an ungodly hour in the morning. There were tramlines down the cobbled centre of the silent London Street, and people sleeping in doorways, wrapped in newspaper. I had never seen people sleeping in doorways. At the end of my interview I was sent outside to await the verdict. The Principal,

Claude Rogers, ex-Euston Road, soon emerged. He was short and stout, and leant back to counterpoise the weight of his protruding stomach. His hands were in his pockets and his dark eyes seemed small, behind round glasses. 'We're prepared to offer you a place', he said. I expect I thanked him, as I was well brought up, then I went home and forgot about it. The next football match was far more important. I had no feeling for what I had done, other than that it was what I had been told to do. I experienced no sense of achievement, because neither had I any desire to go to Reading nor any sense of how well I had performed to get there. I just wanted to go home.

When I left Exeter for my first day at Reading my mother and father took me to the station. They stood on the platform and waved as the train left. Clearly, they were aware of the significance of the occasion. I had no idea that it marked the end of my coherent life. Of all the departures from St David's station, I remember it only because of the abnormality of their presence. In my cell in the new hall of residence in which I found myself at Reading I spent much of the first two weeks lying on the bed crying, as the reality of what had happened to me sank in. For the four years I was at university there the train journey home would be the best thing about the place. The line ran due west for an age alongside the Kennet and Avon canal, until at last it turned more south westerly, through Wellington tunnel and then downhill all the way. Through the window in the vestibule at the end of the compartment carriage I smelled the damp air of the valley as we met the River Exe and glided round the curves through Stoke Canon and Rewe. From the station it was a long walk uphill, past General Buller, to the middle of town. In the summer there was the smell of buddleia flowering in the cracks in the red sandstone walls, and reunion with the particular proportions and texture of the paving stones and the Dartmoor granite kerbs – the minutiae of which a returning exile is uniquely aware and that he or she experiences in the gut with the profound joy of belonging.

I do not remember precisely when exile became irreversible, but at some point the smell and the shape and the colour of home no longer unselfconsciously enveloped me. It had transmogrified into an evocation of something past, which I could observe with longing but no more enter. I had been looking away at the breaking point, and when I turned my head, it was too late. I think, though, that the break was the cumulative effect of many small fractures. They began when I was thirteen, when we left the council prefabs and moved to the private estate of banal brick semis. Topographically it was a move of about a mile but socially I had been carried to a different planet, and to a sense of isolation deepened by the simultaneous onset of introspective adolescence. It may have been in the following year that for some reason I sat in front of the tall mirror of the dressing table in the spare room and drew a picture of my face. I became deeply engrossed, and when I emerged from that mysterious state of concentration, the drawing that I observed objectively in the sketchbook on my knees was unlike anything I had previously done. I saw on the paper not a child's symbolic construction of a face, but a drawing of me. I knew that something had changed, though I had no sense of the significance of the fact that my first intense experience of self-exploration had been made through a visual image.

My childhood was entirely regulated by other people. I was brought up to do as I was told, and without a sibling I had no ally or model for complaint. I was involved in no choices or decisions, even about the most basic things – what I ate or wore, or where I went. Life was controlled most immediately by my mother, latterly, I believe, mainly to avoid the possibility of social contamination, the fear of which had motivated with increasing intensity her long march of thirteen years to escape the council houses. Obedience was secured by fear. At school, also, I did as I was told. My only protest was at having to play rugby rather than football which, it transpired, was a dirty word in the grammar school, that I had entered through the back door. The 11+ examination at primary school was the great parting of the ways. Posh children went to Hele's grammar school, unless they were unusually dull, in which case they disappeared at this point, never to be met with again, into the private grammar school. The rough ones went to the secondary modern, and nonentities, such as myself, were dispatched to the technical school. It was my luck, good or bad, to arrive there in the year that this tertiary system was disbanded, and to find myself instructed by the begowned Oxbridge graduates of Hele's. They had been transplanted from their Victorian establishment into a new building over the road from the U.S. Army Nissen huts that housed the lathes and saw benches of the technical school. They brought with them their alien game, of which I had only the dimmest sense, since it was played by people of a kind that I had never met. It was imposed on us by Harrison, a south-Walian Coach Popper.[7] The rules were not explained – it was simply assumed that we knew, and if we didn't, no doubt we deserved what we got as a consequence, for being who we were. It was a simple case of sink or swim and, as with everything else during the next five years, I sank but never quite drowned. It did not occur to me that for Harrison rugby was the game of the people. Now, I wonder what he was doing in that place. Curiously, when the world resumed its proper shape at 3.15 on Saturdays, the positive focus of my passion was another south-Walian – Graham Rees from Pontypridd, inside left for Exeter City.

At the next divide, when those deemed to be composed of the right stuff were selected to study for O levels in such things as English Literature, which they would pursue at Oxford or Cambridge, the rest of us were dumped into science. I was instructed in physics and chemistry, mathematics and computations. By virtue of art, technical drawing and history, I staggered through enough O levels to emerge in the sixth form, and to experience liberation by teachers who were able to focus my mind. They brought me to the two things about which I would have something to say. These were politics and art, though by reason of the dullness of my intellect it would take a very long time for me to grasp the intimate connection between them. Politics was called British Constitution, the facts of which were efficiently drummed into my head by our master only as a foundation for engaging in the political debate that arose from them, and which it was the purpose of his teaching to encourage. Dakin took full advantage of the two general elections fought in the years of my sixth form, 1964–6. Domestically, in a household in which political education consisted of the *Daily Express* and my father's periodic outbursts about bloody communists, I had moved as far left as the wet end of the Conservative Party. Under the circumstances, I think this was a considerable achievement. The sight of the Prime Minister, Alec Douglas-Home, standing in the drizzle on a wooden box in the pedestrian precinct in Exeter, vainly seeking the attention of indifferent passers by, probably hastened the leftward trend. He looked deeply unhappy. Nevertheless, during the general election of 1966 I heckled at a few Labour Party meetings and, on one occasion even succeeded in landing an effective rhetorical blow on Gwyneth Dunwoody, standing for the Exeter seat. It proved to be the high point of my political career. She glared at me as at something scraped from the pavement by the street cleaner's shovel. Dunwoody had much of the Commissar about her, that might have found fuller expression in another time and place.

Back in school, political debate in the British Constitution class sometimes generated excessive heat, directed on one occasion, unfairly I'm sure, at Dakin. During an art period the next day, my teacher, Peter Thursby, approached the big tables at the back, vaguely waving a note that he had received from Dakin complaining of my 'artistic temperament'. Peter looked puzzled – not, I imagine at my temperament, but about what Dakin thought he might do about it. I carried on painting.

Peter was one of those remarkable teachers who, apparently by doing very little, change your life. I had never met anybody like him. He looked different to the other teachers, since he wore no gown, and was given to yellow knitted ties. In the manner of the period, he had style. He talked to us about art and artists and ideas, and by doing so implied that he took us seriously. For the first time in my life I felt included in an adult world. However, Peter's respect for his students involved a quid pro quo, which was that we were required to respect ourselves, and to demonstrate the fact by work. It was a condition of studying A level art that we went independently to life drawing classes in the evening at the College of Art. Peter knew that the effect would be not simply to improve our draughtsmanship, but also to accelerate our growing up. Female nudity proved to be surprisingly prosaic. Minutely observing the model in a life drawing class is a disappointing way to experience the naked female for the first time if, like most straight boys attending single sex schools in those days, you have constructed an unrealistically romantic image of the opposite sex.

Drawing at the College of Art also relieved Peter of much of the burden of teaching skills to pass exams, so that we could concentrate on working creatively in the time available at school. This required a knowledge of 19th and 20th century art history, and of the current avant-garde. *Studio International* and the *ICA Bulletin* arrived on the big tables every month – plenty of Bridget Riley and not a whiff of the Renaissance. I painted cool-coloured, eight-foot long, non-figurative reliefs that were exhibited, with the rest of the department's work, in the city art gallery. The annual London trip consisted of Peter leading us briskly down Bond Street, where we called at every private gallery. We never went near the National Gallery, though the Tate was within bounds, where we saw 'Sculpture in the 60s' – Kenneth Armitage, Elisabeth Frink, George Fullard and Geoffrey Clarke. These were Peter's contemporaries against whom he measured his own non-figurative sculpture, carved in polystyrene and cast in aluminium. We visited Willey's iron foundry in Exeter, to see how it was done in nineteenth-century darkness and the pervasive smell of hot sand from the casting frames.

The results of Peter's inspired but eccentric teaching were conflicted. I scraped a low A level pass grade, but had the portfolio and spoke the language that propelled me, without trying, into one of a very few university art departments of the period. He had revealed to me a world of which I had no conception until I met him, and which seemed marvellously attractive. However, pursuing it at Reading was another matter. We were taught, using the word loosely, by men and women only a little older than ourselves who, strictly on a part-time basis, dragged themselves out of London into what they made clear they regarded as an artistic desert.[8] They were in awe of Klee and the pedagogic sketchbook, of Kandinsky, and above all made frequent obeisance to their god, Marcel Duchamp. In tutorials, reclining uncomfortably in a Wassily chair, I stared blankly at Rita Donagh, girlfriend of Richard Hamilton, god's high priest on earth. Draped in limp black cloths, always with a smoking cigarette in her attenuated bony hand, she stared gauntly back between the half-closed curtains of her long straight hair – a neurotic mutation of the peek-a-boo girl. A distaste for trends and trendy people, and for pretentiousness, germinated and grew rapidly in the soil of her uncomprehending gaze. The place seemed to be inhabited entirely by such aliens until, for two weeks, I was taught by Terry Frost. Terry was a grown-up – direct, physical and demanding. I responded by working. He must have observed in class that even if I was a waste of time with a paintbrush I could use a screwdriver, and he asked me to help him hang an exhibition of his big red pictures in a gallery in town. We worked quietly for some hours, and it went well. Then he decided that he needed something from his studio, half a mile away. He turned to me, dug in his pockets to find his car keys, and threw them to me. Nothing was said, but that silent gesture of approval and trust still moves me.

Art history was totally disconnected from the studio world, but seemed equally irrelevant. Peter Thursby's teaching had not prepared me for the quattrocento portable altarpiece, Florence or Sienna. As with rugby at school, nobody bothered to explain the rules. It was not so much the assumption that we all came from cultivated homes and would therefore know those rules (and, probably, also Sienna) that made this teaching a disgrace, but the indifference of the staff to the fact that some of us, clearly, did not. Restoration of faith came at the end of the first year, at a lecture given to the whole arts faculty. At that time I had not heard of the speaker, but he won my full attention from the moment he strode onto the stage below me – tall and elegant, dressed in a grey suit. There was no lectern and he carried no notes, only a long pointer. There were two screens showing parallel images. Sir Anthony Blunt talked with extraordinary authority for well over an hour on the intricacies of Poussin. It was the year in which he published his *Critical Catalogue* of the painter's work. It was also two years after his confession to MI5 that he was a Russian spy, though that information would not be revealed to the public for over a decade. I remember nothing of what he said, but the way he said it left a permanent impression, and I have always tried to model my lecturing on the masterly performance he gave that day.

I failed my first year exams, and when I scraped through the retakes I was given a firm push towards typography, the art department dumping ground for reject painters. In desperation I asked the sculptor Chris Lane to come to my room, where in private I painted. The walls were covered with technically poor but intensely felt self-portraits. Chris invited me to join his sculpture department which, because I could make things, suited me. The technicians, one of whom I came to know as a friend, taught me the few useful things I learned at university – welding, plastics, and casting metals – but the teachers cared more for us too. In discussion with Chris, it emerged that I admired the work of Stanley Spencer. He asked me if I'd visited the Sandham Memorial Chapel at Burghclere. I'd never heard of it, and he told me I must go. I hired a car and map-read my way down miles of pre-motorway A roads and country lanes. When I arrived, I found a building that looked more like a waterworks than a chapel – a tall block in the middle with two low wings. I wandered up the red brick path towards a numberless clock face, mounted on a post. The single hand pointed to the left. At the almshouse I was given a heavy iron key. I walked over to the chapel, unlocked and pushed open the door, and *The Resurrection of the Soldiers* was revealed. The effect was overwhelming. It was my first experience of an interior entirely covered by pictures, and it confirmed my instinct – against all I was being taught – that narrative was essential for meaningful art. I have not changed my mind. The story concerned me – soldiers in hospital blues, like the photographs of my grandfather and his friends, the poems of Wilfred Owen, the Britten *War Requiem*. When I got back, Chris told me that soon after the Second World War, when he himself had been a student at Reading, Spencer had been invited to give a talk to the art club. The great man lived not far up the Thames, at Cookham. He arrived wearing a grubby mackintosh and carrying an umbrella. He hung the umbrella on a hat stand and without removing the mackintosh or waiting for an introduction, began to speak. Spencer was known to be a little strange, but it was not to confirm his reputation for eccentricity that Chris told me the story. The painter was nearing sixty by this time, and famous, but in the course of his talk he never once mentioned a painting that he had done in the past. The point was that he spoke only of what he was going to do.

Other than making painting and sculpture, or thinking about painting and sculpture, life consisted of a series of dysfunctional love affairs and occasional bouts of drunkenness, generally indulged at the instigation of my colleague, Carwyn Rogers. Unlike me, Carwyn was street wise and fully functional. At work, we both disliked the pretentions of the art world, an attitude that derived, I'm sure, from a sense of social dislocation that we shared. Though our backgrounds were different, it was, perhaps, the unrecognised basis of our relationship. Carwyn's other life was conducted through the medium of Welsh, which I would hear him speak on the telephone to his mother and father, and his lovely girlfriend, at home. He took me to stay there, at the social club in Upper Tumble, run by his parents. We drove down in his old Standard, past the blast furnaces at Port Talbot, which impressed me in the darkness much as, I imagine, Turner had been impressed by their eighteenth-century predecessors at Merthyr. It was an unknown and, to me, surreal world, an impression that was reinforced when we arrived at the club. The door opened to a wall of masculine sound, Welsh speaking and hard drinking, supervised by the only woman present, Carwyn's mother. The coal industry was not quite dead, though the local drift mine had closed and the work transferred to the deep pit at Cynheidre. Carwyn took me to the old pit to see the elements that he was reinventing in his sculpture – iron and steel, huge bolts and relics of suspended metal, broken and rusting drams. Carwyn had discovered the sculpture of David Smith, that showed him how to use what would now be called his industrial heritage. I thought perhaps he felt it justified to those at home what seemed to me to be an unusual choice of vocation for someone from his background – though I was greatly mistaken in making that assumption.

David Smith had recently died. He became crucially important to me also, though less for the work and more for the man, 'as delicate as Vivaldi and as strong as a Mack truck.'[9] His enormous energy was focussed through the work on the single passion to assert his identity – his absolute freedom to be David Smith, American, against the world:

You know who I am and what I stand for. I have no allegiance, but I stand, and I know what the challenge is, and I challenge everything and everybody. And I think that is what every artist

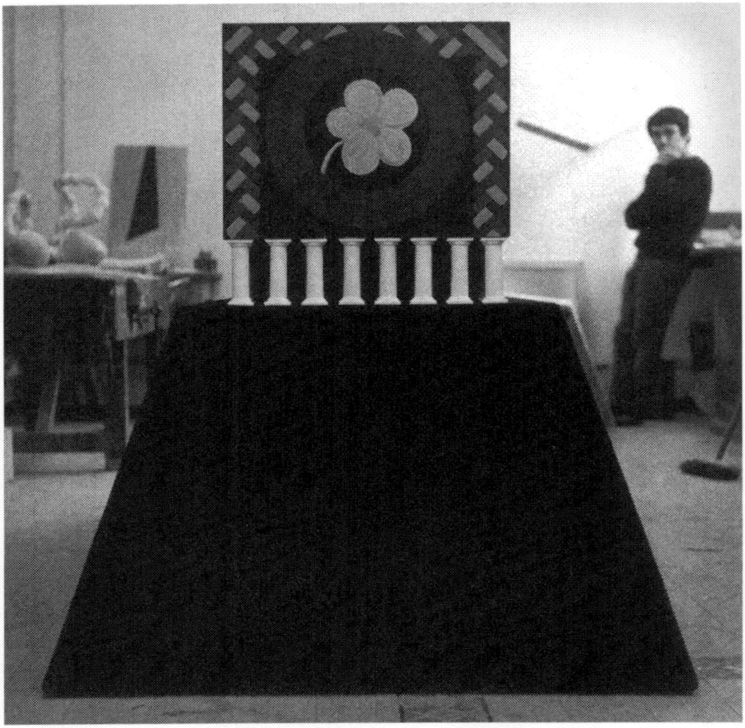

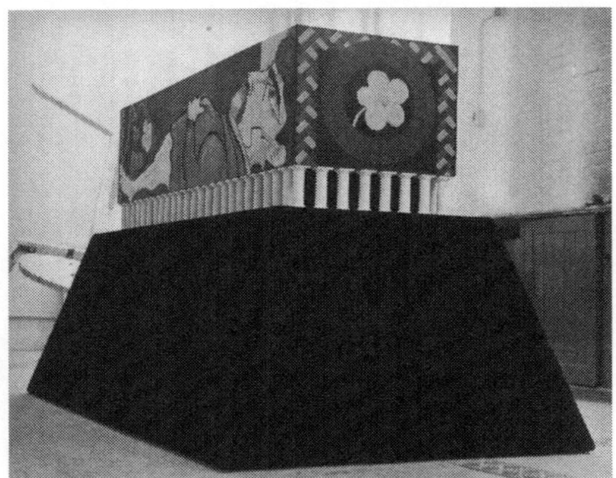

Peter Lord with sculpture,
Reading University, 1970
Philippa Beale

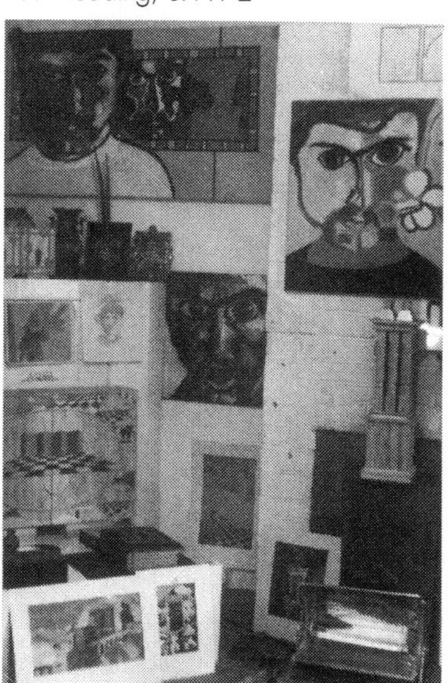

At home, Sonning Common
near Reading, *c.*1972

has to do. The minute
you show a work, you
challenge every other artist.
And you have to work very
hard, especially here. We
don't have the introduction
that European artists have.
We're challenging the
world … I'm going to work
to the best of my ability to
the day I die, challenging
what's given to me.[10]

I empathised with that. I needed to challenge everything and everybody that surrounded me in that benighted art school. 'It is identity, and not that overrated quality called ability, which determines the artist's finished work.'[11]

Inspired by Smith's ideas and passion, in the last eighteen months of my stay at the university my work assumed some coherence. I tried to discipline the paintings, working them to the same module as the sculpture, so as to bring the private and the public world together. The yellow self-portrait – out of Gaugin, Spencer and Smith – is the only survivor among the oil paintings. I had bought the jug for £2 in an antiques shop on London Street. It was my first collected thing, and spoke to me from the little shop window because of its blue enamelled bands. They evoked the blue and white enamel of the milk powder tins of the 40s and early 50s, and the certainties of early childhood.

I left the art school more confused than I had joined it. Departing students were interviewed by the Principal. It was the first time Claude Rogers had spoken to me since he had offered me a place there over four years previously. I was asked what I intended to do next. It seemed pretentious to say I wanted to be an artist, so I affected pragmatism and replied, 'Teach I suppose', though I had no desire whatever to do so. 'Yes', he replied, 'that's probably the best thing.' Then it was over. I've seldom been in an art school since.

4

The Little Girl on the Beach
(Jinx being thoughtful)

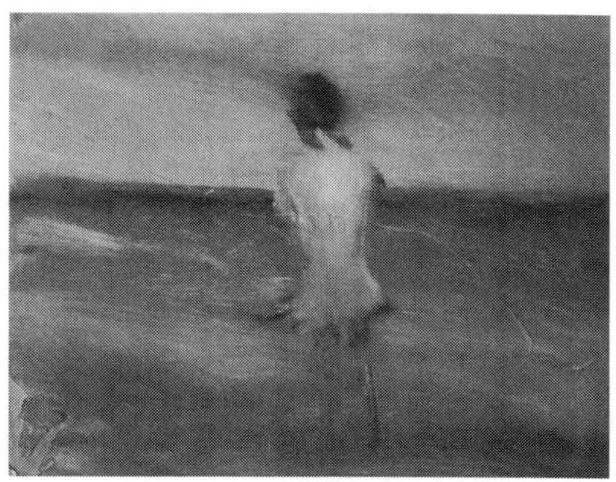

By 1973 I was teaching an art class for adults in the Wylye Valley in Wiltshire. During the first session, as I talked about what work we might do, my eye was drawn to two women, who sat together at the left of the front row. They seemed to be listening with unusual attention, weighing me up. I learned that their names were Eliza and Freda, and after class the second week I was invited to Eliza's home for tea. Topps was a large stone farmhouse in the village of Stockton. Many subsequent visits there introduced me to the world of the country landowner and those who surrounded him. Yet it was difficult to place Eliza herself, who seemed to be both deeply embedded in that community and uneasy. It occurred to me that she might belong with those liberal-minded but idiosyncratic individuals among the English upper class who now and again emerge to embarrass their peers. Eve Balfour came to mind. There were many chickens about the yard at Topps – appropriately independent-minded bantams.[12] In fact, though my thoughts were moving vaguely in the correct direction, they would need to travel much further. Eventually, it emerged that Eliza was the daughter of Sir William Nicholson, the Edwardian portrait painter. His exceptional technical facility and his personal charm had enabled him to move with ease in high society, but he did not belong to it by birth. His family background had been in manufacturing in the English Midlands. His ancestors were artisans – as indeed was he, by instinct – but like all successful painters from the eighteenth century onwards, he had gentrified himself to the degree necessary to earn a living. As a young artist in London he had associated with Augustus John, another social outsider, then in his bohemian phase. John was a product of the professional middle-class but, like Nicholson, would rise to attach himself to high society, albeit somewhat erratically, and eventually aspire to the status of country gent. Eliza told me that her mother, the painter Edith Nicholson, had once been groped by John in the back of a taxi, when leaving the Ritz. It was not an uncommon experience among the women of her circle in the period.

Eliza became my closest friend. We travelled together, and the most important journey for me was to Wales. It was still 1973, the year of Schumacher's *Small is Beautiful* and, though I didn't know it at the time, it was also the year in which Schumacher's teacher, Leopold Kohr, moved to live at Aberystwyth. His is the famous expression, quoted in the title of Schumacher's book. Smallness was on my mind. As a student, I had missed 1968, floundering in a morass of unhappy introspection and an aversion to following trends. On the left-most fringes, Gerry Healy, the demagogue leader of the Socialist Workers' Party[13] had intimidated me when I heard him speak, and humiliated me when I ventured to ask him a question. The angst of the period took me differently – in the direction not of smashing capitalism, but of opting out of it. At the first election in which I voted, my choice had been the candidate of the Wessex Independence Party. My unlikely mix of gurus included Kropotkin, Ned Ludd and John Seymour. I believed in ruralism and the no-growth economy. I had friends of the same inclination. They had recently left Reading for Trefenter, a scattering of houses and holdings on the sea-facing slope of Mynydd Bach, twelve miles from Aberystwyth. My partner and I visited them there and heard about an empty house down the lane from their own that we might buy. When we returned to England I told Eliza about the house, and she demanded to see it, immediately.

As Eliza and I set off together, my partner was hanging out the washing, before going to work. She had a proper job and so couldn't accompany us. There was a deep sense of parting. Eliza drove her swaying Renault 4 non-stop to the desolate house. It had been

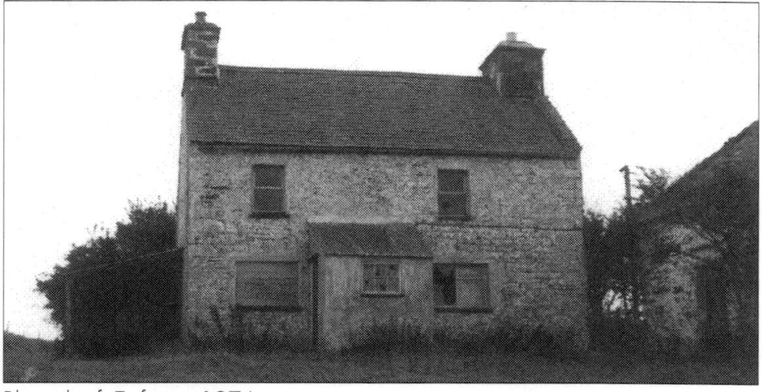

Blaenplwyf, Trefenter, 1974

empty for ten years. We climbed in through a half-boarded broken window, and in the gloom Eliza decided that I was going to live there. She designed the kitchen and we drove home. All the way back we talked. She told me a story about a holiday she had spent once at Maesycrugiau where, on a walk in the hills, she had seen two young men attending to their sheep. They were tall and blond, and she assumed they were brothers, though they spoke no English, so she couldn't say for sure. She told me that they were real Celts, not the short dark Iberians, such as myself, who came afterwards. She was repeating the received wisdom of her father's period – the Celticism of Matthew Arnold, no doubt transmitted to Nicholson by his friend Percival Graves. Near Bath, Eliza asked me to hold out my right hand, palm up. She put her left palm over it, not touching. I felt the buzz of the charge going between us in the very centre of my hand, like an electrified needle.

At Topps, Eliza's kitchen had a long semi-circular window extending round two sides of the room, with a padded bench below. There was a pale blue Aga, where she would stand and press down on the kettle, sliding it forwards and backwards because it boiled more quickly that way. One evening, in the kitchen after class, Eliza presented me with a brown paper bag. Inside were dozens of pieces of broken glass. It was the remains of a picture by the Australian painter Sidney Nolan. It had been smashed by Eliza's teenage daughter, Rosie, overflowing with anger at her mother and the world. Eliza had known that she must keep the pieces, though she didn't know why. She had swept them up, and put them in the bag. When we met, she decided that she had kept them for me. I was able to stick the pieces together, except in one corner, where I fitted and coloured a piece of paper. Two years later Rosie killed herself in London.

Letter from Sidney Nolan
to Edith Nicholson, 1954

Sidney Nolan was a friend of Eliza's. She had lived in Australia after the Second World War and met him when they travelled to England on the same ship in 1951. They remained in contact and, through Eliza, Nolan met Edith, her mother, who was known as Edie or 'E.D.'. Sid gave Edie the picture in 1954 as a thank you, after staying at her house. It came to Eliza on her mother's death, four years later. The subject is the artist's adopted daughter on a beach: 'Do have the little girl on the beach', he wrote, 'Jinx being thoughtful'. Jinx Nolan herself became a painter, and now lives in the United States. That the smashed picture was by Nolan, of all painters, was curious, but characteristic of the way my relationship with Eliza evolved. Nolan was one of the few painters I admired when I was a student. I chose a book of his pictures as a university prize in 1968. His reputation had been founded on the Ned Kelly paintings, and it was those that had attracted me. They are narrative pictures. I never met Nolan, but I stayed in his house on the Thames in south west London. In fact, there were two houses, side by side. Eliza had been asked to guard the valuables while he was away, and I joined her. I drew the view over the river, with the iron railway bridge. The basement of the house was stacked with huge, pristine primed canvasses, all of the same size, ready for paint. That anybody could afford to buy canvasses on that scale impressed me, but there was also the disturbing suspicion of mass production. Nolan was famous at that time. Upstairs, there was a collection of lacquered Chinese furniture, and a solitary small Welsh settle, which made me sad. I saw it as a child, standing naked at the centre of a circle of staring, elegantly dressed adults.

Nolan would live the last decade or so of his life in Wales, near Presteigne. Eliza had been born here, though on the other side of the country, near Harlech. In 1915, William Nicholson's first wife, the painter Mabel Pryde, rented Llys Bach, near Harlech, because friends – the Graves and the Wortleys – lived nearby. The Graves family had built a new house there before the war. Perceval Graves was Irish, and much involved with the Pan-Celtic League and fantasies of Celtic political union. In 1918, his son Robert married Nicholson's daughter Nancy, who would quickly bear him four children, before they parted company under the stress of her feminism, as he saw it: 'My love for Nancy made me respect her views. But male stupidity and callousness became such an obsession with her that she began to include me in her universal condemnation of men.'[14] The Wortley family rented the much grander house of Maes-y-Neuadd. After the death of her husband in 1917, Edith Wortley became involved with Nicholson's eldest son, Ben, who was promptly packed off to America. Then Prydie died, and William himself took up with Edie. Ben returned from America, and was again in the frame. William rapidly married Edie, and Eliza was born at Maes-y-Neuadd, where the Nicholsons were then also in residence. Eliza would remain in ignorance of this complicated familial evolution until quite late in life. She was alerted to the possible implications for her paternity only by an aside made in a lecture about her father that she attended in London. It would be necessary to consult the now reclusive Ben – immediately. Eliza hurried to Rosslyn Hill, and knocked on his door.

Eventually he appeared: 'What do you want?', he demanded. 'Am I yours or father's?' she enquired. There was a distinct hesitation. 'Father's', he replied. 'Thank you.' The conversation was over.

William Nicholson had settled his family at Sutton Veny in Wiltshire, in an ancient manor house. While her father and mother painted, Eliza grew up there in the company of two Welsh-speaking female servants, who had come with the family from Harlech. Outside she heard other Welsh voices – unemployed men from the valleys, singing as they tramped east through the village to find work during the Depression. Inside, the great and the good came to be painted. William Nicholson loved paint – the stuff itself. He would salivate as he worked, producing marvellously sensual images of the most mundane of objects – a lustre jug, red boots. Ben would visit with his entourage, despite the earlier difficulties, and there would be fun – constant punning and games – but even so, he could be a little odd. After one visit, when the family repossessed the east wing that Ben had taken over with his wife, Winifred, and their young children, they found all the furniture painted white – mahogany chairs, tables, everything.

By the time I came to know her, and to hear these stories for the first time, Eliza's unease in Stockton was about to be expressed through a complete change in her way of life. She parted company with her husband and disposed of almost all her worldly goods. They were auctioned in a marquee on the lawn at Topps. Eliza sold everything except the art work of her mother and father, and bought a flat up two flights of stairs in an innocuous terrace off the Finchley Road in London. I have visited her there often. Eliza is wonderful to be with in London, because she knows the place by instinct. Her deep familiarity with it derives from having wandered the streets with her father when she was a child, and from listening to his talk. His reputation as an artist had been established through his co-operation in making woodcut engravings with his brother-in-law, James Pryde. They were the 'Beggarstaff Brothers'. Among the most famous of Nicholson's own woodcuts had been the *London Types* – portraits of the common people, barmaids, costers, news boys – published by Heinemann in 1898. After the Second World War London never felt quite right to Eliza. The smell of horse dung had gone from the streets.

Like William Nicholson, as I imagine him, Eliza has no snobbery. She took me to the Royal Academy where, during her father's retrospective exhibition, she was treated like royalty, but also we went to social housing in Camden, where lived her African companion. Sunshine Ogunde was of uncertain age, earned a little money as a drummer, but mostly survived on state benefits. Eliza would secure the importation of his young wife and children from Nigeria. Eliza's relationships with the many African people whom she came to know in her new life in London, had deep origins. In his memoir, *Goodbye to All That*, Robert Graves reported that a friend had warned him against marrying Nancy by 'hinting, very unkindly that there was Negro blood in the Nicholson family.' I suspect that Eliza rather hoped it was true.[15] One of her ancestors had made a great deal of money mining gold in South Africa, and she was repaying the debt incurred by the human exploitation it had involved. Eliza also became involved with the Caribbean community. At the side of a private swimming pool in the Wylye Valley, the property of the owner of a vast estate, she introduced me to Aubrey Williams, unknown to me at the time. Eliza had obtained a commission for him to paint a mural of exotic fish. I liked Aubrey, though not the mural – a job, I imagine, that had to be done.

When I first knew it, Eliza's flat in north London had two living rooms, a tiny kitchen and a bathroom with a smelly and explosive gas boiler that delivered a trickle of boiling water into the scratchy bath. She studied traditional Chinese acupuncture, and turned one of her two living spaces into a consultation room. It is the most peaceful room I've ever known. One day I arrived in an agitated state, and Eliza decided that I needed treatment. I lay face down on the table as she placed the needles in my back. Four hours later I awoke to the beautiful yellowness of the room, the sun, and the lovely still life of a vase of flowers, painted by Edie, that always hung there. Edie had framed it in what was originally curly Victorian gilt, but she had painted it white, leaving just a little gold at the edges. I lay still and looked. On the mantelpiece was *The Expulsion from the Garden of Eden*, a fancy French ceramic that I contrasted in my mind with a simple English slipware jug, depicting Eve taking the apple, that had been Grannie Horner's.

One day Eliza telephoned from London to say that she wanted to travel. Within a week we were in Turkey. Years earlier, she had lived in Ankara with her husband, who was naval attaché at the British Embassy. I panicked in Istanbul, and wanted to go home – cities intimidate me – but after we crossed the Bosphorus, unlike my grandfather, half a century before, I enjoyed myself. We travelled from place to place in minibuses with the local people. We stayed a bit at Bursa, an industrial town where they made motor car tyres. A young man, who wanted to practice his English, offered to be our Cicerone. He took us to Mount Olympus, which we ascended in a cable car. The only other passengers were a party of orthodox Jews, who unbalanced the car by huddling together in one corner. They stood with their arms around each other's shoulders and chanted. I presume they were praying for deliverance. We descended the mountain on foot.

We ended our journey at Izmir. At that time I was in love. The woman in question seemed to me to be sending ambiguous messages about her feelings, though I suppose I was simply unwilling to recognise them for what they were. I talked about her endlessly to poor Eliza. In the early evening, we sat outside at a restaurant table on the waterfront. She lost patience with me, half turned and pointed to a dim shape on the horizon. 'Do you know what that is?' she asked. 'No', I replied. 'It's Lesbos', she informed me. So I wandered off on my own into the old town on the steep hill above the bay. Shuffling towards me I met a conical decorated Christmas tree – a kind of Shaman figure. I could see nothing of him (I presumed it was a man) but dozens and dozens of tiny packets – spices, perhaps – which I took to be his wares. Then came the remnant of a camel train – two animals. It was followed by some excited children, who seemed to regard it with as much curiosity as I did. We followed it into a cul de sac, where a few people came out to buy. At the head of the cul de sac was a house with a balcony. The doors to the interior were open and because the road led down from where I stood I could see inside. On a colour television set, a family was watching the World Cup. I'm not in the habit of carrying a camera, because photographs ruin memory, and so the impression – the television above and the camels below – remains first hand, and vivid.

Eliza has sent me back my letters, forty years of them. It's the paring down of old age, preparing to move on, as she would see it, without encumbrance, as she arrived. I can't read them, but I'll probably keep them for now, though I too have begun to feel the first stirrings of that need to divest myself of the encumbrance of unnecessary things, and to retreat to the freedom of essentials.

5

Twm Penllwynbedw

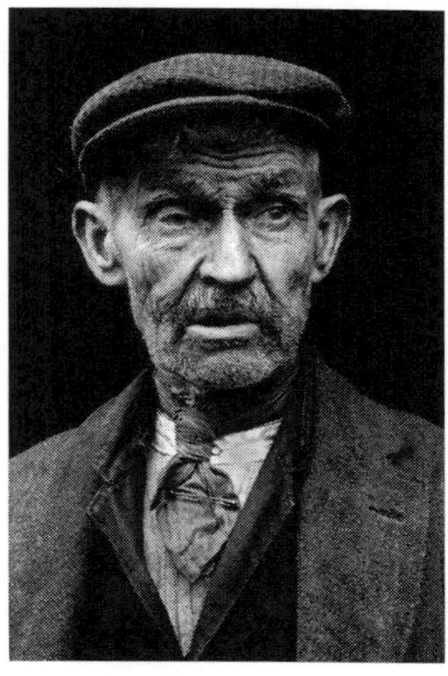

The portrait of Twm Penllwynbedw hangs on the wooden *palis* that divides the stairs from the parlour in the middle of my house. The *palis* is the characteristic room divider in the small Victorian houses of this part of Wales, though the wood is often hidden beneath the layers of flowery wallpaper that denoted aspirations to modernity in the 1950s. I was never inside it, but I know that the rooms in Penllwynbedw itself would have been divided in this way, and Twm's house was similar to mine from the outside also. It was built of dark grey stone, with yellow brick lintels over the sash windows and front door – two windows above and two below, but unevenly distributed because of the kitchen fireplace with the big chimney at one end. Penllwynbedw stood at the side of the narrow road leading up Mynydd Bach from Llangwyryfon, just before the breast of the last rise where Trefenter begins. In 1974, when I first lived there, in a caravan, I used to drive home that way, so I passed Twm's house often. It stood above the road, and from the bank in front of it a trickle of water emerged into a metal basin. Twm lived on his own. Once a week he walked down the hill to the post office in Llangwyryfon to collect his pension. His neckerchief, held to his collarless shirt by a safety pin, was red. His walk was unusually erect – despite his deeply lined face, in old age he was not bent from rheumatism or arthritis, or from childhood rickets, like so many others of his generation. I only ever exchanged a few words with him, and in Welsh, but the little English he had was described to me by someone who heard him speak it in the post office as 'very Victorian'.

Some years after I left Trefenter I heard that knockers had stopped with their van at Penllwynbedw. They asked Twm for water, and in the time it took him to go to the back of the house to fetch it they had manoeuvred a piece of furniture half out of the front door. They were interrupted by a neighbour who happened to be passing. When I heard this story I felt deeply angry, but the truth is that much of the intensity of that anger sprang from my own guilt, because every day that I lived in Trefenter I felt that I was just as much an intruder and a thief as they were. I felt it from the first day, when I arrived to begin work on the empty house that my partner and I had bought. The clouds were down and the fields and buildings were enveloped in drenching drizzle. Standing on the top of the bank beside the track that led down to the house was a figure with a sack over his shoulders, as grey as the rain. He had his back to me as he bent to mend the rusty remnant of a fence, and he didn't turn or speak as I passed. He seemed utterly foreign – but I knew, even as I experienced this alienation, that I was the foreigner, trespassing in this man's place.

Of course, I can't be sure what was in the mind of the man mending the fence. Dai Tŷ'n Ddraenen's thoughts may have been entirely benign. He may have been mending the fence in the spirit of Robert Frost mending wall – though I doubt it. Dai's farm was not far up the road from Penllwynbedw. Between the two was a wooden-clad chalet called Maes-yr-haf, where an elderly and unhealthy-looking couple from the English Midlands lived an unsmiling life. In the pub one day, he got to talking about them. 'They crawled here to die', he observed.

Twm Penllwynbedw was a survivor from another age, though I imagine he was an Edwardian rather than a Victorian. It makes little difference, because neither word accurately evokes his past. Both conjure up ways of being that were unambiguously English. Rural Wales was anything but unambiguous. It was home to a culture facing two ways, looking deeply inward into a tradition divergent from that of England, yet not only bound tightly to that country but, through Empire, connected to the world beyond. It stood both close to and yet far from what 'Victorian' and 'Edwardian' evoke. Had I ever gone inside Penllwynbedw, it would not have surprised me to find Queen Victoria jubilee jugs hanging on Twm's dresser, just as they hung in Grannie Horner's kitchen in Devon. Yet, when Twm grew up before the Great War, to an impartial observer Trefenter might have seemed closer to a village in rural India than to England, with poverty stricken subsistence farms, high infant mortality and some of the worst adult death rates in Europe from tuberculosis. Many of the common people spoke only their own language, and they practiced a distinct and socially demanding religion. Perhaps inwardly Twm's parents would have regarded Queen Victoria from a distance not much less than that which separated my father's Indian *ayah* and her people from the Empress. On the other hand, through sons who had moved away to work in the pits of the urban south, or further afield to the United States or Canada – unconscious imperialists in their way – the perceptions of the people of Mynydd Bach may have been more closely akin to those of the common soldiers of the army, on whom the *ayah* and the *dhobiwala* waited in India. I don't know, because by the 1970s, opportunities for an outsider to gain insights into the state of mind of people of Twm's generation were rare.

Mr Davies was a near contemporary of Twm's, though a very different man, who was as connected to the present through his children as he was to the past through his memory. He had walked up the lane from his farm to see me. One of Mrs Davies's butter hands had broken, and he required me to make a replacement. The work he gave me provided the opportunity for him to tell me a few things that, clearly, he felt I needed to know. Like most of his contemporaries, when Mr Davies was first sent to school he had no English. The teacher would speak no Welsh to him. When he needed to go to the toilet, the teacher insisted that he ask in English. He could not, and he was forced to sit at his desk until he pissed in his pants. I know now that the indignity he suffered was not unusual, but I did not know it in 1975, and I heard of it then not in a history lesson or on a television programme but from a man to whom it had happened, and who had not forgiven the humiliation of it, nearly seventy years later.

On Mynydd Bach folk memory was still a reality. I heard about Rhyfel y Sais Bach – the violent resistance mounted in the early nineteenth century to the enclosure of the common by an English incomer. With an irony that was at first lost on me, the house I was making habitable stood on Lôn Sais. It was 'Englishman's Road', constructed by the Sais Bach to avoid the necessity of passing the houses of the local people when getting to and from Aberystwyth or Cardigan, from where the militia could be called. A few years later Jeremy Hooker wrote a poem for radio about it. 'Englishman's Road' had become his road, the central metaphor in a poem about alienation:

> For this is settled country, its pattern absorbent, deeply engrained,
> but unfinished; without the finality of a coiled fossil, though it
> too is a life wrought in rock. And here these English words play
> on a surface through which they cannot shine, to illumine its
> heart; they can possess the essence of this place no more than
> the narrow road under the Welsh mountain can translate its name.
>
> > Lôn Sais it is called,
> > Not Englishman's Road.

Jeremy lived not far from Twm Penllwynbedw. We became friends at this time. [16]

Jeremy also wrote a poem about Cwrdd y Mynydd – the open air prayer meetings that were held annually on the mountain in the wake of the 1904 revival. Twm Penllwynbedw might well have attended them in their heyday. I had heard that the revival tradition continued, though in chapel and on a reduced scale. One day, as I walked down the lane towards Bethel, I heard many voices singing hymns. I realised that it was Cwrdd y Mynydd. I turned the corner – and met a man in a shiny suit carrying a tape recorder and a loudspeaker. His straggle of half a dozen followers milled around outside the decaying chapel and the chapel house, which was occupied by an English dealer in bric-a-brac. It was a pathetic sight, though the pathos was far deeper than

I could have imagined in my ignorance at the time. A few years ago I heard that the revival had itself subsequently been revived. I suppose that the promoters of the event would suggest that it was a marker of the distinctness both of the local and of the national culture. That would be true, but unfortunately it seems to me that what is most marked in reviving the poisonous myth of Welsh religiosity is the self-righteous complacency and political servility that characterised much of the Nonconformism of the late nineteenth century.

Beyond the chapel was Mrs Jenkins's farm where, every day, I had milk and bizarre conversation. Things began well enough, when all I was capable of in Welsh were benign pleasantries. However, as it became apparent to Mrs Jenkins that I wished to learn well, she turned to English. For months, we conducted conversations in which she would refuse to speak her language to me, and I would refuse to speak mine to her. It was not that Mrs Jenkins was embarrassed by my speaking learners' Welsh to her, but that she resented the intrusion of it. She would not surrender the final bastion of communal privacy that the language afforded against outsiders. Whether the language ultimately lived or died was not the issue for Mrs Jenkins. In the 1970s the country was being ransacked – dressers, settles, tables, jugs flowed out to English dealers and American customers. Farm sales became a spectator sport all over the area. The farm houses became holiday homes for middle-class English speakers. The privacy of the language was the last thing, and the only thing, that could not be bought.

Radicals among the intellectual community took a different view. For them, it was necessary to challenge the erosion of the language. It was the carrier of their sense of self, the symbol of Welsh nationhood, and a thing of beauty in the world. The pragmatists among them concluded that not sharing the language would only hasten the execution of its death sentence. It was these people who invited me inside, a gesture for which I am deeply grateful. But some remained driven primarily by the intensity of the pain of dislocation in their own place. In their heads, they might have acknowledged the necessity of widening the use of the language as a part of a sensible programme to resist decline, but in their hearts, like Mrs Jenkins, they resented sharing it. At a party in Aberystwyth I was told by an angry student from the university to fuck off back to England – though I was told in Welsh, since I spoke the language fluently by that time. The issue seemed simple to her. English inward migration caused language change. Remove the immigrants and it would be possible to pick up the broken thread of the past and reconnect it to a different present and future. She was a daughter of Mr Davies, and I agreed with her.

In fact, the crisis of language change was far more complicated than that. It was an unsettled sea in which local and trans-national currents washed through each other. Among them was social class. A little up the road from Penllwynbedw, past Maes-yr-haf and the turn down to the chapel and the farm, was Waungron, the back door of which had been my point of entry to this place. It was the house that had been bought by my friend from England. He had come to the university in Aberystwyth to develop a computer department. He was a thoughtful man whom I liked, but the bad feelings about myself that I experienced when I considered the position of people such as Twm Penllwynbedw were intensified, not ameliorated, in his house – and especially in the presence of his partner. She combined period feminism with back to the earth aspirations that focussed on an obstinate goat. I was in agreement with her on both issues, and yet I disliked her as much as I did the goat. Her beliefs had been developed in England, in a middle-class urban community, but in the classic manner of the colonist, she chose to live in denial of questions arising when she attempted to apply those beliefs in another place. In particular, whose earth was it, to which she was returning? She had imagined virgin territory in Wales, but found it settled by a deeply rooted and introspective common people. She became one of the many immigrants in the period who congealed into a defensive sub-community, disoriented by the unforseen consequences of the life-style choices that they had made for themselves. Economically stranded, the language symbolised their alienation and many of them focussed their resentment upon it.

Nevertheless, this outpost of the English middle class was not entirely isolated. Eventually, Mrs Jenkins had relented, and she began to talk to me in Welsh. Inside the language she said things that she would not otherwise have said. Her attitude to Professor Gwyn Williams was particularly revealing. The distinguished literary professor had lived a few years in Trefenter in the early 1950s, then worked much of his adult life abroad, at universities in Libya and Turkey. In 1969 he had retired to a house called Trewithan, which looked down on Mrs Jenkins's farm from the hill above, and the symbolic content of this topographical relationship was not lost on her. From Mrs Jenkins's point of view, it was definitely a case of the peasant and the squire. Her resentment was expressed to me mostly in condemnation of his morals – the fact that he had left his wife and taken up with an English woman younger than his son, and produced a second family – though, clearly, there was more to it than that. She couldn't abide him, and I presume her distaste was rooted in old enmities to which I was not privy.[17]

I had seen though never met Professor Williams, but in the light of Mrs Jenkins's hostility towards him I began to make enquiries. It transpired that my acquaintances in the settler community, including Jeremy Hooker and those at Waungron, knew him well. They had not chosen to tell me that they all regularly attended the meetings of the 'Graduandi', a society for university graduates, of which Professor Williams and members of another elevated Welsh-speaking family were the central pillars. It seemed that I was the only person in the area with a university degree who was not invited to Graduandi. Mrs Jenkins had no university degree, but we did have in common our exclusion from this network of what appeared to both of us to be pretentious intellectuals, for whom social class trumped language.

No doubt the prosperous but unsmiling Professor Williams, who had several times passed me on the road, associated me with a third community in competition for occupation of Trefenter. At that time I wore a full beard and dressed always in tee shirt and jeans. If the professor noticed me at all, I imagine that he placed me among the fluid population of Tŷ Newydd, the centre of the local hippy culture. In fact, the hippies were a largely unintrusive background presence in my life, and I had little to do with them. Privacy was among the chief attractions to them of living in Trefenter, since it was crucial to their pursuit of the drug culture of the period. They were blessed with a plentiful local supply of hallucinogens, until Operation Julie resulted in the arrest of Richard Kemp at his home in Tregaron, the source of 90% of the LSD on the British market. However, naturally occurring and free substitutes were available in the form of mushrooms. I first became aware of them following an enquiry, made to a street-wise friend, about a sighting of the usually nocturnal occupants of Tŷ Newydd minutely examining the field in front of the house. I had never sampled an illegal substance. The level of my ignorance of such matters was remarkable for a person who had spent four years in an art school in the 1960s. This missing element of my life experience owed far more to an aversion to fashion than to morality, but whatever the cause, drugs had passed me by. Late one afternoon, there was a knock at the door. I opened it and beheld a dishevelled, John the Baptist, individual. He asked me if I had any grass. This seemed an odd way to describe a field, but assuming he had sheep to tack, or a pony to feed, I responded in a positive spirit and referred him to an organic farm run by a friend a few miles away. He looked puzzled, but left quietly.

It was at about this time, in 1977 – the year of the Julie bust – that I met the photographer Marian Delyth. We soon became friends. Marian was still a student and was working with the added insecurity of one whose chosen field was only beginning to be taken seriously by the art establishment. It was just six years since the first gallery devoted to showing photography, the Photographers' Gallery, had opened in London. Marian has told me that, for her, the initial value of our friendship was the confidence she gained from being taken seriously by a person whom she perceived to be an established artist. For my part, equality was also the crucial characteristic of our friendship, though in a different context. Marian accepted my presence. She spoke in Welsh to me from the beginning, and her confidence in me enabled me to feel at ease inside the language. Marian gave me a space in which I could develop, and she helped to provide the materials with which to inform that development.

Marian photographed Twm Penllwynbedw as a part of her documentation of the settled community of Mynydd Bach, undertaken for her post-graduate degree at Birmingham. She was not a part of the community, but as a Welsh speaker she was welcomed into it in a way that English-speaking incomers were not. She had trained at Newport

College of Art, though as a graphic designer rather than within the radical documentary photography school established there by David Hurn. Marian's decision to train in graphics had been motivated by a prescient sense that specialisation in that field would enable her to stay in Wales and earn a living, as the publishing industry developed. Nevertheless, proximity to Hurn's ideas and the opportunity to attend lectures by Don McCullin and other distinguished figures clearly encouraged her developing interest in the concept of documentary photography. The interaction between documentation (involving the idea of dispassionate or objective observation) and 'committed' or 'creative' photography would become a feature of her work as it developed, and the seeds of her concern with the elusive distinction were sown in the Mynydd Bach project.

Marian set two parameters for her project. Her first could be described, in one sense, as dispassionate, in that she chose to work within a single square mile, imposed on the map, rather than to explore an area the boundaries of which were defined by its sociological or topographical coherence. Nevertheless, she derived her concept from the writing of D.J. Williams, and in Welsh, D.J.'s phrase, *y filltir sgwâr*, has an emotional resonance far deeper than the cold measure evoked by the English words. The expression suggests not the measured square mile, but the networks of relationships among the people that create the identity of a rural community. Marian's second criterion was to record the lives only of the Welsh-speaking people within the *milltir sgwâr*. This was certainly not a dispassionate choice, though at the time it would not have been recognised as undermining objectivity as a defining axiom of documentary photography. The historical and contemporary research undertaken by Marian to inform her work clearly revealed the

Marian Delyth, *Mamgu yn Cae Sgwâr*,
2010. © Marian Delyth

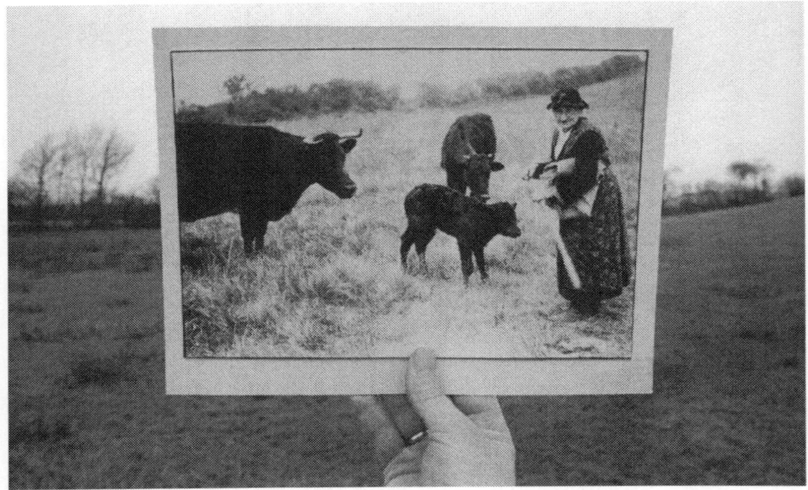

centrality of social crisis to the visual narrative – her vocabulary was of 'decline', 'dereliction', 'exodus' and 'scars', and the responses of local people indicated that inward migration was identified by them as the primary cause. Nevertheless, Marian's visual record did not extend to the pressurising communities, since the relationship of the people to the land and threatened patterns of agriculture seemed to her to be the deeper issues. The work resonated with that of Walker Evans made among the sharecropper families of the southern United States in the 1930s.

Clearly, in creating a visual record of a threatened community, consent was particularly important. In this respect, Marian's portrait of Twm Penllwynbedw was exceptional. The only strategy Marian could employ to obtain a photograph of this shy and reclusive man was to surprise him. It was not her usual way, and she felt guilty about it, since it seemed inconsistent with the respect for the community from which her work as a whole derived.

As a result of our friendship, subsequently Marian and I shared the experience of some of the intense situations and incidents that characterised the polarised cultural politics of the 1980s, both in an institutional and in a private context.[18] Part of the work that we were able to contribute was documentary – in my case, historical documentation of the visual culture, and in hers, photographic documentation of the political activism of others. Nevertheless, in 1993 the opportunity arose for us to act directly ourselves. I was spending much of my time in the National Library, researching documents relating to visual culture. Meredydd Evans came to the table where I was working. He wanted to discuss a campaign to resist the Welsh Language Bill, that had been introduced in the London parliament. The bill had been long awaited, in the hope that it would accede to the demand to grant the language official status in Wales. This it failed to do, whatever the protestations to the contrary of its supporters, including leaders of Plaid Cymru. Mered proposed direct action to make it clear that the creation of the Welsh Language Board was no substitute for official status. It was not to be a protest by student members of Cymdeithas yr Iaith, but independent action by established public figures. However, Mered had experienced difficulty in finding academics and intellectuals who were prepared to demonstrate their feelings on the matter by direct action. He invited me to join him. I saw that my immediate acceptance surprised him, but my perception of his invitation was that I was being honoured. I only wish I had been asked to participate in such actions years before. Among the others who had accepted was Marian. Eventually, seven of us, led by Mered, decided that we should break into the Court House in Carmarthen and cause symbolic damage there in order to draw attention to the failure of the language bill to assure the civil rights of Welsh speakers.

In the early hours of the morning, we approached the Court House on foot. One of the group had chosen to wear sling back shoes, apparently shod with heels of steel. They generated a succession of gun shots which echoed through the deserted streets in the middle of the town. An element of farce seems to be characteristic of the direct actions of intellectuals in pursuit of political change. The damp matches of Penyberth in 1936 came into my mind. As we approached the back of the building down a narrow lane, from the other side of a very high wall came the noise of two accomplices preparing our way by breaking open a back door. As their frustration at the door's resistance increased, so did the level of noise. It seemed inevitable that a policeman would hear us. Marian and I were positioned as look-outs, opposite the entrance to the lane. Eventually silence descended, but in the lane nobody was moving. The attempt to break in had failed. I was called over to assist. I climbed the wall and added my weight to the pressure on the door. The wood splintered and the three of us fell into the building. The accomplices escaped by the front door, allowing the rest of the party inside. I ran up the staircase to the silent court, and on entering at a low level, below the judge's dais, felt the intimidation that it was intended the common people should feel under the law. Portraits formed a prominent part of the display of authority. Thomas Brigstocke's large and imposing *General Nott* caught my eye as I found my way to the judge's chair and applied the Stanley knife to its upholstery. The intended gravitas of the moment was punctured as easily as the beautiful red leather of the chair, which proved to be flimsy plastic. I sensed a metaphor, though in my excitement I couldn't decide for what. By this time, in the manner of Martin Luther, the owner of the sling backs was nailing our statement to the woodwork in front of the bench. Someone telephoned the police, and we settled to await their arrival. This took a while, as we'd locked the door behind us and they couldn't get in. Eventually, the caretaker was brought from his bed with a key, and we were arrested.

By the time Marian and I entered the police van, Mered was already in animated conversation about various acquaintances he shared with one of the policemen who, like most of his colleagues, was a Welsh-speaker. Mered's conversation, and sometimes singing, would continue for most of the twenty-four hours in which we were locked in the filthy, blood-spattered cells of the police station. The experience was deeply revealing. Apart from the taking of statements, absolutely nothing happened. The reason for the delay was clear. Consultations were underway at a political level about what to do with us. In the event, the decision was to do the very minimum. We were released, but the manner in which that happened manifested the complexity of the issues in the confused nation that we are. As we left the police station, the door was opened for us by the inspector on duty, who shook each of us by the hand and congratulated us on our action.

The situation was adroitly handled by the political establishment, through its influence on the press. Our action received almost no publicity whatsoever. The only broadcast notice of it was a brief reference in the Welsh-language radio news, which attributed it to Cymdeithas yr Iaith, the Welsh Language Society. In the atmosphere of the time, in which news of Cymdeithas actions was commonplace, that was sufficient to condemn the protest to instant obscurity. In due course we were charged with criminal damage and sent for trial at the new Swansea Crown Court. I believe it was the first case heard there in the Welsh language. The public gallery was packed with supporters, and the atmosphere was intense. The enclosed and artificially lit space created a world in which the norms of every day life were suspended. I could maintain no objectivity in my experience of it. Since the facts of the case were undisputed, the proceedings were entirely focussed on the judgement. It was more than equal to the occasion. After fining us a token amount, the judge concluded his statement by noting that the damage done to the chair at Carmarthen was as nothing compared to the damage done to the Welsh language over centuries by the power that it symbolised. He rose, and the gallery sang the National Anthem.

As we moved out through the courtroom doors harsh daylight burned away the world of the previous few hours. We filed slowly between a crowd of the next defendants and their supporters, who stared at us as if we were the inhabitants of a foreign country, marked out by our language and class. I knew instantly that their world was real, and ours was a fantasy. The Carmarthen protest was completely ineffective but, considered in retrospect, it was not without significance. It marked the lame end of a troubled era. A fire had been successfully extinguished. Sadly, since then, though there have been occasional puffs of smoke, there have been no flames. Yet it would be wrong to give the impression that I think about it in a negative way. Though it was difficult, it was an exciting time and place to be. Marian Delyth's portrait of Twm Penllwynbedw evokes the confusion and tension of that period, in which his world came to an end and mine began. The picture represents how it became possible for me to stay. I'm glad that I met him.

Chwalfa

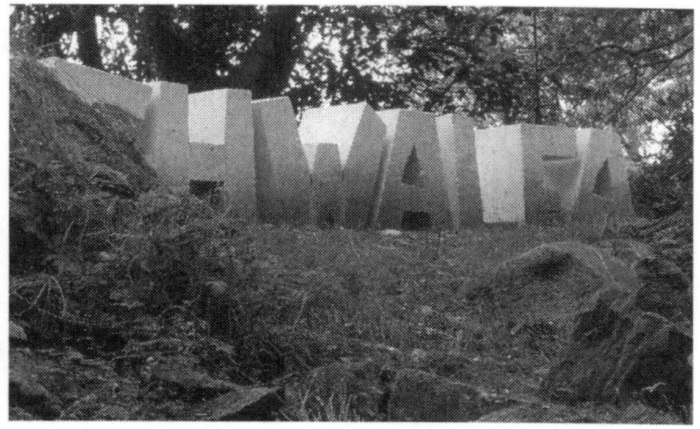

The year 1981 ended badly. During the summer, waiting in sweltering heat in Cheltenham bus station for a connection to London, I had met a French woman who lived in Southern Ohio. She said to call her if ever I went to America. So, a few months later, I did. It was my first visit there. I'd been on the ground at JFK five minutes when my wallet was lifted from my pocket. The theft set the tone for the relationship, which was conducted in an octagonal log cabin of the woman's own construction, during the worst blizzards for years. It reached 40° below freezing and I was stuck. So was she. Eventually the weather lifted enough to get back to New York and I caught the last flight out on Christmas Eve – Laker Airways – to London. The snow had travelled in the same direction. Wales was closed, so I went to my parents' house near Exeter to await the thaw, which was a long time coming. When I was able to return to the holiday cottage on Mynydd Bach in which I had been living temporarily, the pipes had burst and much of my art work had been ruined by water. The house was uninhabitable. I was taken in by friends, but there was nowhere to go next – I had no money, and my work seemed irrelevant to the things that I had come to care about, as well as second rate. I decided to try to live in Exeter, and gave myself a trial period of six months. I left Wales on 1 March. I loaded a van with what survived of my property, and drove off. For the first hour of the journey tears flowed down my face. In Exeter I went to live with my aunt Audrey, and found a studio above that of the ceramicist Laurel Keeley. Everywhere and everything was deeply familiar, but I knew no-one – I moved about inside an echoing shell. Although I loved the place, I had left it, and I couldn't re-enter its life.

A letter arrived from the Welsh Arts Council. It was a design brief for a competition to build a public memorial in Whitland, Carmarthenshire. I remember taking it from the envelope – it was printed as a faux blue-print. The memorial was to celebrate a tradition that in the tenth century Welsh law was codified by Hywel Dda, king of most of Wales, at a place called Hendy Gwyn ar Daf, the Welsh name from which Whitland derives. I knew immediately I was going to get the job – I had no doubt about it. Among the surviving copies of the law of Hywel Dda was a mid-thirteenth-century illuminated manuscript called Peniarth 28, held in the National Library of Wales. I drove to Aberystwyth and went to the Library. In those days, a first visit there was intimidating. The building was reminiscent of the Reichstag, and the door was guarded by porters dressed in black uniforms with officer hats. However, this first impression proved misleading. I asked if I could see the manuscript. Someone directed me to a table in a temporary room – the Manuscript Department was being refitted – and the small bound volume was deposited without fuss in front of me. This was normal practice in that happy era before the imposition of the curatorial fetish of the white gloves – or, indeed, in the case of a relic as important as Peniarth 28, the era of complete denial of public access. Today, I would not be allowed anywhere near the manuscript, yet the experience of handling it at the start of the memorial project was crucial. I remember clearly opening the volume at one of the many illuminated pages and being astonished by the freshness of the colours in the drawings. It seemed impossible that it was old, never mind seven hundred years old. It was intensely moving to hold such a thing in my hands. Ordinary members of the public, of whom I was one on that day, are now often denied the experience of contact with the relics of our heritage, including artefacts that are not rare or fragile – artefacts that are our property and not that of the curators and conservation officers who meanly appropriate them as vehicles for the expression of personal and professional power in some institutions. The inspiration that direct contact provides can deeply enrich writing and making that is concerned with the expression of cultural identity. The electronic media that nowadays mediate the experience of the artefact degrade and dehumanise our perception of the reality of the past, as also they do of the present.

After the Library, on the way back to Exeter, I visited the site at Whitland, which was less inspiring. Work had begun already, and a massive straight stone wall was under construction. It bisected the flattened rubble of the buildings that had previously stood there. I started to draw and to write – but mainly to write. On 1 September, six months to the day after leaving, I drove back to Wales to live.

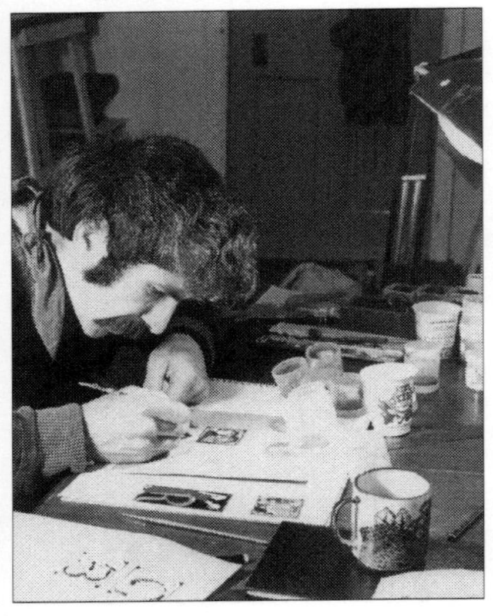

Marian Delyth, *Peter Lord making enamels at the Barn Centre, Aberystwyth*, 1984. © Marian Delyth

I was not at the selection meeting for the Whitland project, and the process by which my proposal was chosen was described to me much later. Present were representatives of the Welsh Arts Council and Carmarthen District Council, and members of the committee of local people who would be the commissioning body. They inspected several well presented sets of drawings, some made by sculptors with an established reputation. My proposal was contained in an unprepossessing A4 ring binder and was scarcely noticed at first. However, it gradually attracted the attention of the committee because it was the only submission that presented a narrative of the event which the memorial was intended to celebrate. The text and illuminations in Peniarth 28 had provided the design idea for much of the artwork, taking the form of calligraphy, champlevé enamel plaques and brick mosaic pavements, which were to be located within a series of gardens. I was told that the local members of the group came to feel that I understood the event in the same way as they did, and I was commissioned. Considering their decision in retrospect, I realised that the pleasure they took in the narrative itself was intensified by relief at the prospect of not having to defend to their fellow citizens the expenditure of public money on a vacuous object on a plinth. Objections were likely to be few since the six gardens in which the narrative was to be related would replace a decrepit cattle market in the centre of the town on a site surrounded by houses.

However, Cofeb Hywel Dda proved to be the commission from hell for all concerned. It became the focus of a bitter dispute for precisely the reason that the committee thought it would appeal to the people of Whitland. The members of the committee had failed to distinguish between the attractions of the narrative form and the potential for dissent created by the content of a particular narrative. The codification of law is indicative both of internal coherence among a people and of their distinctness from their neighbours. Early medieval Welsh law was constructed on different principles to English law, which had been codified in Wessex a little earlier. Since the commissioning body had selected itself, most of its members were predisposed to welcome the national resonance of such a narrative. However, there was a second public in Whitland which was differently disposed. Whitland lies in the parliamentary constituency taken by Gwynfor Evans for Plaid Cymru in 1966. It was the first nationalist seat in Wales and a symbol bitterly resented by the Labour Party. A public park with a national narrative, which from their point of view was indistinguishable from a Nationalist narrative, was a disagreeable prospect to most of them. Indeed, they felt it was an affront to their British sense of Welshness.

At first the construction of the memorial was slowed only by minor impediments. Council officials were uninterested and, in one case, corrupt, and they treated me like a benign idiot. On site there were two stonemasons – one was incompetent and the other, though able to lay stone, could not read a drawing. It poured with rain all winter, and the low-lying site became waterlogged. However, public opposition to the project lacked a focus and was confined to directing anger towards members of the committee, the workers and myself. It bordered on hatred. The prime mover of the project, a

Marian Delyth, *Woman crossing the unfinished
Hywel Dda Memorial, Whitland, c.1985*. © Marian Delyth

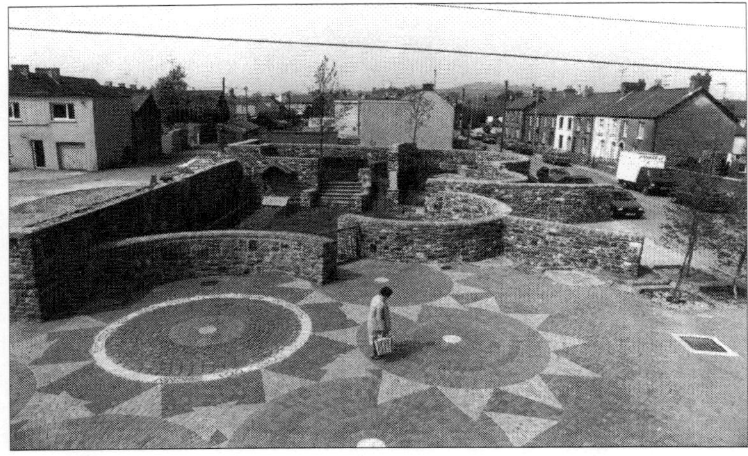

resident of Whitland and an officer of Carmarthen District Council, died well before the memorial was complete. The gardener, who had come to Wales to find a less stressful life, returned to England. The more outspoken members of the memorial committee suffered years of abuse. A single incident will serve to illustrate my own experience. The site was adjacent to the dairy which was the main employer in the town. Many workers went home for dinner every day and so walked past me when – on my hands and knees – I was laying the mosaic pavements which covered what had been a narrow lane leading to the centre of the town. One man was in the habit of stopping every day, his feet in close proximity to my hands, and saying 'Why don't you fuck off back where you came from.' The performance of this ritual persisted for the week or so that I was working on that part of the site. The question was, of course, remarkably resonant, though with a twist. This time, the thrust of it was not that I return to England, but to Aberystwyth – Welsh Wales, and in particular Welsh-speaking Wales, as he dimly perceived it.

Eventually a more potent outlet for opposition to Cofeb Hywel Dda was presented to the objectors by what seemed at the time to be the incompetence of council officers. I now realise that the opportunity was probably engineered by opponents who were in a position to exert an influence on those officers, whose reluctance to engage with the building of the memorial had seemed to me inexplicable. A central element in the scheme (pre-dating my involvement) was the closure to traffic of the lane which became the location of the mosaic pavements. While the work of pedestrianisation was underway the lane had been closed under a series of temporary orders. At a memorable meeting of the committee the chief executive of Carmarthen District Council announced (though so quietly that he had to be asked to repeat his statement), that there would be no permanent closure. The following morning many delighted local people drove backwards and forwards over the art work, some of them expressing their relish by honking their car horns at me and the other workers as they went. The memorial, which they clearly perceived as a nationalist icon, was defaced and members of the local Labour Party proclaimed a great victory for democracy.

In an attempt to bolster their confidence, immediately after my appointment the Commissions Officer of the Arts Council had written to the Hywel Dda Committee to assure them that they were in 'safe hands' because I was an experienced sculptor. This was untrue, since at that time nobody was experienced in the kind of work involved at Whitland. It was unknown territory both because of its large size and its vague management structure, which was divided between the Committee, the Arts Council, the District Council and the sculptor. Four years later, having completed Cofeb Hywel Dda and three other projects, I could indeed have been described as the most experienced sculptor in Wales at public art projects, which may account for my appointment to design a scheme for a visual celebration of the literature of Gwynedd at Parc Glynllifon, near Caernarfon. I took a narrative approach to the design of the scheme in the same way as at Whitland. The literature of Gwynedd was presented as a story in the form of a series of sites, each related to a theme – children's literature, drama, the *canu cenedlaethol* or patriotic poetry, *gwerin y graith* or the literature of the slate quarrying communities, and so on.

On the face of it there were few similarities with the situation at Whitland. There was no resident community around the site, which was enclosed within seven miles of ten-foot high wall. The park had been the home of the Newborough family, who were the most powerful landowners in Caernarfonshire. However, as I began work on the report with my colleague, Delyth Prys, a worrying spectre of Whitland arose in the form of the mysterious internal machinations of local authorities. The project was largely the idea of the Chief Executive of Gwynedd County Council, Ioan Bowen Rees – a thoughtful and cultured man. He had with him the Planning Department but it soon became apparent that together they were in a state of internecine strife with the Education Department, which was the occupying force in the park. Glynllifon housed their agricultural college and they resented the attempt which was being made to challenge their status as sole occupier. I therefore devoted a substantial part of my report to describing management structures which would resolve this conflict before it undermined the project. My recommendations were ignored, with entirely predictable consequences in both the short and the long term. The immediate difficulty was that the design of the scheme itself was adopted only in part, because the two departments would not co-operate. Half of the sites identified for development were under the control of the Education Department.

The report was presented in 1986, and at that point I withdrew from the development of the scheme so as not to prejudice my position, should I choose to apply for one of the site commissions at a later date. By 1992, two sites had been developed though the second remained unfinished. The competition was announced to present schemes for *Gwerin y Graith*. This had always been the theme to which I was most drawn. When Delyth and I began work on the outline scheme, large areas of the park at Glynllifon had been covered with dense conifer plantations and much of the remainder was a jungle of rhododendron and bramble. The remnants of the water features and sculpture created by various Lords Newborough from the late eighteenth to the late nineteenth centuries had to be discovered, like the ruins of Rome. One of the few routes open through the park ran from the house alongside the river Llifon at the bottom of a steep-sided and narrow valley. One day Delyth and I scrambled upwards beside a stream which descended into the dark valley bottom from the north. At the top we emerged quite suddenly into an open landscape of fields set against the distant background of Snowdonia. The tips of the quarries at Rhosgadfan were visible against the mountains. This was an unforgettable revelation. Rhosgadfan was the home of Kate Roberts and the setting of her book *Y Lôn Wen*, which had been the first piece of the canon of Welsh literature that I read when I was learning the language, fifteen years earlier. Although I had ceased to work as a sculptor by this time, I felt so strongly about the potential of this site that I decided to try for the commission. I wanted to express not only its particular meaning but to demonstrate through the narrative principle an approach to the design of public memorials that could make them active in the culture. I designed a diffuse site with elements that gave me the opportunity to commission other artists to co-operate with various levels of design responsibility. I had adopted this principle at Whitland, where the architect David Thomas had been commissioned and, through him, the sculptors Maggie Humphrey and David Petersen and the graphic designer Glyn Rees. In another project, at Llanbadarn Fawr near Aberystwyth, I had commissioned seven artists to work in wood, glass, textile, ceramic, metal and stone, and to design calligraphy.

I got the job at Glynllifon. The site was to be unified by the symbol of a jug, fallen on its side and spilling its contents. My idea was to suggest the continuing flow of the literature, through which a sense of tradition persisted despite the breaking of the community from which it arose by various forms of economic, political and

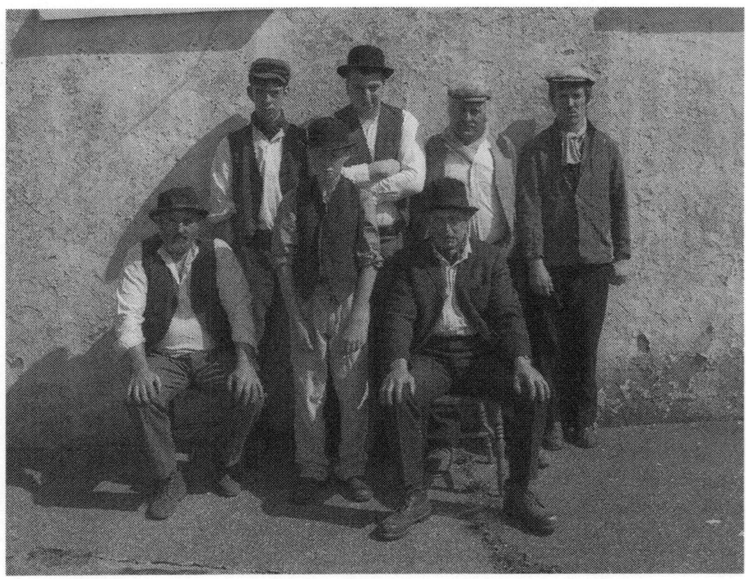

People of Trefenter posing for *Gwerin y Graith* mural, Glynllifon, c.1992–3

social pressure in the twentieth century. I gave the main commission to the ceramicist Morgen Hall. Morgen came to the site, visited Rhosgadfan, read Kate Roberts and made superb pots, some of them on a monumental scale. I designed and Martin Bellwood made the patterns for, and then cast, red bronze to flow into the soil and into the water of a small lake from which a waterfall descended to the floor of the valley. The site was funded by the Transport and General Workers' Union, descendents of the North Wales Quarrymen's Union, which had led the Great Strike of 1900-03.

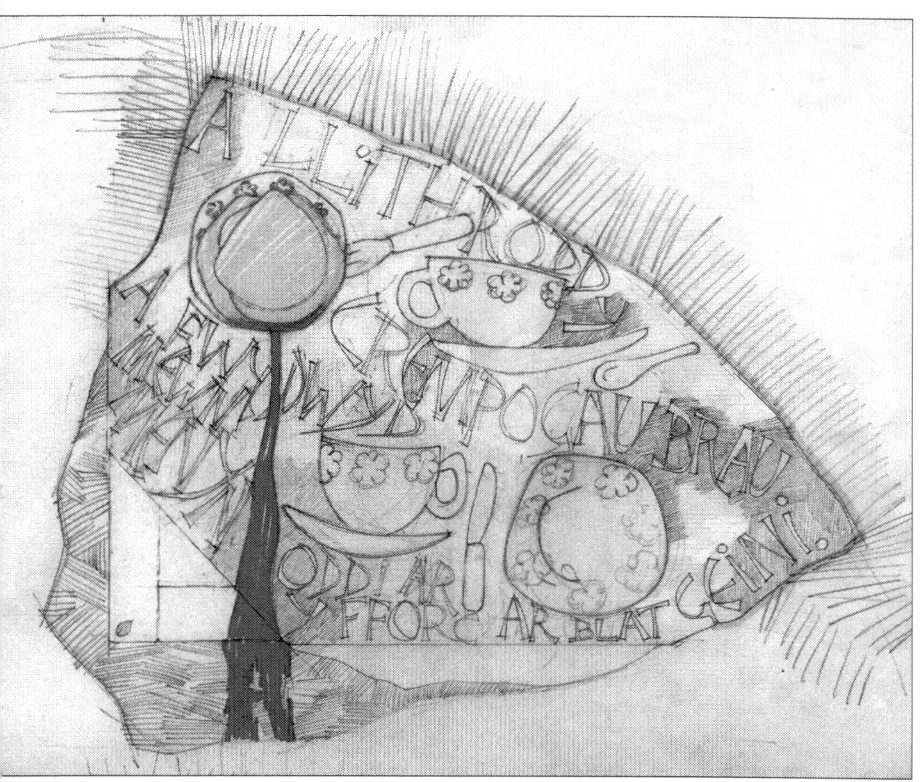

Peter Lord, *Gwerin y Graith*, Glynllifon, c.1992

Soon after the opening, I received a letter, enclosing a poem:

DWYLO

Lle gynt bu clochdar adar drud
   ar 'dir y lord' ym Mharc Glynllifon
bu dwylo'n creu y rhandir hud,
   aelwyd i'n llên, lle dal murmuron
ein cyni a'n cân, lle daw ynghyd
   leisiau ein doe a'n gwyrdd obeithion.

Y dwylo a adawodd le
   uwchben y wal i weld tomenni,
a lle i Wini ddwad i de
   'fel awal' o'r grug drwy ffens o lechi,
i Meri Ifans ffraeth a chre
   roi proc i'r tân a rhwb i'r llestri.

Dwylo a fu'n ysgythru'r gair
   gan wneud y trwm yn ysgafn erom,
dwylo fu'n casglu'r poer i'r pair
   ac yn distyllu'r dagrau drosom,
rhoi llif ein bywyd ni mewn crair
   a llaw yn y llyn i'w estyn atom.

Daw plant ein plant i ben y bryn
   i holi am graffiti'r streicia,
am gemeg y dagrau sy'n y llyn,
   am jygiau cain sydd ar eu hochra,
a dod yn dalog i'r fan hyn
   i ddringo dros lythrennau'r CHWALFA.

Enid Wyn Baines, 1993

HANDS

The strutting birds have left
his Lordship's land, Glynllifon,
where new hands recreate a magic home
for words that hold the murmur
of distress and song, connect
past voice and present hope.

The hands make room
above the wall to see the tips
and room for Wini, come for tea,
a breath of heather, through the fence of slate,
and Meri Ifans, sharp-tongued and strong,
who pokes the fire and shines the jugs.

Hands etch the word,
bring lightness to its weight
hands gather kisses to the cauldron,
distill the tears for us to make a reliquary
of our life-flow, passed through
a hand above a pool.

Children will climb the hill
and ask about the strike graffiti,
what is the chemistry of tears that salt the lake,
why the fallen jugs rest on their sides –
will play care free on the letters of
DESTRUCTION

Enid Wyn Baines, 1993 (translated by Peter Lord)

I feel that *Gwerin y Graith* was a beautiful concept and that, given care and the time to mature, it could have become a powerful place. I was very proud of it. In the event, it lasted about six months. One Monday morning I received a telephone call and was told that it had been vandalised. When I arrived I found that the site had not so much been vandalised as systematically demolished. The ceramics had been broken, including a jug held in a bronze hand rising from

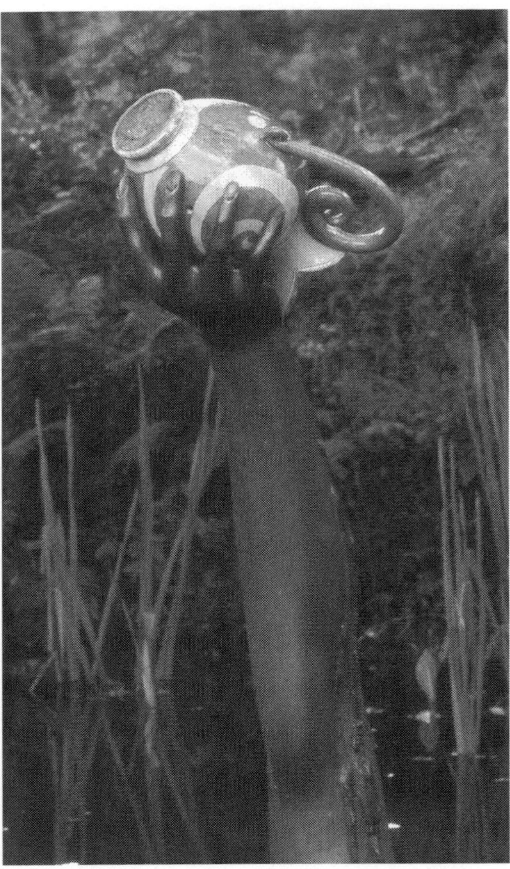

Peter Lord,
Morgen Hall and
Martin Bellwood,
Gwerin y Graith,
Glynllifon,
*c.*1993

the middle of the lake. The only survivors were three jugs on top of a tall column. The mystical Brenhines yr Wyddfa passage from Caradog Pritchard's *Un Nos Ola Leuad*, etched on toughened glass, had somehow been smashed. The bronze castings had been levered from their mountings. For reasons not disclosed to me, Gwynedd County Council thought it best not to pursue the matter and the police were not asked to investigate. The wreckage was removed and the incoherent remains were left to decay.

I do not know who was responsible for the destruction of *Gwerin y Graith*. It may have been students from the agricultural college or the work of someone living in the locality, perhaps at Y Groeslon or Penygroes, the two nearest villages. These communities were created by the slate quarrying industry whose people and literature the site celebrated. At the time of the attack they were suffering the consequences of high unemployment and a depressing built environment, to which the action at Glynllifon may have been a response. If so, it is doubly sad that the fact that the memorial was funded by the voluntary contributions of working people and that its narrative of nation and language was congruent with a narrative of class conflict did not have the power to overcome the anger arising from the social deprivation they felt. The location of the memorial within the walls of a place associated by the powerless with the powerful was apparently not perceived as ironic, but rather to have reinforced a sense of alienation from visual art as a form favoured by elites. Furthermore, *Gwerin y Graith* was made mainly by social and geographical outsiders. Apparently, destruction seemed to be the appropriate response. The fact that the most prominent remaining feature of the site is the word CHWALFA, cast in massive concrete letters, intensifies the sad irony of it all. In Welsh, *chwalfa* is a resonant word which means dispersal or destruction. It is the title of a novel by T. Rowland Hughes which describes the Great Strike and its consequences. The cast letters, which lead away from the site and into the evolving woodland, were intended as a metaphor, but the destruction of the rest of the work has changed its meaning. To those few who know what has been lost (nothing indicates to the casual visitor the history of what happened there) perhaps the ruins of *Gwerin y Graith* retain the power to move the emotions. Indeed, it has been suggested that for some the site has more power than if it had been maintained as it was conceived.

Of course, in one sense the destruction of *Gwerin y Graith* meant that my hopes for it had been fulfilled. It had certainly become 'active in the culture'. Unfortunately, I had misjudged that culture or, more precisely, failed to pay attention to the fact that culture is not monolithic but multi-faceted, and formed by fluid and sometimes volatile interactions of forces. Given the experience at Whitland, I should have known better. The destruction of the piece does demonstrate that narrative content gives artwork both immediate life and, through the dialogue generated, however disagreeable its form, the potential for subsequent incorporation into new narratives of our history. But personally, I don't want to go there again.

The Surgeon Apothecary

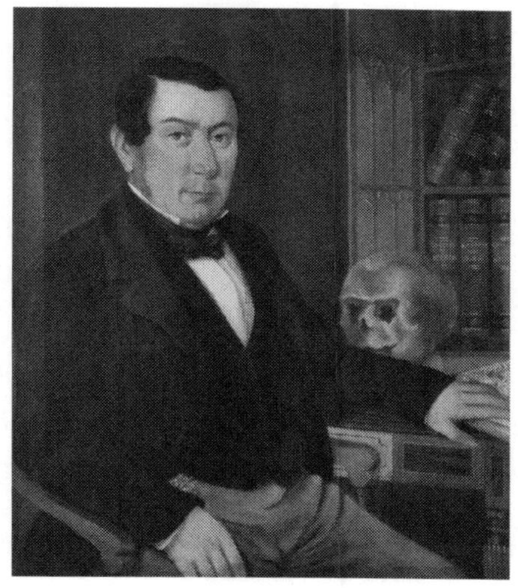

Over a decade ago, a portrait of a surgeon was sent for sale at auction from the house of a family in Pwllheli, with no information other than that it had been there as long as anyone could remember. Clearly, the picture was a statement of well-being. When it was new, I imagine it was hung in the parlour, over the fireplace – the finishing touch in an assembly of Regency and early Victorian architecture, furnishings and decorations that would act within the family as a mirror of personal stability and, addressed to visiting friends and acquaintances, as an advertisement of professional achievement. The surgeon chose to identify himself professionally through the display of his medical books and his specimen skull, and socially by sitting himself at his splendid bookcase-cum-desk, made in the style of the English manufacturer Gillow. It exemplifies the taste of the prospering middle class of the 1840s, a date for the picture that is confirmed by the sitter's clothes. By the time that I acquired the portrait, over a century and a half later, his name was long forgotten, and so I called the picture simply *The Surgeon Apothecary*. There were a surprising number of surgeons listed in the street directories for Pwllheli and the surrounding area in the period, an indication of the size of the town's rising middle class. The most settled of them appears to have been Hugh Hunter Hughes, listed from 1835 until 1850, and he may be the sitter. The painter of the portrait was as confident as the surgeon, and was well able to meet his requirement for a striking display of status. This suggests a professional. However, his or her limited interest in anatomy – considerably less developed than that of the client, one hopes – indicates that the painter had not been academically trained. He or she may have been an itinerant, staying in the town for a week or two to paint portraits until the local demand was satisfied, but there is reason to believe that the painter was a resident artisan called John Roberts. He was certainly capable of undertaking the work, and he is unusually well documented – indeed, he is the subject of the only substantial biographical essay about a Welsh artisan painter written by someone who knew him. The author, John Jones, Myrddin Fardd, was a generation younger than his subject, but lived and worked as a smith at Chwilog, close to Roberts's home at Llanystumdwy.

John Roberts was born in the parish of Abererch in 1810, and although he went to London for a period to gain 'inspiration for his talent', he spent his working life in the Llŷn peninsula. Myrddin

Fardd makes much of this: 'He loved the place of his birth greatly, along with its people, so that he could not think of moving his tent to any other place on earth.'[19] In the frustrating manner of the many memoirs written in the period (especially the memoirs of worthy ministers of the church, which are the model for the essay), at the expense of facts about the life and work of the subject the author discourses at length on his appreciation of the beautiful landscape of Llŷn, on his subject's good character, and on his physiognomy. The interest shown by the writers of the *cofiannau* in the appearance of their subjects does not necessarily reflect a limited capacity for the reproduction of engravings or photographs in their publications, though in the case of John Roberts, no photograph accompanied the essay, nor does it appear that one has survived. The fascination of the writers derives from their idea that physiognomy and character are closely linked – indeed, that the one is expressive of the other. We are told in some detail about the eyes, nose, mouth, and the manner of walking of John Roberts. For the record, he was tall and slim, but well proportioned. He had dark eyes and a shapely proboscis of moderate size. His lips were thin.[20]

More helpfully, Myrddin Fardd does inform us that John Roberts's inclination to draw emerged early. He did not have the benefit of a family background in craft practice, and learned his trade as the result of a happy accident. He was spotted at work by a passing itinerant painter:

He was more than a little surprised when he saw the main walls and partitions of his father's house covered with drawings. He felt somehow that John possessed abilities that deserved support, and he entered into conversation with the family about what he could do for him – he promised to take him as an apprentice – John began immediately on the task of being one of those birds of passage, and before long he far surpassed his master.[21]

The implication that the presence of itinerant portrait painters in Llŷn in the period was not unusual is interesting, though it would have been useful also to be told the name of this particular individual. We do not know whether he was a specialist portrait painter, as were most itinerants, or a generalist artisan. Whatever the range of skills he learned from this unidentified master, John Roberts subsequently practised as a generalist, painting pub signs, heraldry and inscriptions, as well as making easel paintings of landscape, people and ships. Indeed, painting pictures of the sailing vessels that traded out of Pwllheli and Porthmadog in the period may well have been a more important source of income for him than painting the portraits of their owners or captains. However, like many generalists (who, by and large, considered themselves tradesmen), John Roberts was not in the habit of signing his work. Only two portraits survive that have a deep tradition of attribution to him. *Robert Owen, y Crudd* (the Shoemaker) is a simpler portrait than that of the surgeon, though not sufficiently different to present a difficulty in attributing both pictures to him. The shoemaker may perhaps have been painted a little earlier. When the picture was given to the National Museum in the 1960s, a letter was appended that expanded upon the information given by Myrddin Fardd about the painter:

A design of his making is to be seen in the parish church of Llanystumdwy. John Roberts painted the writing above the east window … and he also drew the two angel faces that are in the middle and divide the words … I was told, many years ago by one who was present at the time that he had made it all up himself, that is, not copying at all.

It is said that he painted a picture of a ship above the pulpit in Rhoslan Chapel (Llanystumdwy) but that somebody painted over the picture when redecorating the chapel. I don't know if this is true, but if it is, the covering should certainly be removed.[22]

One of two surviving portraits of the poet Robert Williams, Robert ap Gwilym Ddu, is traditionally given to John Roberts. The other – a fine full length drawing, known only from a photograph – is unattributed, but distinctive in style. Both men lived in the same area of Llŷn and it seems likely that it too was made by Roberts. Until 2010 these appeared to be the only survivors of his work as a portrait painter, but in that year I received a letter telling me about a picture of a cattle drover, Lewis Thomas Lewis, still in the possession of his descendents on a farm at Llangybi. This severe looking gentleman had unsettled generations of children. Adults often recall having been frightened in childhood by the family ancestor portrait, whose eyes followed them silently about the room – generally the gloomiest room in the house. Hanging behind the door in the cold and rarely used drawing room of my maternal grandmother's house, at the far end of a long, narrow and dark passage, was the picture of two lions that she herself had painted in the 1920s, in Landseer mode. For years I suffered a recurring nightmare about being chased by them, round and round the house, faster and faster, closer and closer, until I woke in a sweat. The portrait of Lewis Thomas Lewis that intimidated generations of his descendents at Llangybi was painted a century earlier, probably during the decade 1827–37, and the image resonates strongly with what I take to be John Roberts's full length

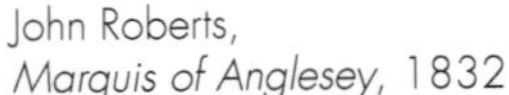

John Roberts,
Marquis of Anglesey, 1832

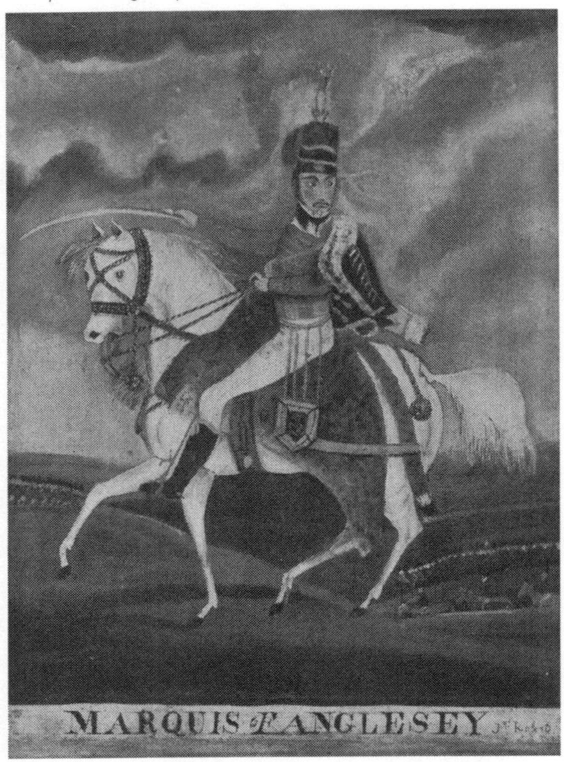

drawing of Robert ap Gwilym Ddu. Nevertheless, since the portrait of Lewis Thomas Lewis, like the others associated with Roberts, is not signed, there can be no certainty about the identity of the painter.

The only surviving portrait that carries the signature of John Roberts confuses rather than clarifies the issue. It does not look at all like the others. *The Marquis of Anglesey* is signed on the front and inscribed on the back 'John Roberts hen Walia Fecit Fedy. [sic] 1832', but it is painted on a small panel and is distinctly less sophisticated than the larger (and later) paintings on canvas. The

Marquess became famous for his role in the Battle of Waterloo, and by 1832 had acquired a considerable iconography at the hands of academically trained painters and engravers. At the time of the battle he had been merely Lord Uxbridge, and received his grander title in compensation for the fact that his right knee was shattered by grape-shot while riding at the side of the Duke of Wellington. The incident was the subject of a frequently repeated anecdote: 'By God, sir, I've lost my leg!' exclaimed his lordship. 'By God, sir, so you have!' replied Wellington, pressing on. The leg became an international tourist attraction at the farm where its remnants were amputated after the battle. Like the painters of the signs that adorn the pubs named in his honour, John Roberts seems to have combined elements from various engravings to make his image, though the white charger is mysterious.[23] For whom John Roberts painted the picture is equally unclear, but if it was not simply a celebration to be framed and hung on a wall, the chamfered edges of the wooden panel suggest it might have been intended for a piece of furniture or wainscoting, perhaps in an appropriately named pub. The question is, of course, was the John Roberts who painted the Anglesey portrait the same as he who painted the later portraits in Llŷn including, perhaps, the surgeon?

The problem of sorting out who did what and why in the case of artisan pictures such as these is fascinating. Perhaps the uncertainties in the case of John Roberts will be resolved in time, if more pictures emerge. However, the very attractiveness to me of the work of Roberts and other artisans gives rise to a deeper and more troubling problem. I like artisan paintings – portraits especially. I am clear about that. Why I like them is another matter. The American anthropologist John Michael Vlach, much of whose work concerns the material culture of folk societies, has argued for thirty years that the work of artisan painters (or 'plain painters', as he calls them) is simply a failed imitation of academic art, made by individuals who lacked the training or the talent to do better. 'Plain painters are best understood as novices experimenting with a complex apparatus', he wrote in 1988, and I don't believe that he has changed his mind in the meantime.[24] Am I, then, simply a misguided lover of bad art?

Huw Griffith of Bodwrdda with his Children, Margaret and William

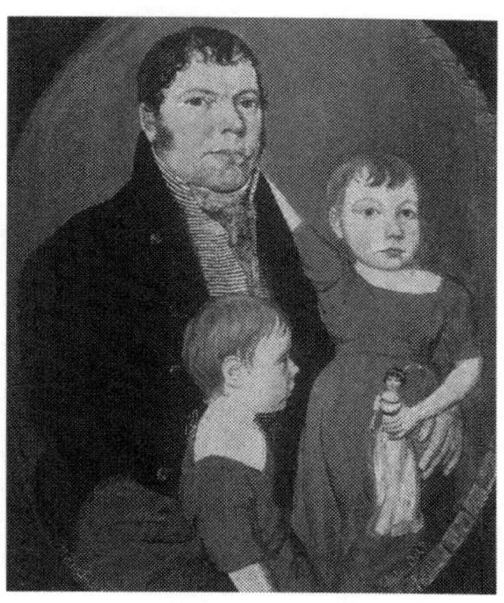

The difficult experience of building the Hywel Dda Memorial at Whitland in the years after 1982 had the unexpected consequence of securing my elevation to membership of the Art Committee of the Arts Council. At what I think must have been my first meeting, the most pressing issue concerned Eric Rowan's book, *Art in Wales*. It had been commissioned by the Arts Council some years earlier, but had gone substantially over budget, and a further subsidy to the University of Wales Press was required to secure its publication. The officers recommended a large grant and so, being a newcomer, I took their advice and voted in favour. Shortly afterwards, I read the text. The story it told bore no relation whatsoever to the story of the literature that by this time Delyth Prys and I were seeking to interpret at Glynllifon – a story which was closely integrated with the wider history of the culture. We discussed the issues at length – why, for instance, the great strike at the Penrhyn quarries had a substantial literature, but according to Rowan, did not feature in the history of painting and sculpture in Wales. What lay behind the absence of such a seminal event from the visual record? It appeared that a similar disconnection between visual imagery and core issues of the culture afflicted all parts of Wales. Apparently, neither the coal strike of 1926–7 nor the great depression of the 1930s had left any visual trace. According to this official Arts Council version of Welsh art history, the most important features of the inter-war years were the influence of Ernst, Picasso and Matisse on the abstractions of Ceri Richards; the work of Eric Gill at Capel y Ffin; and the encouragement given by Ben Nicholson to David Jones to join the Seven and Five Society in London. Eleven pictures by David Jones were reproduced in the new book. Painters without London reputations, such as Evan Walters, were not reproduced at all. Indeed, Walters was dismissed in two sentences, the tone of which clearly revealed the author's English metropolitanism and his contempt for Welsh identities:

> Evan Walters, for example, who studied in London and spent some years in America, chose to paint the people of Wales and the landscapes around Llangyfelach. Yet with his creative energy and his interest in the theory of optics, there is no telling what direction his art might have taken, had it been fostered in a more intense and metropolitan milieu.[25]

It was clear that Welsh imagery needed a history that valued it for its expression of the cultures from which it sprang, rather than metropolitan aesthetic fashions, and I decided that I would try to provide one. I stopped making sculpture and began to research and to write. It seemed to me that the issues needed to be addressed simultaneously at two levels – theoretical and practical. In other contexts, equivalent critiques of prevailing mainstream art history had been developing for a decade or so, though my awareness of the awkward squad was limited at that time to John Berger and Marxist analysis. In fact, a better parallel for our own situation was the issue of female marginalisation in mainstream art history. Linda Nochlin had asked her celebrated question, 'Why have there been no great women artists?' in 1971.[26] If we were to follow the consolidated received wisdom of the twentieth century, for both women and men in Wales there was an even more fundamental and stark question to be answered: 'Why has there been no Welsh art?' As an official governmental report put it, in 1927:

> For good or evil, whether from causes innate in the Welsh
> nature, or for historical and economic reasons, Wales has
> no art but literature and music.[27]

It was apparent that most of the many authoritative assertions of this sort concerning the visual deficiency of Welsh cultures emanated from the Anglophile establishment. Like Nochlin, therefore, initially I drew the simple conclusion that we had been written out of history for reasons that were to do with prevailing power structures, and tried to address the issue firstly in a paper written for the Arts Council, called 'Cultural Policy', that concerned the funding of new art, and then in a pamphlet called *The Aesthetics of Relevance*, that dealt with art history.[28] However, ultimately the theoretical argument would only prove persuasive if a substantial body of unrecognised Welsh pictures and artefacts could be shown to exist, and so I began to look.

At this time I worked in a studio at the Barn Centre in Aberystwyth – an arts and social collective housed in a fascinating group of buildings that had started life as Green's Foundry, from where mining machinery was exported all over the world. My colleagues were a stimulating lot, to say the least. Brith Gof worked – sometimes explosively – downstairs. There was Colourscape, Cwmni Cyfri Tri (Jeremy Turner's first theatre company), Cliff McLucas and many other creative individuals working in visual arts, music, dance, theatre and television. Among those with whom I discussed ideas was the photographer Keith Morris, who told me that he had seen a large group of portraits in the Methodist Theological College in the town. It was a fortuitous place to begin the search, since the Principal, Elfed ap Nefydd Roberts, was interested in pictures and at that moment engaged in a programme of restoration of the portraits from the colleges in Aberystwyth and Bala that had come into his care. The collection was large and included a few familiar names. Lewis Edwards had been painted full length and life size by Jerry Barrett, well known for his *Florence Nightingale Receiving the Wounded at Scutari*, among the most celebrated Victorian visualisations of imperial history. Most of the pictures were less imposing – and less pompous – but proved to be the work of painters whose names had been forgotten.[29] Nevertheless, a particularly attractive pair of portraits stood out, not least because one of the sitters was a woman – the only woman I remember in that gallery of rather dour male worthies. Jennett Davies and her husband, John, were unusual people, because they had been among the minority of mid-nineteenth-century gentry with Nonconformist sympathies, and had suffered social ostracisation as a result. Furthermore, the name of the painter of their portraits was known. Elfed fetched the *Dictionary of Welsh*

Biography and we stood at the foot of the staircase above which the portraits hung and read the entry on Hugh Hughes. R.T. Jenkins had made rather more of Hughes's activity as a polemicist than as a painter and engraver, but it was a start. However, it proved to be a most inadequate preparation for the avalanche of pictures by Hughes that flowed in my direction over the next couple of years.

Finding pictures by Hugh Hughes proved no more difficult than picking apples from a fruitful tree. There were dozens of them – it was just that, until that point, it appeared that nobody had bothered to look up into the branches.[30] The process began very soon after my first visit to the Theological College. I had been told of a dealer in Cardiff called John Owen, who had an interest in Welsh pictures. I visited him at his small shop, and spoke about Hughes. He assumed an air of familiarity, though I suspect that this was the first time he'd heard the name. Nevertheless, two days later he telephoned. 'Did this man Hughes paint landscapes?' he enquired. 'Yes, certainly', I replied, though I had no idea whether or not this was the case. 'Well I've bought one for you.' The day after my visit to Cardiff, he had attended a sale somewhere in the borders and bought a signed Hughes landscape – a rarity, as it would turn out – and it became my first picture by the painter. The second was found, soon afterwards, in service as a draft excluder in an Aberystwyth fireplace. Others appeared in the cellars of the National Museum, the attics of the National Library, illustrated in the *cofiannau* and in histories of Methodism, and in private homes. At Llanidloes I visited Shirley Hooson to inspect a group portrait of the Glanyrafon Hunt, about which she had told me. On an adjacent wall hung a small but vivid picture of the nineteenth-century pig fair in the town: 'That's a nice picture – do you know who it's by?' Shirley replied that the picture was signed but she couldn't remember the name. It had been bought for its local interest in a shop in the town, many years earlier. I took the picture down, and on the back was an inscription and the signature of Hugh Hughes.

There were also manuscripts, held at the National Library. Among them was a group of letters which made it clear that my first impression, that no-one had previously investigated Hughes, was incorrect. The painter T.H. Thomas, prominent among the cultural nationalists of the late nineteenth century, had become interested in his work a century earlier. It was largely the research undertaken by Thomas that had informed the short biography of Hughes published in 1912 in the Rev. T. Mardy Rees's *Welsh Painters, Engravers, Sculptors*, the pioneering volume in the field. In response to one of his enquiries, another painter, John Deffett Francis, had written to Thomas in 1887 to say that he had met Hugh Hughes at the Carmarthen home of the printer John Evans, sixty years earlier, when he was twelve years old. Francis had been fascinated by a picture, painted by Hughes, of Mr Evans and his whole family sitting at the breakfast table. It had been 'the cups and saucers together with the table ornaments' that 'entranced' his child's eye.[31] The picture had been hanging above the mantelpiece, in front of which he had observed Hughes and Evans in conversation, prior to dinner. The reference was both exciting and frustrating, because the picture described by Francis was clearly of a different order to the single portraits I had found thus far, but I had no idea where it might be. A year or so later I gave a lecture in Carmarthen, and took the opportunity to mention the picture, hoping that somebody might know of it. No-one did. However, John Evans, the subject of Hughes's portrait, was of particular interest to the local newspaper, the *Carmarthen Journal*, since he had been its publisher and printer in the 1820s, and so in its brief report of the lecture the paper described the missing picture. Among the audience attending the lecture had been a gentleman who was in the habit of sending a copy of the *Journal*, every week, to a relative living at Grosmont, on the border with Herefordshire. The relative read the report of my lecture with some surprise. A picture fitting the description belonged to his elderly next-door neighbour, Mrs Innes. I was invited to visit her at Grosmont shortly afterwards. It was, indeed, the missing picture of the family of John Evans – large and finely painted. Although she had no idea of the identity of the painter, Mrs Innes was able to name all the sitters. She was a direct descendent of Louisa, one of the Evans daughters seated at the breakfast table. Louisa's mother was placed at the centre of her large family, her husband to her left. On the opposite side, one of her sons was reading a copy of the *Carmarthen Journal*. There were boiled eggs for breakfast, served in silver tableware accompanied by the blue and white china that had fascinated the young Deffett Francis. The picture was hanging in Mrs Innes's parlour, immediately above a sideboard on which was arranged some of the same silverware painted so vividly by Hughes over a century and a half earlier. On the wall, in a gilt frame, was hanging a silhouette of a gentleman, also depicted in Hughes's picture where it was set on the Evans's mantelpiece, immediately to the left of the surviving original.[32] The proximity of image and reality was surreal, an effect intensified by the disconcerting sense of being directed that I was experiencing as I researched Hughes.

The sheer quantity of work and the number of new painters coming to light by this time was remarkable. As anticipated by the theory, there were, indeed, hundreds of Welsh pictures of all kinds.

Somehow Delyth Prys discovered the whereabouts of the original version of the memorial image of the poet Hedd Wyn, familiar from a postcard reproduction and, in another form, as the frontis and paper cover image of his *Cerddi'r Bugail*. I wrote to the nieces of the painter, Kelt Edwards, the sisters Ruth Ahmed and Lillian Guy, asking if I could see the picture. I wrote in Welsh but the sisters proved not to be fluent Welsh-speakers, which turned out much to my advantage. They misunderstood my request, and concluded that I wanted to buy the picture. During a long polite tea in the house they shared at Rhosneigr, *Hiraeth Cymru am Hedd Wyn* was not mentioned. However, when finally I broached the subject, the picture was rapidly retrieved from behind the sofa, lurking in a brown paper bag that had

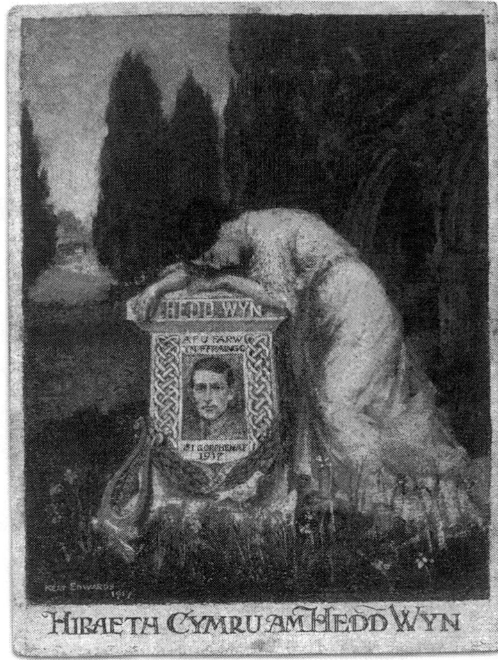

Kelt Edwards, *Hiraeth Cymru am Hedd Wyn*, 1917

been its home for many years. The sisters found it depressing, and were keen to get rid of it. The transaction took all of ten seconds. I offered £500 to which they responded immediately with a demand for £700. The sisters were aged, but pretty sharp. They had obtained the advice of a friend on the value of the picture. He proved to be Kyffin Williams. '£600?'. 'Done'. As I left, the sisters kindly gave me a copy of the postcard print of the picture and two other cards designed by Kelt Edwards during the First World War, one inscribed in his own hand. Later, they sent me the original photograph of the painter and his cousin, Elias Davies, with the Chair of the Corwen Eisteddfod of 1920. The painting was part of a life.

Although pictures of all kinds were coming to light, it was clear that at the core was a large group of portraits, made coherent by the fact that almost all had been commissioned outside the familiar framework of gentry patronage, and that they had been painted by professional painters who had not been academically trained. Hugh Hughes had been the first to emerge, though it transpired that the most prolific of them was Hughes's younger contemporary, William Roos, from Amlwch.[33] He was the only one of them with a small record of sales at auction houses. Among a wider group of more elusive artists was John Roberts, painter of the Pwllheli surgeon apothecary. The experience of discovering these painters and of exploring the stratum of society that had commissioned their work was intensely exciting because although their practice had gone almost unrecorded by historians, it dovetailed with well documented understandings of the wider cultures of Wales. Most obviously, it was apparent that the portrait painters were closely associated with sitters who were central to the intellectual and literary evolution of the nation in the early nineteenth century. It was Hughes's portrait of Thomas Charles, for instance, painted in 1812, that had been the foundation of all the subsequent engraved images of the Methodist leader, so familiar from histories of Nonconformism, in which he was a central figure.[34] Both Hughes and Roos had also painted Christmas Evans, and it was the same story with the literati. Indeed, it was the link between the painters and the *beirdd gwlad* – the folk poets of the first half of the nineteenth century – that led Delyth Prys to suggest we called them '*arlunwyr gwlad*', which I rendered in English as 'artisan painters'.

Hugh Hughes was central to the exploration of the story because, as R.T. Jenkins had pointed out, in addition to painting and engraving, he had written extensively on a wide range of subjects – though not on art, an omission suggestive of his craft-based approach to his work. Hughes had risen from a childhood of poverty and social marginalisation to become a public intellectual with a radical vision, even if his views were sometimes eccentric, a characteristic of the autodidact that manifested itself also in the erratic quality of his painting. In his writing Hughes placed the middle-class at the centre of all social and spiritual progress, a fact that deepened the import of his group portrait of the family of John Evans. Clearly, it was the portrait of an idea, as well as that of a family. I decided to write a biography of Hughes, and entered into one of those intimate relationships with a subject that are so familiar to first-time biographers. I had many long conversations with Mr Hughes, especially on trains, in which I explained to him the mysteries of a modern world by which he would have been both fascinated and appalled.

I carried my excitement about Hugh Hughes to the National Museum, where my research was assisted by the new Registrar, Tim Egan. When he was appointed, Tim had been horrified at the dire state of records about the collection, and began the long process of imposing order on the chaos. I had found a reference to a Hughes portrait of Thomas Beynon, Archdeacon of Ceredigion, painted in about 1825, that was supposedly in the Museum collection, but missing. Tim located the painting at another museum, loaned at some time in the past with no record made. I visited Cardiff to look at the retrieved portrait, and was enthusing about it when the Keeper of Art, Timothy Stevens, passed by. He enquired what I was doing and I began to explain. He offered a single observation on the subject: 'Well', he said, 'there's no rubbish like your own rubbish, is there?' and passed along.

Leaving aside the personal insensitivity of the remark, Stevens' attitude brought into focus an aspect of the issue of which I had not fully taken account at this early stage. In the prevailing political context, the marginalisation of Welsh visual culture by an establishment concerned only with the promotion of metropolitan values was unsurprising. It reflected the colonialist attitudes that pervaded every other aspect of the English relationship with Wales. Often blatantly expressed from outside by the likes of Mr Stevens, it was equally entrenched within, since those who acquiesced in the colonial relationship profited by it. Nevertheless, it had not occurred to me that the rediscovery of so many pictures by Hughes and his contemporaries would be regarded by everyone as anything other than a welcome enrichment of the culture. Following the feminist argument pursued by Linda Nochlin in the United States, once the work was revealed, surely there could be no possible argument for failing to accommodate it in tradition? However, it soon became clear that there was an additional problem, which arose from the particular nature of the emerging body of artisan pictures. The Curator of Art at the National Museum had dismissed them summarily as 'rubbish'.

The work was not excluded simply because it was Welsh, but also because, apparently, it was bad art. This moved the argument much nearer to a feminist position expressed by the South African art historian Griselda Pollock, who had pointed out that the prevailing mainstream tradition could never accommodate large parts of the work of women since that work had been created within different value systems. It was congenitally distinct. The problem lay with a dominant tradition that was, and only ever could be, exclusive, and designed to affirm the superior quality of its own favoured material.

I cannot remember who told me of the existence of a portrait of Huw Griffith of Bodwrdda and his children, but I remember well the excitement of visiting Meillionydd Mawr, the beautiful farmhouse in Penllŷn where the portrait lived. It turned out to be a small picture, rather dirty and a little damaged, and it hung in a dark passage, but it was well respected as a part of family history. The discovery was important in two respects – firstly, because it was among the few pictures clearly signed and dated by Hugh Hughes, and secondly because its style was distinct both from other works by Hughes that I had seen, and from the academic art tradition. The portrait was painted on tinplate. One of the children was depicted in profile – a device commonly used by artisan painters to capture a likeness. It was an early work. In 1812, Hughes had travelled from his home in Liverpool to paint in Llŷn, where members of his father's family still lived. He worked in Pwllheli that year and, on a return visit the next, it appears that he travelled further west to paint his portrait of Huw Griffith. It would have been important to Hughes that Griffith, a tenant farmer on the Nanhoron estate, was a fellow Calvinistic Methodist who frequently wandered far afield to attend religious gatherings. It's possible that Hughes had met him at such a meeting

– perhaps even at the *sasiwn* at Bala in 1811, when the Methodists had emerged from the Church of England as a new denomination. Hughes was certainly present at that seminal event. He painted his portrait of Thomas Charles in its immediate aftermath.

Shortly after seeing the portrait of Huw Griffith, I visited St Fagans to look at paintings in the collection of the Welsh Folk Museum, as it then was. Among them, dirty and stored in a drawer, were three small oil portraits of the children of William Hughes, a High Street shopkeeper in Pwllheli – a characteristic middle-class patron of the artisan. The painter of the portraits was unknown, but it was immediately apparent that the pictures were the work of Hugh Hughes. They were identical in style to the portrait of Huw Griffith and his children. All three were profiles, and they were painted on tinplate, which almost certainly dated them to 1813. Considered together, the Pwllheli group confirmed the existence of a genre of historically significant and, to my mind, visually delightful Welsh pictures. Their character was exemplified by the forthright gaze of Huw Griffith, his yellow striped waistcoat, the tokens held in the hands of the Hughes children, the overall flatness of the pictures, and the absence of illusionary backgrounds. However, it was a genre with no place in the prevailing story of high art, at any rate in its account of matters since the early seventeenth century. In terms of the methodological problem this presented, the most significant thing about the Hughes portraits was their location at St Fagans, rather than at the Art Department of the National Museum. Had the portraits been the work of Sir Joshua Reynolds, undoubtedly they would have been appropriated by the Art Department when first offered to the nation. The fact that they were kept in a drawer at a folk museum indicated the scant regard in which the genre they represented was held by visual culture specialists. They were fine examples of Mr Stevens' rubbish.

Coming to this kind of work in the 1980s as a practitioner, rather than as a connoisseur, it did not occur to me to find the visual characteristics of the early work of Hugh Hughes and painters like him as anything other than attractive. Directness and clarity seemed to me to be virtues of many artisans' aesthetics. I enjoyed their pictogramic approach more than attempts to immitate the appearance of the seen world by the application of illusionary conventions – Renaissance perspective, and all the other paraphernalia acquired in an academic art training. The enhancement of an image by the use of colour and design in a way that was meaningful within the context of the picture, rather than in pursuit of the appearance of an external reality, was an established principle of modern high art, and celebrated in the mainstream tradition. Dismissal of artisan painting as a lesser thing, appropriate for a folk museum but not an art museum, therefore seemed to me paradoxical. The application of particular visual conventions in the early nineteenth century by artisan painters was regarded as rubbish, apparently because it derived from a tradition of sign painting. The application of the same conventions in the name of Modernism by the likes of Ceri Richards – celebrated on the walls of the National Museum and in Rowan's *Art in Wales* – apparently resulted in serious art. That there was a conflict of art historical methodologies was immediately obvious but only gradually, as I was exposed increasingly to the arrogance and snobbery of the high art establishment, did it become apparent that it was rooted in a conflict of social values.

Artisan painting is not defined by style but by its place in a network of social and economic forces. However, aesthetics become entangled in that net because in some cases – though by no means all – the social context in which artisan painting flourished tended to throw up a consistent pictogramic style, resulting from the application to portraiture of the visual conventions of the craft practice of painters of signs, inscriptions and decorations. By the early nineteenth century these pictogramic conventions – suggested in Hughes's paintings of 1813 – were quite distinct from the illusionary conventions of high art portrait practice. In the broad European context, the parting of the ways had been bound up with the wider evolution of attitudes described as the Renaissance, but in the context of London, most immediately relevant to Welsh practice, the profound change had occurred in the early eighteenth century, when English painters became upwardly mobile. Practice became gentrified, and an artistic elite emerged aligned with the economically and politically empowered. Through his theoretical writings the portrait painter Jonathan Richardson exercised a considerable influence on this development:

> A Portrait-Painter must understand Mankind, and enter into their Characters, and express their Minds as well as their Faces. And as his Business is chiefly with People of Condition, he must Think as a Gentleman, and a Man of Genius, or 'twill be impossible to give Such their True and Proper Resemblances.[35]

Along with the new artists' aspirations to social differentiation from the craft community came a concomitant claim to differentiation in terms of quality of mind. In his discourse upon connoisseurship, of 1719, Richardson sought to ingratiate himself with the empowered by suggesting that the appreciation of pictures required a special sensibility and understanding on the part of his gentleman patrons. Implicit in the suggestion was the notion that temporal authority was justified by moral authority, deriving from this refined sensibility.

Notions of refinement of taste and the possession of a special sensibility that implied a spiritually qualitative difference between the artist (along with the gentleman patron) and the common herd became embedded as a fundamental myth of high art practice. From Richardson to Clive Bell, writing two hundred years later, mainstream art history was the product of the empowered, reinforcing psychologically and morally the status quo of a hierarchical society. According to Bell:

> Only artists and educated people of extraordinary sensibility and some savages and children feel the significance of form so acutely that they know how things look. They see because they see emotionally.[36]

Curiously, the money that sent young Bell to school at Marlborough and to university at Trinity College, Cambridge, came from his father's coal mines at Merthyr and Neath.[37] The profits from the labour of the Welsh proletariat would help to fund the Bloomsbury Group, of which Bell was a central pillar. Economic enslavement financed decadence. It was not until the second half of the twentieth century that the divisive social implications of this hierarchical myth, with the notion of the genius of the individual artist at its core, began to be challenged by the political left. This is John Berger:

> It's depressing. The rain's set in. It's wet, but we can't grumble. It's grey and dull … All true painters naturally see and feel in a way that is a hundred times more acutely visual and tangible than the last, or indeed, any comment, can illustrate. But what they see and feel is – normally – *the same as everybody else*. To say this is, I realize, platitudinous. But how often it is forgotten. Indeed, has it ever been consistently taken for granted since the sixteenth century?[38]

To admit artisan painters into the mainstream of art history and into the high art museum would have been to undermine the myth of the special sensibility of the artist – to acknowledge, as Berger pointed out, that the painter was no different to anyone else, other than in his or her visual sensitivity. The community of curators, connoisseurs and critics – the doorkeepers of high art – had even more to lose by modification of the high art myth. Their professional empowerment depended on their claim to an equivalent sensibility to that of the creators of high art, a sensibility that enabled them uniquely to appreciate it and that justified their appropriation of the right to judge it – to determine 'excellence', a word repeated mantra-like as the sole determinant of value by the believers, working in their museums and arts councils.

The concept of high art was deeply embedded in the social and political structures within Britain among whose beneficiaries were those who had, firstly, denied the existence of a Welsh visual culture and, subsequently, when the existence of the material became a matter of documentation, denied the value of one of its core components. It was now to be excluded because it did not meet the mysterious criteria for excellence upon which their validation depended. Indeed, they alleged that my affirmation of the material denied the notion of excellence – that is to say, of relative quality in art – but this was not the case. I was seeking to distinguish between quality and value. It was always clear to me that variation of quality existed within artisan painting as in every other manifestation of material culture. What was being challenged was not the concept of quality but the mystical basis on which judgements of quality were made within high art methodology, and its role in underpinning disagreeable political and social realities:

A people or a class that is cut off from its own past is far less free to choose and to act as a people or class than one that has been able to situate itself in history. This is why – and this is the only reason why – the entire art of the past has now become a political issue.[39]

Through the 1980s, it became apparent that the core body of painting in Wales during the first half of the nineteenth century had been the work of artisans, rather than of academically trained painters. As the indifference of the art establishment to what was being revealed turned to hostility, I became increasingly interested in the equivalent work of artisan painters in the United States, and especially in the very different attitude towards it that seemed to be expressed by the American art establishment.

The Young Physician

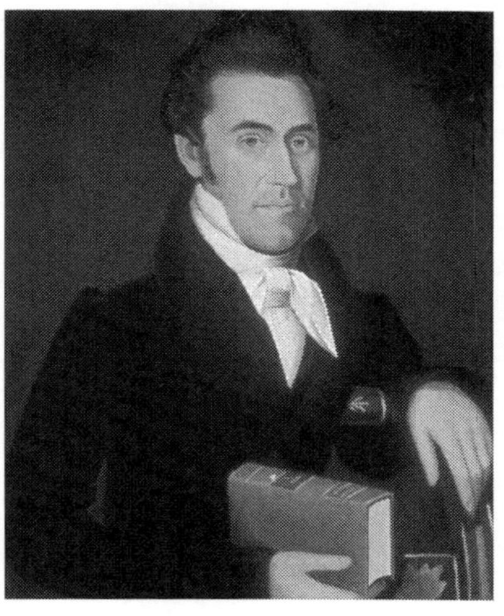

In about 1830, probably in Duchess County, New York State, the artisan painter Ammi Phillips took the portrait of a young physician. Nothing is known of the circumstances, though since Phillips's first wife died in that year, the picture may have been related to her illness. The physician's name has not been recorded, and his profession is assumed only from the fact that he holds a copy of *Cooper's Surgery* in his hand.[40] *Cooper's Surgery* was a standard text of the period on its subject – on both sides of the Atlantic. The same book is displayed prominently in the bookcase of the *The Surgeon Apothecary*, painted by John Roberts in Pwllheli, and it is far from being the only link between the two pictures. In fact, they are close in almost every way. Clearly, they serve the same purpose, and they deploy the same conventions to do so. They are the same size, the sitter is posed in a similar way, and both men display their fashionable furniture, albeit with rather more subtlety in the case of the American. The manner of painting is similar in terms of its degree of finish and level of skill – both faces are well executed and expressive, though reflecting different characters. The American is distinctly suave, with urban tastes, I fancy. The ruddy-face of the Welshman suggests that he was, perhaps, more inclined to country life, if not to alcohol. The painters have been less interested in the torsos of their sitters, which are too small for the heads in both cases. Hung side by side the two portraits would seem entirely compatible – they could represent partners in the same practice. There is, however, one significant difference between them. It does not lie in the nature of the patronage that generated the commissions – in the expectations of the sitters, their social standing or how much they are likely to have paid for their pictures. Neither is it to be found in the practice of the painters – the range of their businesses, their painting styles or the levels of training and skill they exhibit. The difference lies in the perception of the pictures (and of the kind of painting they exemplify) by their respective modern audiences.

John Roberts's picture *The Surgeon Apothecary* is unknown to the public and to art historians working in Welsh institutions. It hangs in my house and, until 2011, had never been exhibited or reproduced.[41] Neither of Roberts's pictures owned by the National Museum is on display. On the other hand, I first saw *The Young Physician* reproduced in one of the many lavish publications that deal with the subject of American artisan painting within the framework of folk art. I would not see the original until 1999, when I was making the televison series 'The Big Picture', with Ceri Sherlock. To explore the parallel between Welsh and American artisan painting, and the difference in its valuation between the two countries, we filmed at the Abby Aldrich Rockefeller Folk Art Center at Williamsburg in Virginia, a prestigious museum which owns the most extensive and historically important collection of artisan portraits in the United States. It is visited by thousands of people every year. Many other pictures can be paired in the same way as the two doctors to demonstrate the striking disparity in the status of artisan painting between the United States and Wales. Both as a portrayal of a national military leader and in its formal conventions, Roberts's *Marquis of Anglesey* closely resembles American artisan portraits of Washington and other heroes of the War of Independence. The sociology of Hugh Hughes's group portrait of the family of John Evans, another privately owned Welsh picture largely unknown to the public, is closely reflected in Erastus Salisbury Field's *Joseph Moore and His Family*, which is among the most widely reproduced of all artisan paintings. It is held at the Museum of Fine Arts in Boston. The affirmation of these works provided by exhibition in such museums, and the associated assessments published by art historians, is reflected in their market value. In 1985, the American Folk Art Museum in New York was presented with the Ammi Phillips portrait *Girl in Red with Cat and Dog* by a donor who had paid over a million dollars for it.[42] Its graphic quality encouraged its use as an emblem of the institution and the art historical construct that it represented. At the height of the Museum's development, in its pupose-built home, significantly adjacent to the Museum of Modern Art, the painting was set at the far end of the long and otherwise empty entrance hall. Icon-like, behind protective glass, it was embedded in the wall at the point of ascent to the riches above.[43] The work of the Pennsylvania coach-painter Edward Hicks reached even more spectacular heights. In 1999, one of the sixty or so versions of his *Peaceable Kingdom* fetched $4.7 million dollars at auction. These are Picasso prices.

At Williamsburg I asked the curator, Barbara Luck, what it was that her audience gained from their visit to the painting galleries at the Folk Art Center. I sensed a certain defensiveness in her restatement of a position in which ideological cracks had begun to appear by this time but, nevertheless, she remained clear that 'By and large there's an enormous sense of validation about these people's personal past. Finally they realise that *their* past, *their* inheritance has been deemed worthy by someone in a museum setting. I think it's a very gratifying experience.'[44] Working in Wales in the aftermath of the debacle of the devolution referendum of 1979, it seemed to me that the absence of such institutional and intellectual validation of our own cultural product was among the root causes of the psychological dependency that the referendum result signified. I felt that I could contribute to encouraging the psychological shift necessary to secure political movement by working in the field of art history. In the United States artisan portraits were surrounded by a rhetoric of national confidence and assertiveness. If the story of Welsh art could be changed, so would our valuation of the material. If we changed our valuation of the material, then as in the United States, it could contribute to, and be a sign of, a change in our valuation of ourselves. That is why, along with many other people, I made so much fuss about the ethos of the Art Department of the National Museum in the 1980s.[45] Raising self-esteem and self-confidence was the key to shifting the political mood of the period towards rejection of the colonial status of Wales within the British state. The American experience seemed to provide a model.

There was no doubt in my mind about the legitimacy of changing history. Indeed, the interpretation of artisan painting presented a clear example of history as a mutable cultural construct. This understanding presented the only explanation for the utterly different status of the same category of pictures in two places. The conventional wisdom of high art history and criticism with which I was brought up – the 'mainstream' – had for centuries promoted the idea that visual art was a universal language. As early as 1715 Jonathan Richardson wrote:

> And this is a Language that is Universal; Men of all Nations hear the Poet, Moralist, Historian, Divine, or whatever other Character the Painter assumes, speaking to them in their own Mother Tongue.[46]

Furthermore, the idea of its universality – that it sprang not from the need to satisfy the practical and psychological demands of a particular social context but from the mysterious access of the 'great artist' to truths of a supernatural nature – implied that

> to create and to appreciate the greatest art the most absolute abstraction from the affairs of life is essential. And as, throughout the ages, men and women have gone to temples and churches in search of an ecstasy incompatible with and remote from the preoccupations and activities of laborious humanity, so they may go to the temples of art to experience a little out of this world, emotions that are of another.[47]

Despite an incoming tide of argument to the contrary through the twentieth century, the embeddedness of the idea that, on the basis of its belonging to another world, great art in Europe was also great art in America and, for that matter, in Japan or Nigeria, secured it against being washed away. The idea that 'It is the mark of great art that its appeal is universal and eternal'[48] still lurks, a hard rock just beneath the surface, inside the mind of the art museum community throughout the western world. However, if the value of pictures truly derives from such universals as these, then either American or Welsh historians have something very wrong in their different assessment of artisan portraits. They cannot both be correct. The pictures cannot be, at the same time, 'rubbish' in Cardiff and as good as Picasso in New York, unless the notions that underlie the mainstream of art history are misconceived. During the 1980s and 90s I made often the theoretical argument that, indeed, they were not only misconceived but mischievously conceived, and I deployed the American parallel in support of the theory. However, I did not do so without an increasing awareness of certain difficulties with the American understanding of artisan painting. At that time the priority was the potential impact on national psychology of the inspiration of the American example. The public exploration of the problematic aspects of the construct I set aside.

Two of the problems were methodological. Firstly, Americans categorised the artisan painted portrait as folk art. My understanding of the folk, rooted in Welsh and broader European tradition, did not lead me to feel that the middle-class patrons of artisan portrait painters were to be included among them. Indeed, if Hugh Hughes himself was to be believed, their whole sense of self depended precisely on their success in differentiating themselves, economically and socially, from the folk. Looking over their shoulders from whence they had come, in fact it had been they, the middle class, who had created the myth of the Welsh folk.[49] Secondly, the American construct of folk art asserted that the material celebrated – within which artisan portraits held a central place – was uniquely American. In fact, that belief had provided the *raison d'être* for the construct, and was persistently emphasised in the interpretation of the material to the public. Observing not only from Wales but also from a wider European perspective, this was clearly not the case. The material was far from unique and, indeed, it could be shown that much of it derived directly from European antecedents.[50] The American critics and historians who promoted the uniqueness of American folk art had failed to distinguish between a retrospective narrative of pictures that was, indeed, unique, and the pictures themselves, that were not. Although these problems were pretty obvious from a European perspective, when I first began to think about them I was unaware that they had also been noted in the United States itself and, indeed, had been the subject of a passionate debate that began there in the mid-1970s. That debate had not emerged from academic circles with a sufficiently high profile to affect the perceptions of the general public or the art market, which remained dominated by the affirmative rhetoric broadcast in a continuing flow of lavish publications and exhibitions. The economic power of the folk art establishment that they expressed was, in fact, a signifier of the deepest of the problems underlying the construct.

Received wisdom points to an exhibition mounted at the Whitney Studio Club in 1924 under the uncontroversial title 'Early American Art' as marking the public starting point of the construction of the American Folk Art tradition. The roots of the exhibition lay with a group of young artists associated with the Ogunquit artists' colony in Maine, who had interested themselves in the non-academic visual culture of rural communities in the north eastern United States. They found it manifested in many forms, including the decoration of everyday objects, sign painting, weathervanes, decoys, furniture – and artisan portrait paintings. The founder of the Ogunquit colony had been the wealthy artist and collector Hamilton Easter Field. He had travelled in Europe before the Great War, where he became familiar with both the avant-garde and the non-European sources that inspired many of its leading exponents.[51] In fact, the enthusiasm of the Americans at Ogunquit was entirely characteristic of a long, if spasmodic, European tradition of engagement with the idea of 'the common people' by young artists trying to de-contaminate their aesthetics from prevailing metropolitan academisms. In France, both Brittany and Normandy had provided fertile territory before the Great War,[52] as had Cornwall in England. There, it was an on-going trend – Ben Nicholson and Jim Ede would meet Alfred Wallis only four years after the Whitney Studio Club show to form their lop-sided alliance of the 'primitive' and the sophisticate. However, in the United States, such young artists – some of whom, significantly, were first generation immigrants, such as Elie and Viola Nadelman – chose to find in their discoveries the potential source for a particularly American modernism that would challenge European domination of the art world. By 1926, the Nadelmans had accumulated a collection large enough to open to the public as the Museum of Folk and Peasant Arts, at Riverdale, New York State. Their choice expressed a wider desire among radical intellectuals to assert a national identity that would break the last vestiges of what they regarded as the colonialised mentality of the old American elite, that still looked to Europe as its cultural model – the philosophy of 'I'd rather go to Europe than go to Heaven'.[53] It would assert a powerful artistic creativity in America which matched the economic and military power that had, as they saw it, recently salvaged the old world from barbarism in the Great War.

In less than ten years the new tradition would be stamped with the highest establishment approval available and a corpus crystalised that remains in place in the twenty-first century. In 1932, the exhibition 'American Folk Art. The Art of the Common Man in America', was held at the Museum of Modern Art in New York. The cover of the exhibition catalogue had no words printed upon it, but carried simply a small coloured image of the American Eagle. Some years ago I bought a copy through an American rare-book dealer, and when it arrived I found that it been prominently inscribed with the words 'Property of Tom Funk'. Tom proved to have been, in 1932, when he saw the exhibition, a young New York designer, a characteristic representative of the audience to whom the narrative appealed. I can imagine his excitement. Artisan portraits were the exhibition's primary exhibits, a preface to a display of many kinds of naïve pictures, calligraphy, weathervanes, decoy ducks and ships' figureheads, reclassified as 'sculpture'. The fact that, from the first, the American construct of folk art was more strongly influenced by aesthetics than by sociology, since it was defined by visual artists and connoisseurs rather than by sociologists and anthropologists, would have long-term implications. The middle-class artisan portrait was associated with a group of works to which it did not belong.[54]

The 1932 exhibition was significant not only for its definition of the corpus, but for its politics. Conservatives, threatened by the rise of socialism and communism in response to the disaster of the Wall Street crash and the Depression, found the construct appealing both as a personal escape to a more stable age and as a potential prop to contemporary social cohesion – a restatement of the unifying foundation myth of the eighteenth-century constitution. For the left, the construction of a tradition that placed the 'common man' at the centre and which pointed a way forward on that basis had obvious appeal, and the moment was opportune. The exhibition opened in the year of Roosevelt's election victory and the promise of a New Deal through 'Relief, Recovery, Reform'. From a Welsh point of view, the willingness of the left to claim the same national and, indeed, nationalist heritage as the right seems curious. Broadly speaking – though there were, of course, notable exceptions – the Welsh left in the 1930s was anti-nationalist. Fundamental to this different reaction was America's condition as the first post-colonial society. The United States was understood to be the fruit of a democratic revolt against the aristocratic oligarchies of the old European world. In 1934 the claim of the left to the heritage was stated by Lewis Corey, the founder of the Communist Party of the USA, who accused the right of having usurped the true radical tradition – the spirit of American individualism had been perverted by laissez-faire capitalism. The ruling class had:

> donned the guise of the pioneers' rugged individualism as a screen for predatory practices and a disregard for the masses' need.[55]

The progressivism of the left was a restatement of the defining revolutionary principles of freedom and democracy. Looking forward was consistent with looking back – though for some visual artists and musicians on the left, paradoxically steeped in a European tradition in which there was a deep linkage between progress and the stylistic avant-garde, the philosophy was not without its difficulties. They experienced a conflict between proletarian or populist political convictions and the pursuit of an art that was unintelligible in form to lay-people. In visual culture, abstraction was problematic, for instance. Stuart Davis, among the most prominent of radical young painters in the period, would remain committed to non-figurative aesthetics, and so found it necessary to protest that 'Social content in art is not dependent upon descriptive naturalism in method'.[56] Initially, the composer Aaron Copland took a similar line, writing revolutionary pieces such as 'Into the Streets May First' in a modernist idiom, but after 1932 he abandoned his Schoenberg-like avant-gardism for the accessibility of the folk-inspired pieces 'Billy the Kid' and 'Appalachian Spring'. He defined the principle that he applied as 'imposed simplicity'.

The organiser of the 1932 'Art of the Common Man' exhibition was Holger Cahill, a left-leaning intellectual of Icelandic origin, who had visited Scandinavian folk museums a decade earlier. He would play a central role in the development of the art programmes of Roosevelt's Works Progress Administration. Through its Federal Art Project – the FAP – he facilitated the development both of new practice in the social realist public mural painting that flourished briefly in the years before the Second World War,[57] and the Index of American Design. The Index project provided work for many unemployed artists in recording images and artefacts chosen by its editor, Constance Rourke, as exemplars of her sense of the American-ness of American visual culture, with a strong emphasis on the same material – the 'democratic arts' – that was gathered together within the folk art construct.[58] Crucially, however, Cahill was also instrumental in the promotion of folk art among wealthy connoisseurs of a different political complexion to his own. He was involved romantically with the New York art dealer Edith Gregor Halpert, whose Downtown Gallery represented young modernist American painters and sculptors, such as Stuart Davis. She had been successful in attracting the patronage of wealthy collectors, the most notable of whom was Abby Aldrich Rockefeller, among the richest women in the United States. Aware of the excitement surrounding the recovery of folk paintings and artefacts, Halpert had begun to collect early on, and opened the first commercial gallery specialising in the material above the Downtown Gallery.[59] Promoting folk art as the ancestor of modern American painting, Halpert succeeded in interesting Mrs Rockefeller in the material, and she also began to collect on a large scale, buying mainly through the gallery. It was from the Rockefeller collection that Cahill, by this time Curator at the Museum of Modern Art, drew his material for the 1932 exhibition.

By the mid-1930s a powerful alignment of forces was in place to promote the idea of American folk art, though it could not be described as a coalition. On the one hand there were radical young visual artists and musicians, supported by left leaning intellectuals who, for a brief period found themselves empowered in government. On the other, a growing community of wealthy collectors that came to include members of the most notable industrial dynasties in the country – the du Ponts and the Fords, as well as the Rockefellers – was supplied by the beginnings of an art market that their collective demand could sustain. Together they stimulated the development of a body of theory and research that reinforced the nationalism of the folk art concept. The most influential of the writers was Jean Lipman, editor of *Art in America* from 1940. In *The Magazine Antiques*, another powerful organ for the promotion of the concept, in 1941 Lipman published a seminal affirmation of the artisan portrait – 'American Primitive Portraiture: a Revaluation':

Most critics have consistently based their estimates on
academic English or Continental standards, naming those

American painters the greatest who were the least American and most imitative in their approach. The bold, abstract American style has been criticised as lacking in finesse of characterisation and in subtlety of coloring and design. It is a strange blindness that has caused these critics to look for skilled academic refinement in the art of a sturdy pioneering people who had colonised a wilderness through fresh vigorous enterprise and robust vitality – qualities with which the native art was necessarily endowed. But, as Willard Huntingdon Wright commented in his *Misinforming a Nation*, 'in our slavish imitation of England – the only country in Europe of which we have any intimate knowledge – we have de-Americanised ourselves to such an extent that there has grown up in us a typical British contempt for our own native achievements.'[60]

The 'intimate knowledge' of England assumed by Wright (and by Lipman) was, in fact, confined to English aristocratic taste. Clearly they did not know England, and certainly not Britain. It might be suggested in their defence that their ignorance was based largely on the narrow understandings of contemporary English art historians. Had they known better, perhaps they would have been less ready to make the facile association between 'pioneering spirit' and non-academic style that so confused the notion of American folk art.[61] The date of Lipman's essay is also significant in terms of understanding its anti-English sentiment. Neither the United States nor Russia had entered the Second World War at this point, and isolationism remained a powerful political instinct both on the right and on the pro-Soviet left. However, for the left, the end of an era had already arrived – marked, ironically perhaps, by one of its most lasting expressions, Aaron Copland's *Fanfare for the Common Man*, composed in 1942.[62] The long ascendency of the right, that would extend through the Cold War, had begun. In fact, Holger Cahill had been named in a letter to Roosevelt as a Communist sympathiser as early as 1937.[63] In the 1950s Cahill and Copland were among the many leading pre-war intellectuals and artists who would come under 'investigation' in the un-American activities frenzy. In this atmosphere, patriotic identification of the folk art material with the political right intensified and, with it, renewed emphasis on connoisseurial critique. Social elites require elite art. In 1974, fifty years after the Whitney Studio Club exhibition, its successor, the Whitney Museum, facilitated the publication of what was intended as a definitive survey of the field, under the title *The Flowering of American Folk Art*. In her introduction, Jean Lipman restated her original patriotic position but with a significant rebalancing towards the connoisseurial notion of 'excellence':

> In 1942 and again in 1946, in my two books on American
> folk painting, I expressed the opinion, 'radical though this may
> seem,' that a number of gifted folk artists arrived at a power and
> originality and beauty that were not surpassed by the greatest of
> the academic painters. I have never changed my mind and am
> convinced that the entire field of activity of the folk artists was
> absolutely not, as has often been said, a charming postscript.
> I believe it was a central contribution to the mainstream of
> American culture in the formative years of our democracy.[64]

A decade later, Lipman, again affirmed her view, this time in the context of her own collection, stating that she had developed it according to 'the same standards of excellence that we would have demanded from Calder or Picasso'.[65] The connoisseurism of American folk art tradition in the post war period was deeply ironic, given the motives of those who had established the corpus by decrying European high art tradition as decadent and oppressive. The very museums, critics and collectors whose attentions began to validate American folk art in the public mind in the 1930s unashamedly developed their promotion of the corpus by reinventing old world connoisseurism as a critical methodology. Writers such as Mary Black, editor of *The Magazine Antiques*, who was among the influential tradition builders of mid-century, mimicked the European mainstream by constructing hierarchies of artists, by tracing the evolution of style through top-down artistic influence, and by projecting the artistic aspirations of modernist painters backwards onto nineteenth-century artisans.[66]

In 1975, these tendencies reached extreme heights in their development when the art historian and collector John Gordon curated an exhibition entitled 'Masterpieces of American Folk Art', in which many artisan portraits were included. His introduction to the catalogue presented in strident mode both the patriotism and the connoisseurism that inflected folk art rhetoric – just as the post war settlement between labour and capital and 'the grand governing narrative' of American history was breaking down under the stress of the civil rights movement, the women's movement and Vietnam.[67] It was a moment of critical political coincidence. The Bicentennial celebrations approached as the war reached its humiliating climax:

> From the earliest examples to the most recent, all two hundred pieces have directness, strength and great simplicity in design and restrained decoration, that immediately evokes the American character.

The non-academic paintings and sculpture, unshackled by the strictures of school learning, follow paths of individuality of style and result in artistic expression at least on a par with the highly trained, most developed talents in the academic field … An uncomplicated forthrightness communicates its intention and beckons with the spirit of frontier friendship and simplicity … A no-nonsense art by the people, for the people, produced in an ambience of private conscience and outspoken mind. The artist's concern for expressing what he sensed and felt, rather than what he saw, made the difference. Genius does not involve itself merely with description; it penetrates to revelation.

The American craftsman worked as a free man … and the result was democracy at work. Freedom nourishes the artist's muse. A tradition developed that was not tired or repetitious of the standards and techniques of previous generations. The peasant art of Europe seems to strain for the epitome of repeating the accomplishments of the past; in America each craftsman produced the fresh statement.

Here, in the only democracy at work, a classless and free society granting gifts of opportunity, the miracles did happen. The flowering of free spirits produced a meaningful and abundant outpouring of expression that clearly revealed American life. The atmosphere nurtured the spirit … And is this wondrous output not the great democracy's distinct contribution to world art.[68]

Gordon's rhetoric, deployed in affirmation of the American-ness of American folk art, carried unmistakably the resonance of the political right in the United States. He signed off his defiantly bombastic essay six months after Saigon fell to the Viet Cong. For people of the antiwar generation, the resonance of this rhetoric was problematic, to say the least, and it was folk culture specialists and art historians of that emerging generation who, at last, challenged the received wisdom. Among them was Kenneth L. Ames who, in 1977, drew attention in particular to Gordon's essay:

> Gordon's 'wondrous output' buttresses the mythology of folk art and is too fatuous to merit an extended rebuttal. Perceptive writers have long seen the distortion in calling folk art the real American art and the true expression of the American people ... But just as the myth of the melting pot supported the belief that when immigrants came to this country they threw off associations with their native lands and retooled as that new product known as the American, the myth of nationalism maintains that American material culture at an early date became distinct from and superior to that produced in the rest of the world.[69]

Ames's observations on Gordon's essay formed part of a wider and seminal challenge to the received wisdom, *Beyond Necessity. Art in the Folk Tradition*, published in 1977. At the Winterthur Museum in Delaware, where he was teaching, Ames was given responsibility for the catalogue of an exhibition of the folk art collection of its founder, Henry Francis du Pont. However, Ames chose to write an iconoclastic document that seemed to conservative readers to have little to do with the exhibition. It created an intense atmosphere for a conference held subsequently to discuss the issues arising. The conference report, that emerged a further three years later, described its impact:

> Ames's essay shocked the world of folk art. Often brash and irreverent in tone, always penetrating in its analysis, the essay

is a trenchant examination of values relating to museum and collecting practices … Ames did not ignore the objects in the exhibition, but he used them in an unconventional manner for a museum catalogue. They became foils for analyzing concepts … No one within the museum field had so openly challenged so many assumptions about collecting and exhibiting folk art … It established the tone for the conference which became a sociological phenomenon in its own right.

The conference atmosphere was electrically charged. Participants readily took sides and clustered with their ideological peers, almost as if at a political rally …[70]

Art matters, because different understandings of it embody fundamental personal identities that are not socially – and, by extension politically – compatible. As Ames saw it in 1980, new parameters of study such as those that he had proposed would mean dealing with 'conflict, for from my point of view the manifest and latent functions of the study of folk art point to explicit as well as implicit conflicts within our society and, at another level, perhaps within our own minds as well.'[71] Ames was participating in a wider socio-political project. The folk art argument expressed the 'implicit conflicts' in American society that he experienced, as would the issue of art at the National Museum of Wales, a few years later, when it became the superficial focus of a deeper debate.

Although he had yet to meet Ames, among the iconoclastic party at the Winterthur Conference was the young John Michael Vlach, at that time working on folk culture in Texas. In 1983 he published *Folk Art and Art Worlds*, which included a succinct précis of his position:

The approach to folk art that I am advocating is one which recognizes artists' intentions first and the qualities of their works second. This is a view which some might distinguish as sociological rather than humanistic, but I see no profound disadvantage or disservice to art in grounding the study of art in the lives of the people who create and use it.[72]

Shortly afterwards Vlach turned his attention to the particular anomaly of artisan portrait painting within the American folk art corpus, as an exemplar of the problematic nature of its wider philosophical foundations. I was excited by *Plain Painters*, published in 1988, because of its pioneering attempt to deal in an intellectually coherent way with material of importance to me, and I agreed entirely with its central thesis, that artisan painting – 'plain painting', in Vlach's terminology – had no place within folk art constructs, American or otherwise. As an expression of the aspirations of the white middle class, artisan portraits clearly had little to do with the 'common man', understood by the left as an ethnically diverse working class. However, his depreciative insistence that artisan painting was no more than a failed attempt at academic art – 'novices experimenting with a complex apparatus' – was more difficult for me. It seemed to confirm that this part of Welsh visual culture, by which I set great store, was not being undervalued in Wales after all, and that the National Museum's assessment of the pictures as 'rubbish' was correct. Even after reading his persuasive book I continued to feel that there was more to it than that – not simply in terms of the social significance of the pictures, a point which Vlach entirely accepted, but that the best of artisan painting went beyond under-achieving academic art. Considering Vlach's arguments with care, and aware that my use of the qualifier 'best' seemed to propel me towards the connoisseurial camp, a direction in which I certainly did not wish to be propelled, a feeling remained that the baby was being thrown out with the bathwater. Unfortunately, at the other end of the theoretical spectrum, that warm but contaminated amniotic fluid continued to nourish the nexus of art museum and art market in the promotion of artisan portraits within American folk art. Eleven years after *Plain Painters*, the myth was as virile as ever. Sotheby's New York reported that:

> Fuelled by patriotic and nostalgic fervour, the market for American naïve painting is booming. Works by Edward Hicks and Ammi Phillips are among the most desirable. A flood of new collectors have entered the market in recent years and are paying top prices.

In *Beyond Necessity*, among the cultural strands that Kenneth Ames had identified as contributing to the myth of the American-ness of American folk art was anti-intellectualism, to which Sotheby's sales pitch continued to make direct appeal:

> This art is not intimidating. Naïve paintings are immediate. The people who made them did not, on the whole, have a formal training. They are a reflection of American culture and social history but you don't need a classical art education to understand American folk art which is very comforting. In addition, for Americans, this art is a kind of subliminal celebration of the qualities that we like to see in ourselves and in our history – independence, industriousness, self-reliance and creativity.[73]

In 2010 I travelled to the United States to discuss the present state of the folk art argument. John Vlach welcomed me at his small office in Washington as 'comrade', and I considered myself honoured by that epithet. His 1960s Berkeley credentials are sound, and he remains keen to acknowledge himself as the awkward squad – indeed, as a 'hated figure' in folk art circles. He identifies as an outsider, a position rooted in his early experience as a pioneer of African-American folk studies, which he experienced as on-going, living tradition. It was in this capacity that he had gone to the Winterthur meeting in 1977.

> There was a blow up at this meeting … I was the young wild man, came in from Texas, and I was doing my African-American thing, and there were no blacks in the audience – I was the blackest person there – but they were interested because it was an opening … I wasn't first but I was up early in the day and the market was really interested – we'd already had the [Watts] riots and now folks are calming down and trying to figure out … There must be beauty in there somewhere? … So I was bringing a whole new set of collectables to their attention …
>
> I would say in the United States the museums are actually the producer of the desire [to collect]. When academics and museum types get into it they don't try to connect with the market but they do connect with the market whether they like it or not because people read that and then they take it to the market place and say 'This is going to be hot – we got to get a lot more of this …'[74]

Vlach used the example of the market in the quilts made by the black community of Gee's Bend, Alabama, 'thirty five thousand, forty thousand – some of them they've allowed to be mass produced in Japan, so you can get a replica … Welcome to America!'

At Winterthur – 'polite at the beginning and towards the end hissing and moaning from the crowd' – the meeting had ended with everyone retreating into their respective corner and going home: 'There was no conclusion,' he observed. 'But you came back?' I suggested. 'You wrote *Folk Art and Art Worlds*':

> I was an advocate … I was dealing with the needs of the art community to recognise that it was a lot more complicated than just finding and being lucky to find some great things in a flea market. The notion that you would actually go to folk producers was alien. Partly they could get away with it because they would say, 'Well, folk is a nineteenth-century phenomenon.' Well, that means that you're missing some of the great opportunities because traditions still live, people make the same old thing, and also new versions of the same old thing, and new things they never thought of before – it's in a kind of experimental flow, some of it may drop out, some of it may survive, you don't know until you see it all, and if you have say a certain collection – say it was pottery, the span was maybe a century and a half and you had the sequence right – you could be able to see how some of these ideas are being experimented with, rising, failing, emerging: the kinds of dynamics that happen in lively societies of creative people.

> For these guys, folk art was dead art that we were recovering. Bless us all! All us collectors!

I asked what was signified by what they were recovering:

> Patriotism. I would have said patriotism first and secondarily then the market values because you could go to a flea market

and get prime folk art from somebody who is a purveyor of junk and who'd say OK! 'I'll give you five dollars', 'Yes OK, you take it. I ask you ten but you take it', and so you have a know-nothing purveyor at that point, then it's all a bunch of giggling ... Because most of the stories in my experience they would tell is the find that everybody missed ... everybody came into the flea market or to an estate sale and walked right by it and walked right by it and *I saw it* and knew what it was – it was a limner portrait! So ... you call it a limner portrait rather than an awkward painting by an amateur (which doesn't necessarily make it a bad thing), but your language is already romanticising the effort and so you are king for the day because you found the best new discovery ...[75]

'Whose patriotism is it?', I asked:

Right wing republicans. They're interested in a nicer America. It's just the nature of American conservatism. 'We're fine, you're not, I'm sorry for you ...' The sense of a kind of enfranchisement from the womb. [It] derives ultimately from class privilege.

'So your intervention, and Ames's intervention, back then, was a total failure?'

Yea, didn't change them, but on the other hand, you know, we are teaching the children ...

John Vlach manifests his feeling for these issues by intense and immediate patterns of expression – the issues live and are personal for him. Ken Ames appears more reflective, detached perhaps, thirty years on from the Winterthur conference, though he remains equally marked by the concerns of his generation – 'the Vietnam stuff'.[76] Ames had been a student at Pennsylvania State University in Philadelphia

– 'a fairly animated school, not quite as lively as Berkeley, but a lot going on there.' However, it was his move to Winterthur that had made him aware of the issues with which he would deal in his early career: 'I don't think I had ever had a sustained class confrontation … It was a really pretentious place, but it also pretended not to be pretentious, which is kind of interesting … It was pretty conservative.' Like Vlach, Ames identified anti-elitism as an important motive for the attack that he was about to launch:

> The shift actually had to do with an impulse to democratise the material studied and to move away from an oppressively elitist orientation …

> So the exhibition went one way and for good or ill I had free hand at what I wanted to do. I did a course with students who were smart and we read lots of stuff. We read conventional folk art stuff and we read W.E.B. Du Bois – we read all over the place, you know, and it was one of the few classes I've ever had where people were shouting and weeping in class. There was a fair amount of animation about this stuff … excitement and disagreement and a fair degree of passion about things and, you know, I read enough to decide a lot of it was significantly wrong headed and I tried to say something about it.

> It was the wilful ignorance of the staff of the American Folk Art Museum. 'We don't want to know anything, we just think it's beautiful and we want to make up what we think about it' – and they still do that … It's a strange operation, but what I learned from it was that some people are passionately attached to a whole lot of things you don't understand and they're

passionately attached to a whole lot of things that don't make any sense – quasi-religious things.

The elevation of the artisan painter had reached its quasi-religious apotheosis at the American Folk Art Museum in 2008, in the exhibition 'The Seduction of Light', which set pictures by Ammi Phillips and Mark Rothko side by side. Speaking of Phillips, the Director of the Museum, Tracy C. Holander, was moved to employ the language of mysticism that identifies the great artist in the mainstream tradition:

> The earliest extant canvases were painted in 1811, and though some of Phillips's key themes are in place, the works themselves are awkward and immature. The portraits that came from his brush just a few years later, however, are miraculous and ethereal visions filled with transcendent light and beauty, as though Phillips had been touched by God in the intervening years.

> In their paintings, both Phillips and Rothko opened portals to a dimension where form was suspended in an ether of suffused atmosphere, and where the mysticism of light was coaxed into being primarily through the vehicle of color. For neither artist was color a simple tool to compose pleasing arrangements, instead it was a complex language of its own, used to invent and investigate the depths offered by the deceptive flat plane of the canvas.[77]

Hollander's exhibition of pictures by Mark Rothko and Ammi Phillips in the same art gallery had no doubt been conceived as progressive, in the sense that it sought to unify American visual culture, but in its attempt to mystify the artisan Phillips by linkage with the high artist Rothko, rather than to demystify Rothko by comparison with Phillips, its most important revelation was the institution's aspiration to the same level of connoisseurial authority (with all that it implied socially and politically) as its neighbour, the Museum of Modern Art.

Aware that I had recently visited John Vlach and Ken Ames, when I met Stacey Hollander for the first time at the American Folk Art Museum my reception was frosty. Her response to my initial questions was reminiscent of the defensiveness that I had experienced, a decade earlier, when interviewing Barbara Luck at the Williamsburg Folk Art Center. A sense of intellectual embattlement suffuses these institutions. Nevertheless, as Ken Ames had suggested, I would leave her with no doubt in my mind as to the sincerity of the mystical beliefs that apparently underpin her love of this material. Ames thinks about this strain in American folk art critique in terms of misplaced values – cherished ideals that, if a 'person of any sense' looks around, will not be found in our world, so 'they'll have to imagine them elsewhere ... place these ideals in a safe historical or quasi-historical or imagined historical niche where I can claim or demonstrate that if they were once possible, it's possible that they're here now, too':

> It's a kind of displacement thing, it's projection – you project that on all this stuff – things you want to believe in, and so anybody who tried to say, well, wait a minute, there are other readings to this ... 'I don't want to hear that!' If it gets close to your ideological core, 'Go away!'

I wonder where this all leaves us now, apart from generally confused? The one certainty seems to be that we all use yesterday's images to make today's arguments but, looking back, perhaps I was wrong to sideline the difficult methodological issues arising from the use of the American example as an inspiration, if not as a model, for change in Wales? In the mid-1980s things seemed simpler – politically simpler – as they had seemed simpler, no doubt, to Holger Cahill in America's crisis half a century earlier. In 1932, in pursuit of his progressive goals it had not been apparent to him, for instance, that the way in which he promoted the work of artisan painters and craftspeople might have 'actually demeaned the very people it sought to affirm'.[78] Despite the on-going and often penetrating deconstruction of his idea of American folk art and its entanglement with high art values and contemporary politics that was initiated by Ames and Vlach, there has been no change in the appeal of the material as manifested in the art market, and only minor modification to the promotional rhetoric. Perhaps Lipman was justified in her claim, made in 1986, that 'the critical battle for folk art as *art* has been won'.[79]

The parallels that existed between American and Welsh artisan painting practice extend to modern parallels in revisionist critiques. They extend even to the naiveté of those of us who applied those critiques, and ventured to criticise prevailing wisdoms, thirty years ago. Ken Ames had been as surprised at the reaction to *Beyond Necessity* as I was surprised by the hostile reaction to my own early work. When I spoke to him in New York I quoted to him a sentence from his book: 'Folk art has been used by a small but vocal faction against the rest of society and exploited as a means to personal and financial aggrandizement.'[80] I asked if it hadn't occurred to him that such a statement might upset some people? 'It didn't dawn on me enough', he remembered. 'I thought it was just fairly straightforward and even handed.' That was exactly as I had thought about 'Cultural Policy' and *The Aesthetics of Relevance*. I empathised with almost everything that was said to me by Ames and Vlach, but I was left with the paradox of their having come to different conclusions from my own about the value of the particular group of works – artisan portraits – in which I had invested heavily.

Perhaps the resolution of this paradox lies in rigorous adherence to the principle which I have expressed so often – that art is not universal. Perceptions of value come from an interaction of attitudes, both knowingly and unknowingly acquired, some of them rationally refined, modified or abandoned, some cherished for reasons too deeply buried in one's sense of self to be meaningfully explored – but all particular to times and places. Even if there are aesthetic universals in the form of human instincts that might respond in consistent ways to visual qualities such as redness or circularity, for instance, they can never be isolated, despite the efforts of generations of artistic essentialists to descend to imagined states of naïvety or to rise to states of mystical hyper-sensitivity. Art cannot be universal while cultures remain differentiable, but the idea that it can have no absolute and universal meaning is disconcerting, of course, because the need that gives rise to the search for absolutes and universals in high art is a manifestation of the same deep human uncertainty that gives rise to religion, its first cousin. The desire to make art universal is as mischievously conceived as the desire to spread Christianity, or any other religion, in order to exploit human uncertainty in the interests of empowerment or material aggrandisement, whether personal or imperial.

Driven by my own affection for the material, I regret that people whose views I respect do not share my perceptions of it, and, indeed, may be hostile to them. Early in his career, John Vlach studied and wrote about Philip Simmons, an African-American blacksmith working in Charleston.[81] His respect for the man remains deep – it is significant that he tends to refer to him in conversation as Mr Simmons. For John the work he made exemplified a wider idea of folk art, 'of collectively held views about what is decent, beautiful, helpful' – an elegant group of descriptors, but a group that as well expresses the doctrines that the artisan painter Hugh Hughes espoused in affirmation of the nonconformist middle class in Wales, as it defines the art of the common people of the United States.[82] The blacksmith died just a few years ago. Is the work of Philip Simmons now to be despatched to the category of 'dead art', to cohabit with that of Ammi Phillips and all the other nineteenth-century artisans promoted by the collectors to whom John is hostile? It seems to me that absolutely to elevate making over the thing made is to betray the creativity, skill and care that Simmons invested in his work, when he made it – a betrayal of the admired maker. Certainly the distinction must always be drawn between the living maker and the thing made, but unless we bury the artefacts with their maker, the thing made also lives, albeit in a different sense – in the sense of its evolving relationship with those who experience it as audience or custodian. Indeed, it lives in this different sense as soon as it leaves the maker's workshop, even in his or her lifetime. The maker owns the work only in a partial way. If his or her offer of the work is accepted – if the piece becomes a part of the consciousness of a culture, a process facilitated by the likes of John Vlach and myself, as well as the market and the rich collector – then it becomes mutable. Indeed, it must change, just as we all must change, as the times around us change. Perhaps John feels that American collectors have irretrievably contaminated the material they collected by their particular construction of its meaning. They were not primarily interested, as he was, in the people, in society and in what was wrong with it. That was my interest also, but I felt that what, perhaps, had become contaminated art in the American context could, in Wales, be interpreted positively so as to contribute to social and political change.

There are specific historical issues that I think mitigate against a universal application of the American revisionist devaluation of artisan painting. For instance, there is considerable evidence to suggest that the use of pictogramic conventions by some artisan portrait painters and the attraction of those conventions to their patrons, derived from a living tradition, contemporaneously expressed in sign painting. Without tradition, it is difficult to account for the consistency of non-academic formal traits of the kind visible, for instance, in Hugh Hughes's early portrait of Huw Griffith. In that light, modern appreciation of these pictogramic qualities in the work cannot be dismissed simply on the grounds of misrepresentation – of the retrospective application of modernist high art aesthetics. However, the central cause of confusion in the evaluation of the material seems to me to lie not in disputed understandings of the field that necessitate, in John Vlach's words, 'a different approach to folk art',[83] nor indeed in the narrower questions surrounding artisan portrait painting, despatched to an uncomfortable no-man's land of distasteful bourgeois aspiration. Rather, they lie in the understanding of the material to which both groups of artefacts are contrasted – high art. Until the belief that high art is qualitatively special is recognised as no more than a phase in the evolution of art history it will not be possible to understand the totality of visual culture in a coherent way. In the art museum, for instance, interpretation will not progress beyond the tokenism that grants Alfred Wallis a place in the Tate Gallery, legitimised by the authority of those high art practitioners who patronised him. This is not an attack on the material presently described as high art, and certainly not an argument for removing it from art museums. It is an attack on the mainstream narrative that uniquely appropriates to it a quality not present in 'lower' forms. It is an argument for understanding high art in a different way. The stratification of visual culture that uniquely appropriates excellence to the product of the empowered, institutionalised in mainstream connoisseurial art history and in the high art museum, is a cipher for legitimising an anachronistic social stratification.

It seems to me that the history of visual culture is more coherently described for the present state of western society as a horizontal spectrum – a continuum, characterised by fluid interactions between personal, social and political identities of class, gender and ethnicity, and the imagery and aesthetics arising from the expression of those identities. The methodological and historical case for integration is strong. It may be argued both negatively and positively – on the one hand demonstrating the absurdity of granting to the neo-classical statues of a Canova the accolade of high art while dismissing the ship's figurehead to the folk museum, and on the other describing the extensive transfers of imagery, technique and style between social and political domains and geographical locations that, in fact, characterise the history of all visual culture, including the artisan portrait. We need to turn the argument on its head, so as to demystify – to de-sanctify – high art, realising that its quasi-theological aura has been promoted to underpin social and political elites, to justify the status of the powerful against the weak. If we consider material culture as a horizontal spectrum rather than as a hierarchy, we will free ourselves to find quality – even excellence, if we can rehabilitate the term in this new and, as yet, hypothetical context – at any point along the spectrum. Such an integrated tradition does not deny the concept of relative quality. In writing about images, to deny a place to the concept of quality would be perverse, since the need to compare is built into the very grammar of our thought. However, it does require compared images to have been created within a similar purposive framework and, crucially, it requires a distinction to be made between quality and value.[84] Neither does integration imply homogeneity of interpretation throughout the western culture group – as the case of artisan painting demonstrates. Those aspects of the American and Welsh material that display close parallels of social origin and outward form continue to stimulate distinct interpretive narratives because the purposes which those narratives serve legitimately express both the history of successive investments of meaning in the work – the mutability of the work – and the present function of interpretation in nations with different contemporary political and social agendas.

I conclude that it is legitimate for me to like this work – artisan painting both American and Welsh – and to value it highly, here and now. Furthermore, it is legitimate for me to propose that you, too, also here and now, allow yourself to like it and to value it highly – indeed, if you wish, to find the best of it beautiful.

8

L.S. Lowry drawing the Stockport Viaduct

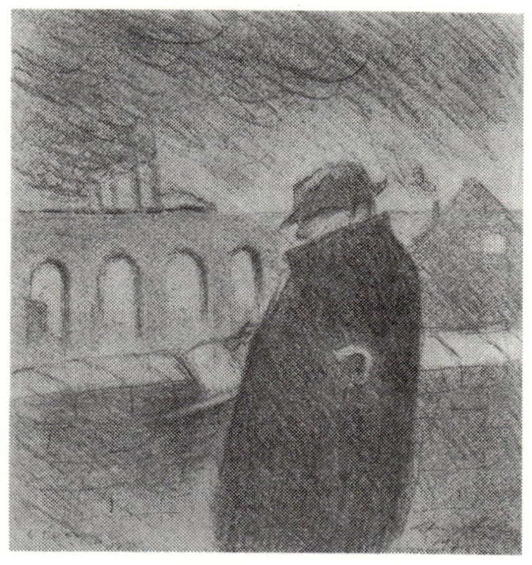

Generally speaking, artists like to hold court in their studios. However, it was Mervyn Levy's custom to receive visitors at the Chelsea Arts Club. His preference reflected the assessment he made of himself that he'd 'always been more of a writer and a talker than a painter.'[85] I didn't meet him until he'd turned 80, and his physical presence came as a surprise, since he was both unusually short and unusually handsome, even at that age. The form of his fine bearded head displayed his origins. His grandfather had left Russia in the 1890s and the family had eventually re-established itself among the shopocracy of Swansea. The languages of the home were English and Yiddish. He told me that one of the few people that he remembered hearing speak Welsh was Dylan Thomas's father. I don't believe he said this for effect, in order to emphasise Thomas senior's failure to pass the language on to his son. Levy and Thomas had grown up and gone to school together. Levy's reputation as a superb draughtsman (he won the Herbert Read drawing prize at the Royal College of Art in 1935) was sustained by the exhibition and reproduction of his many portraits of his friend. They became nice little earners, and Levy saw no reason to cease production after Thomas's death. Similarly, heavy demands would be made on him for the next forty years to recount Dylan anecdotes. Nevertheless, the ease with which he slipped into Dylan mode surprised me. He showed no irritation or resentment at what seemed to be the obscuring of his own personality by that of Thomas. When I met him for the first time, the stories soon began to flow, and wonderfully entertaining they were too, though mostly irrelevant. I broke in: 'Look Mervyn', I said, 'I haven't come all this way to talk about Dylan Thomas. I want to talk about you.' He seemed surprised by this, and the mood changed. Talking about Dylan was easy. Greater consideration was required when talking about himself, since it was not his habit to do so. The few autobiographical pieces he wrote were largely oblique – he preferred to reveal himself through his observation of others. He was generally scornful of autobiographical artists:

> It is fashionable today for artists to make statements: long-winded, arrogant, complex, mock-esoteric nonsense flows easily enough from the lips and pens of creative pygmies.
> The bigger the artist, the less, it seems, he has to say.[86]

Levy was trained at Swansea School of Art, one of a procession of talented individuals, from Evan Walters, through Archie Griffiths and Ceri Richards, to Alfred Janes, who were brought on by William

Grant Murray. In addition to art, he taught himself a BBC accent and in 1932 departed for London. He lived in Chelsea with Thomas and Janes, 'ankle-deep in cigarette cartons'.[87] At the Royal College, William Rothenstein was his teacher, with an inclination to debunk the *vie bohème* that he had adopted. 'Do you paint with your beard?' Rothenstein enquired one day. 'Why no sir!' replied the bewildered Levy. 'Then why not have it harvested and made into brushes.'[88]

I met Levy when I was researching the visual imagery of industrial society. I was particularly interested in the effect of the social traumas of the 1920s and 30s on Welsh painters. He grew up at the southern end of the Swansea Valley at that time, when thousands of people were unemployed, depressed and increasingly angry. I asked him for his sense of it all. His answer was unexpected: 'Do you know,' he said, 'it passed me by.' It was starkly honest and thought-provoking, because it taught me an important lesson about the danger of over-simplifying the experience of a culture, even in times of what seem to be all-consuming crisis. Levy once observed of history that 'the past is only the present seen from another view-point.'[89] His present, and that of his arty friends in Swansea in 1932, was straightforward: 'What we wanted to do was to go to London and if possible go to Paris and somehow or other to identify ourselves with the French and continental avant-garde.' His scholarship to the Royal College enabled him to fulfil the first part of that ambition quickly, but the second part would take some time:

When eventually I was sprung from the day dream of the Royal College into the hideous jungle of the real world I pretty soon learned that a beard was not in itself an open sesame to fame and fortune. No one was prepared to accept it as a bona fide testimony of my genius. So I shaved it off and took a job as a cellulose sprayer to a firm of interior decorators working on a contract for the Plaza and Carlton Cinemas in the Haymarket. It was night work. For six months I ate my dinner at 3 a.m. and gambled over grubby cards with men like teak and sandpaper: tough and rough. Men without masks. Salubrious humans who forced me by the example of their refreshing innocence to rethink the whole question of the bohemian myth. Under the lofty, echoing ceilings, I met for the first time, honest men who sought nothing but a reflection of their own identity in the water of being.[90]

Working in cinemas was something of a family tradition, since grandfather Rubenstein had opened the first picture house in Swansea.

Now the war intervened, but Levy enjoyed it. 'I had a wonderful time going round in Humber Snipes looking after the education of the ATS and Anti-Aircraft Command.' Furthermore, his experience in the army as an education officer provided him with a sense of direction that he would follow for many years. He became part of a movement, characteristic of the post-war period, to make art accessible to all. From 1947 he worked in education, mainly in the west of England, and in 1954 he produced the first of his many books, *Painter's Progress*. It was followed the next year by his book for children, *Painting with Sunshine*, which achieved considerable success. In 1958 he published *Painting for All*, but his most important contribution was to pioneer the teaching and interpretation of art on television. Levy was the first – before Adrian Hill with 'Sketch Club', and long before Kenneth Clark with 'Civilisation'. Levy's programmes, all broadcast live, were popular, gaining audiences of millions. He was excited by the ability and vision of the amateur painters who sent him their work, which he exposed to a wide public both in his programmes and in the annual Housewives Painting Exhibition, sponsored by *The People* newspaper.

Levy was a populariser – but, in the tradition being forged by the Arts Councils in the period, he was unashamedly a populariser of high culture. He interviewed for television or wrote about the likes of Edith Sitwell, Duncan Grant, Wyndham Lewis, and – in Paris at last – the designer Erté:

Why do the images and the personalities of these particular people - Sitwell, Erté, Lewis, appear so often in my fragments of mirror? Why have they so indelibly marked my imagination, my thought processes, my ideas, my feelings? They have marked me simply because each of the characters I have mentioned so far symbolises the highest level of cultural achievement. What other level is worthy of one's deepest attention?

The human race is largely dross, genetic waste. If this is an autocratic philosophy, then I am an autocrat, but not in the Nietzschean sense of 'Overman' or 'Superman'. I am interested only in those relatively few figures who have had the power to shape the nature and identity of a culture. And, since I am a Western man, I am primarily concerned with the mores of Western culture. I acknowledge only the autocracy of the cultural élite ...[91]

Levy did not lose contact with his own country. He both broadcast on the Welsh region of the BBC and contributed essays to *Wales*, the magazine edited by Keidrych Rhys that was the main medium in the English language for the exchange of ideas among artists and intellectuals in the period. Among his essays was a devastating attack, made in 1958, on David Bell's book *The Artist in Wales*, which I have often had cause to quote. It was reading this essay, and empathising so wholeheartedly both with its analysis and its aggressive anti-establishment spirit, that first led me to write to Levy. It had indeed been a 'blackguardly performance' – 'abrasive' and 'ill-bred', as the irritated Ralph Edwards complained to Keidrych Rhys from his comfortable ivory tower at the Victoria and Albert Museum.[92] Levy had forgotten the essay by the time I wrote to him, but was delighted to be reminded of it. In reply I received a postcard of a Sunset Boulevard street sign above the shadow of an elegant female hand, aiming a pistol. He had inscribed it: 'For David Bell':

Dear Peter,

Your welcome packet finally arrived 10 days late! No, Keidrych Rhys didn't tell me about the Ralph Edwards letter, which I am delighted to have provoked! You are right of course, I *destructed*, but left the construction to someone else: You! I simply did a Bomber Harris wipe out! …

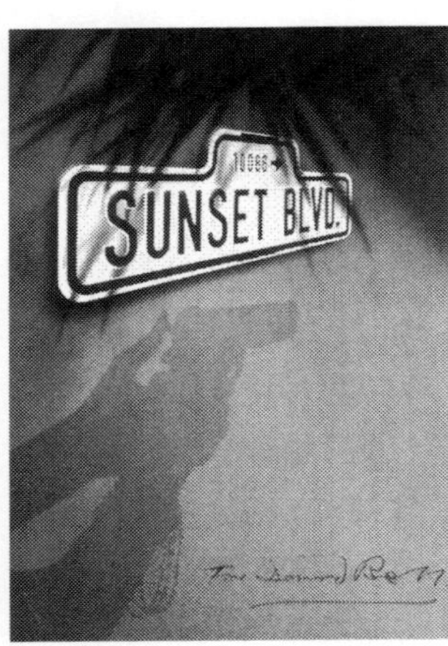

Postcard annotated
by Mervyn Levy

Look forward to seeing you …

Yours,

Mervyn

At the end of our first talk at the Chelsea Arts Club I asked Levy if I could buy a piece of his work. Some months later we met again, in the garden at the back of the club, where he opened a portfolio. It was full of very bad drawings – the good ones had long ago gone to his archive at the University of Texas in Austin. However, planted in the middle of the mediocrities was a wonderful image of the painter L.S. Lowry, drawing the Stockport viaduct. Levy had been a friend of Lowry's and had written three books about him. I was being tested. 'Well Mervyn', I began hesitantly, 'obviously I'd love the drawing of Lowry, but I don't think I'll really be able to afford it.' He fingered the drawing and explained that if he sent it to Austin, he would get four figures for it, which was clearly true, and my hopes sank. He looked up. 'But to you, two hundred quid!' I bid him up to two-fifty and we agreed. I can only assume he liked me. I certainly liked him, and his approach to life. His attitude to money – when he had any – was typical of his wider philosophy: 'My confirmed policy has always been, much or little, dispense it quickly and cheerily over the face of the earth. To treat it seriously is fatal.'[93]

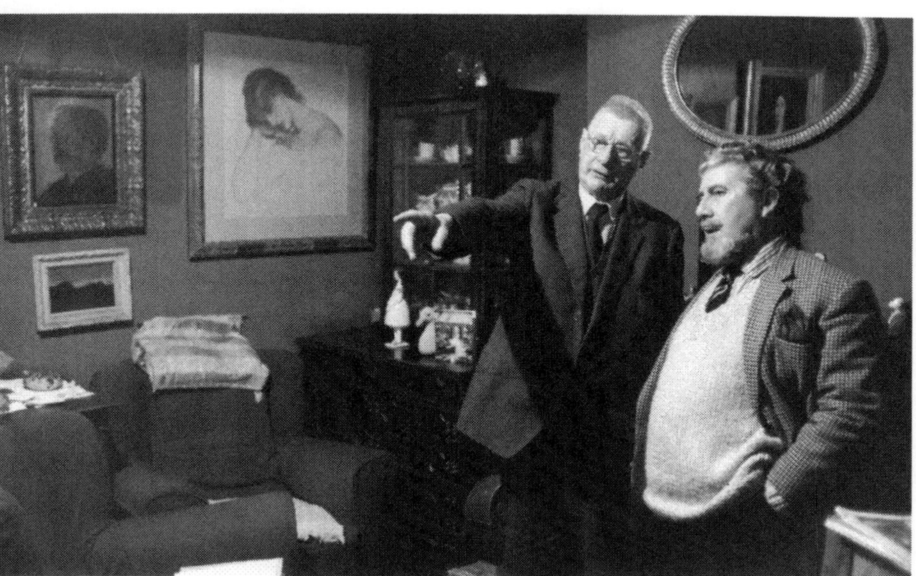

Crispin Eurich, *L.S. Lowry and Mervyn Levy, c.*1962
© Crispin Eurich Photographic Archive

Levy developed his admiration for the work of L.S. Lowry in the 1950s, and soon came to know him. He would publish the first of his books about the painter and his work in 1961. Coincidentally, their friendship covered most of the period in which Lowry painted in south Wales – his first visit was in 1958 – but Levy was not the link. Lowry was introduced to Wales by his most important patron, Monty Bloom, who had been born and brought up in Ebbw Vale. Levy made little of this Welsh connection in his writing, though he might have done so, and for reasons deeper than the fact that he was himself Welsh. David Alston has pointed out that by bringing him to Wales Bloom rekindled Lowry's interest in 'locality', at a time when both the material environment and the urban industrial culture of the 1920s that the painter had exploited in his early work was disappearing.[94] Levy noted Lowry's 'fixation in time, the preservation of the fly of the twenties in the amber of his imagination'. He had asked him about it. 'His answer was simple and perfectly logical. "I was happiest in the twenties, and I don't see why I should take my leave of them! Not in my painting at any rate."'[95] However, Levy does not seem to have sensed revival in the Welsh paintings. It's not hard to find the reason. Levy's fascination with Lowry was primarily psychological and philosophical – the same fascination that drove him to Salvador Dali, who he also knew. Levy was deeply interested in psychoanalytic theory, and particularly in the Freudian understanding of sexual symbolism. When he first visited Lowry's house he was struck by the large number of Rossetti ladies that adorned the walls, and was moved to speculate about his sexual history. He concluded that Lowry was a virgin with an Oedipus complex. 'Hence the compensatory (safe!) mother-lover-wife phantoms of Rossetti.'[96]

In 1966 I had visited the Lowry retrospective exhibition at the

Tate Gallery. I left depressed and with a headache – though, curiously, it was the whiteness of the pictures that I found oppressive, rather than any dark, industrial gloom. Levy also observed this paradox. For him (a sociable man), the work was an entry into meditation on human isolation, whether manifested in the crowd or in Lowry's dispassionate observation of individual grotesques:

> In his art, Lowry conceptualises not only reflections of personal loneliness, but also the wonder and the mystery of the creation, in which man is set as an unwitting pawn – defenceless, stupefied, and occasionally noble. Thus, beyond and through a view of the apartness and oddity of the individual man, the artist creates at his greatest – and he is at times a very great artist – a view of humanity which *must* show man as a mere ant in the totality of the universe.[97]

Levy held Lowry in the highest regard. He thought him 'one of the two most significant painters these islands have produced this century.' The other was the Scottish painter J.D. Fergusson – 'Fergusson because he extended, revitalised and redirected a tradition; Lowry because he created an allegory of man, in its way as unique as that of Hogarth.'[98] It was on a visit to his friend in 1975, less than a year before his death, that Levy drew him at work before the Stockport Viaduct. Both men signed the picture, because the choice of location was significant. Levy regarded the viaduct as the 'most compelling of all the images that ever held his mind in thrall', and Lowry seems to have agreed:

> 'It often appears in my pictures,' the artist once told me. 'As I make them up, I suddenly know I must bring in the Stockport Viaduct … I love it … it is a part of my life, my dream.'[99]

In his last book on Lowry, published in the year that he made the drawing, Levy described the significance of the viaduct as it appears in the Tate Gallery's picture, *Industrial Landscape* (1955):

> As it stands at Stockport, the Viaduct is set relatively low in the townscape, but its grandeur is unmistakeable and unforgettable. By its lofty elevation in the painting, the artist has heightened its majesty, and its air of mystery, endowing it with a quality of the unreal – part fact, part fantasy. We sense its structural strength, and its complementary delicacy, and we hear, as if with the artist's own inner ear, the long, distant scream of the train as it races across the stone trellis. It is the lonely desolate cry of the heart.[100]

Reading these words fifteen years after Levy's death, I begin to realise his generosity in all but giving me his picture of *L.S. Lowry drawing the Stockport Viaduct*. It is clear that it meant a great deal to him. He passed it to me as a gesture of encouragement and trust. Perhaps also it had crossed his mind that I might write about it one day.

9

A Portrait of Jack Jones

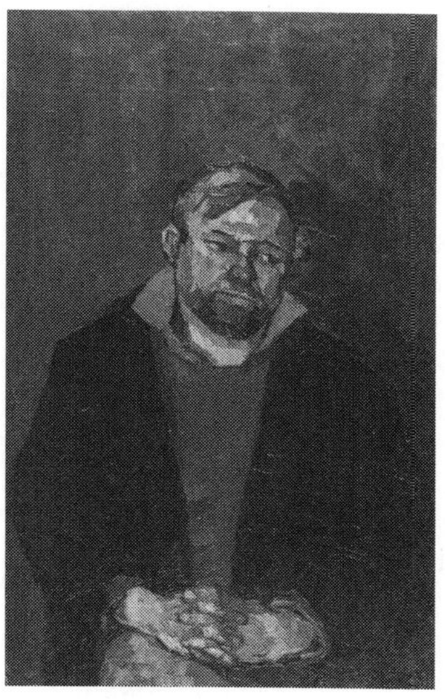

Had I been able to buy a picture painted by Kyffin Williams, it would have been a portrait, rather than a landscape. It seems to me that often Kyffin's portraits have a startling directness and penetration, and sometimes also originality of conception. Kyffin himself would have denied it – he often protested that achieving a likeness was difficult enough, never mind the psychological stuff. The painter and writer Jack Jones sat for him in 1969, some ten years after they first met, and the result was a brooding and intense picture. Kyffin remembered that 'everyone who knew Jack well said what a ridiculous interpretation it was, since he was a jolly fellow, downing his pints at the London Welsh Rugby Club and telling wild and outrageous stories.'[101] However, at the time he was painted, Jack Jones's world was about to enter a downward spiral. Huguette, his French wife, would spend long periods in mental institutions, and it emerged that their son Shôn had serious learning difficulties. Jones would drink increasingly heavily, and by the late 1970s had himself succumbed to clinical depression and alcoholism. Kyffin's portrait was prescient:

> I felt very lonely sitting in the studio which was then in a sad basement. He hardly spoke at all. I felt he was struggling to make his first marks on the terrible white expanse of canvas. I did not dare speak to him. He looked at me every few seconds – moved to his canvas, made a stroke with his brush and moved back again. He squeezed his paint out of great fat tubes on to his palette and he began to attack the canvas. The studio was silent. We seemed remote, as if we were the only two people in the world. I lost all sense of time. He must have been working for hours, but there was nothing on his face that told me how the portrait was going. I felt very lonely. He wasn't painting any old object – he was painting me. I felt tired – very tired and sad. I don't know why. I think the troubles of all my days were driving through my mind. And when I saw the portrait almost finished I knew he had captured not only my head but what was in my head and in my heart. For on that particular day I was sad, and sadness was in the face he painted. The portrait was not only beautiful – it was true.
>
> I have lived with this picture in my home for four years – and it has not died on me. My friends say it's not like me – it's too sad,

much too sad. But they are wrong. The artist was right. He got it right the first time – spontaneously – for there seemed to be no obstacle between him and me.[102]

The relationship between the painter and the sitter, cemented by the intense experience of the painting, continued for many years – which, perhaps, was surprising, given the directness and immediacy of Kyffin's views of the mountains of Snowdonia, and the contrived nature of Jones's conception of Swansea. Socially, too, in their origins they were miles apart – Kyffin's family moved among the country gentry, while Jones was urban and brought up by his working-class grandmother, who, until he was sixteen, he took to be his mother. He was the illegitimate son of a man who never acknowledged him.

It was the experience of Swansea during the Depression and, subsequently, of the armed forces during the Second World War, that determined the course of Jack Jones's career. Like many others of his generation, the end of the war presented him with the opportunity to go to college, which otherwise he might not have done, given the poverty of his childhood. That early experience of material deprivation perhaps then inclined him towards the financial security of a career in teaching on completion of his formal education. Like several Welsh contemporaries in the arts, he taught in England rather than in Wales. Whether that was a matter of choice or a function of circumstance is not clear, but it would appear that his distance from home clarified his vision of Wales, as indeed it did for Kyffin, even if at the same time it fixed the country of his pictures in a mythologised past.

Initially Jones had studied English. Describing the deprivation experienced by the people of Yr Hafod in Swansea, where he grew up, he later remarked that he did not see a painting until he was in his mid-twenties. The Glynn Vivian Art Gallery, he observed, was for the posh of Sketty. This was a characteristic over-generalisation from his particular experience. In fact, in Swansea in the 1920s and 30s, working-class young people had better opportunities both to see pictures and to become artists than in most other places in Britain. Nevertheless, it was only after the war, when studying at the Sorbonne in Paris, that visual art moved towards the centre of Jack Jones's consciousness. He took a course in art history, and in 1953 himself began to paint. It is tempting to interpret the naïve style of his paintings as a consequence of this late and untutored development of his career, but that would be a misconception. In fact, he was closely familiar with contemporary painting, not least through personal acquaintances, who included Ray Howard-Jones as well as Kyffin, and evidence of the influence of new trends is apparent in subtle changes in his manner, within his naïve aesthetic framework. In the 1960s, the

Kyffin Williams, *Swansea Street I and II*, mid-1970s
National Library of Wales

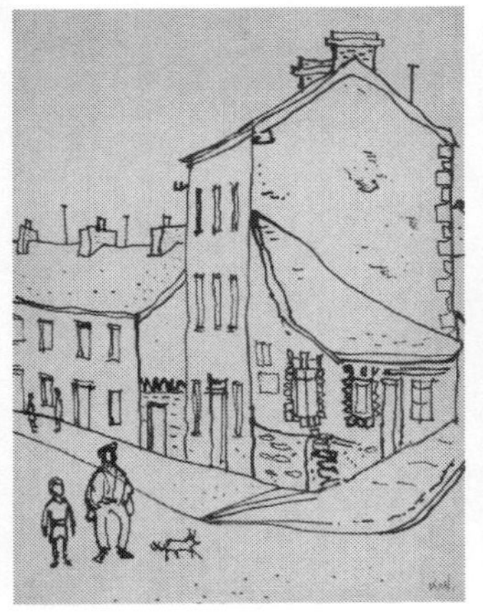
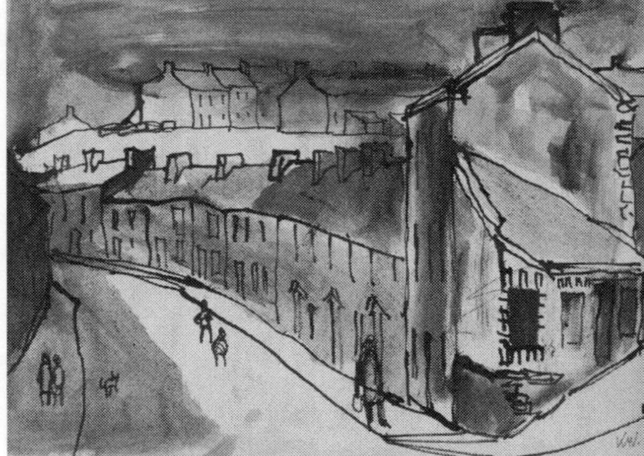

influence of the fashion for bland non-figurative painting is apparent in the increased emphasis on surface pattern, which for a time seemed to dominate content. There were also occasional ventures outside his usual conventions, where the influence of Kyffin is clear. In the mid-1970s he painted fluid and elegant watercolours in the manner of an academically trained painter. Jack Jones could draw properly, when he chose to do so, but as a rule, his rectilinear compositions made a curious contrast to Kyffin's oblique views of Swansea streets, drawn on visits to his friend. He infused the terraces with the mannerisms that had iconised the upland farms of the north west.

Nevertheless, there is no reason to doubt repeated assertions made by Jones that he began to paint as he did before he had heard of L.S. Lowry, or seen any of his pictures. Critical reaction to the similarity between his work and that of Lowry clearly troubled him. In a letter written to Jones in 1974 Kyffin made an acute distinction

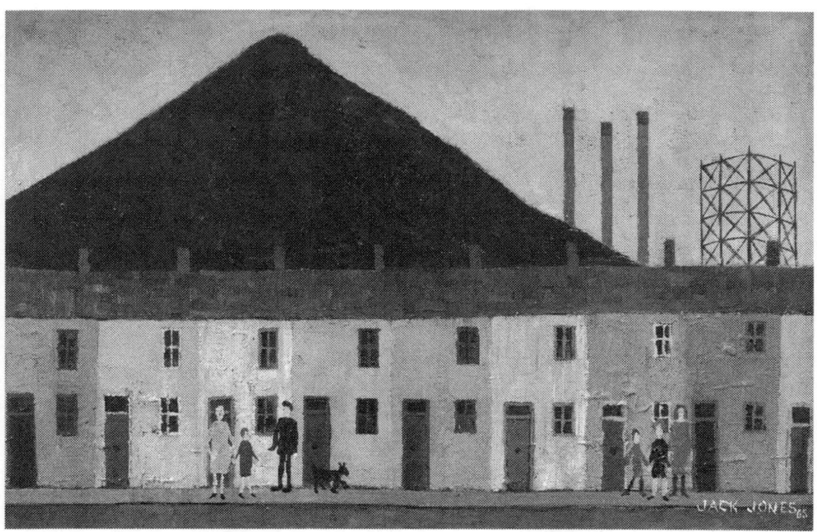

Jack Jones, *Slag Heap and Terrace*, 1965
Attic Gallery, Swansea

between two other painters, who were often critically conflated at that time: 'Will Roberts is a very good painter – better in my opinion than Joe Herman as he paints people, real John Jones[es], and not THE People. Little Joe is in danger of becoming a bore.'[103] Six weeks later, Kyffin tried to reassure Jones about the integrity of his pictures in the context of the popularity of Lowry, which was then near its high point, with reproductions of his work to be seen everywhere: 'A strange man, Lowry', remarked Kyffin. 'A selfish old bugger maybe, but then I suppose that is essential for a painter – certainly you and he are as different as possible.'[104] Nevertheless, Kyffin chose his words carefully. Jones and Lowry were indeed very different kinds of people, but similarities both of content and style between the work of the two men made repeated public comparison inevitable, especially in the newspapers, and the critical esteem and widespread popularity of Lowry's work did leave Jones under suspicion in the art world, even at home, within Wales.

In the course of his difficult life, Jones was plagued by inner contradictions, which all but destroyed him. The simplicity of his manner of painting manifested his struggle to resolve the complexity of his personality. This sophisticated and troubled man surely chose to paint faux naïve and rigidly ordered pictures as a way to cope. Jones attempted to present a clear and simple image for his audience but, more so, for himself. The return to childhood of his pictures was both a mask presented to the world, and a personal retreat from his inner struggle. In this context, the related question of the sincerity of the painting of a faux naïve does not arise.[105] He did not pretend to be innocent. Rather, he sought innocence and, in the end, saw the appearance of innocence in his pictures as a symbol. He would recover from his mental illness through Christian belief, which confirmed for him the rectitude of this vision. In an interview late in life he observed that innocence was a prerequisite for entry into the Kingdom of Heaven.

In a deluge of statements made in his writings and in interviews, Jones always presented his childhood as idyllic. 'Never have I been as happy since', he said, but this was a deceptive reflection, given that few among the people who saw and bought his pictures appreciated the depths of despair that he experienced as an adult. Despite material poverty, the security which he frequently stated that he had felt before the revelation of his bastardy at the age of sixteen, must be seen in terms of the desperation that would follow: 'My paintings are concerned with small people in an immense and sometimes frightening world', he said. It would seem that he continued to feel himself a small person in a frightening world for most of his life. Jack Jones was not a documentary maker – at least, not a documentor of society, whatever he might have pretended in his public pronouncements. Notwithstanding his insistence on its cheerfulness, his record was of a deeply felt sense of personal dislocation.

Perhaps it was the starkness of the contrast between this sense, manifested in the contrived nature of his work, and Kyffin's unfractured sense of location, revealed in the immediacy of his response to landscape and to the common people, that so attracted Jack Jones. As a critic, he was out of step with many of his contemporaries in the 1960s in his championing of the work of Kyffin, who seemed to many commentators to be regressive, at a time when innovation was valued above all else:

The drawings and paintings which sell at from 30 guineas up are an excellent investment of anybody's money. One day, when all the hysteria of pop-art, junk-art, plastic sculpture and the rest has died down, there will be a re-valuation. People will turn away from the sensational and will look desperately for the works of real craftsmen and artists who respect their materials. Then the works of painters like Kyffin Williams will be highly prized.[106]

Jones's art market prediction would prove to be accurate, of course, which is all the more remarkable since, in the period when it was made, Kyffin was in the curious position of finding himself periodically derided both by radicals and conservatives, a fact that gave him particular cause to be grateful for the reassurance offered by his friend's acclaim:

My Dear Jack,

I have just received the *London Welshman* and am overwhelmed by your peons of praise. You really didn't ought. But nevertheless very many thanks for your kind words …

My portrait for the Caernarvonshire magistrates of Lord Morris of Borth y Gest was rejected unanimously, one elderly gentleman saying that it would make 'damn good target practice for the T.A.' I have now got it back in my studio and really rather like it.

I hope Dorothy Thomas [of the Attic Gallery] has continued to do well for you and that you are turning out many more pictures. I will be back in the middle of September and hope to see you, Huguette and Sionni Bach then.

Until then my very best wishes and thanks.

Ever yours,
Kyffin[107]

Nine years later, Kyffin's radical portrait of the National Librarian, Sir Thomas Parry, disturbingly set against a rent and oppressive background of grey-blue, similarly embarrassed the academic establishment. Kyffin's relationship with that establishment, particularly as represented by the National Museum and its Art Department, was curious. They didn't quite know what to do with him. Since, in the 1970s, the place was infested with congenital snobs, Kyffin's gentry background attracted them. He had close connections with prominent Welsh figures in the arts, notably the Angleseys. In 1970 he became an Associate Member of the Royal Academy, and four years later a full RA. He was the right type to be granted insider status, and was duly appointed to serve on the Art Advisory Committee. Unfortunately for the Museum, he proved to be both patriotic and idiosyncratic, not a combination that sat easily within an institution which preferred to deny its national raison d'être and was rigidly mainstream in its taste. Kyffin was definitely awkward squad. In 1974 he wrote from Anglesey to Jack Jones:

> I am currently smitten by some flu bug that has put me in a
> fever and prevented me attending a meeting at the Nat[ional]
> Museum and consequently robbing me of the pleasure of
> staying with John and Glenys. It is probably a good thing
> as I am certain I would have said wild provocative statements
> that would have done no good. I had better give it up and paint.
> Let the ambitious ministers and the ignorant and cowardly clots
> have their way. Here is so far away and I begin not to care.
> Selfish you see.
>
> I think I care more about Wales doing well at Rugby.

'Some flu bug' was Kyffin's code for an attack of *petit mal*, the epilepsy that afflicted him all his adult life.

It was in this period of the mid-1970s, when he came home to live, that I first became aware of Kyffin. He was frequently quoted in the press, and in particular on the subject of the lack of patronage for painters in Wales. This struck me as odd, since the homes of so many of the middle class Welsh-speakers that I entered displayed their Kyffin landscape on the wall, and in more than one case, a row of them. Later, when I came to know him a little, it became apparent that Kyffin's complaint was rooted not only in the understandable insecurity of a man who, in mid-life, had given up his day job in the hope of living entirely from his painting, but more deeply in the fact that he had unquestioningly absorbed the mythology of the Welsh as a uniquely unvisual nation. This fiction had been promoted with perverse pride by influential figures among the nonconformist intelligentsia who appropriated the national agenda in the nineteenth century. Kyffin was vulnerable to the twentieth century residue of their scorn not only as an artist, but also as the son of an Anglican parson, from a family with gentry connections. For many nonconformists, a blanket rejection of the Welsh gentry as an insidious manifestation of the English church and Toryism was as fundamental an article of faith as their belief that the Bible revealed the word of God. Social class was, therefore, deeply implicated in the tension between Kyffin's patriotism and his apparent negativity towards aspects of the national culture. It resulted in a sense of internal exile that I have observed in other men and women from predominantly English-speaking gentry backgrounds.[108]

Kyffin's occasional but intense use of religious iconography in his work suggests that Christianity, transmitted through a family inheritance of Anglicanism, was important to him, whether or not, in the end, he would have considered himself a believer. He painted both a Crucifixion and a Deposition from the Cross. Perhaps such intimations of belief were an element in Jack Jones's allegiance to him, though as far as I am aware Jones refers to it nowhere. On the other hand, in the tone of Kyffin's description of Jones's religious experience, one senses sincere respect. Kyffin described how, in hospital in Swansea, Jones had 'met a priest and was converted to Roman Catholicism, an act that changed his life. His new belief became the cornerstone of his life, and he returned to London to paint and to live a life of continual worship.'[109] I do not know to what extent worship was a part of Kyffin's life. He was an outgoing man in public, but he communicated little of his inner life through his public engagement, or even in his autobiographical writing. To his close friends he may have done so – but I was not among them and so, to me, there was a contradictory mystery about him. I remember a dinner, following the opening of an exhibition, when he must have been well into his eighties. He kept the company entertained with hilarious anecdotes for several hours, then suddenly decided it was time to go. He stood briskly up, his back as straight as a guardsman's, and strode off alone into the night.[110]

I suspect that, perhaps within the wider context of religious belief, Kyffin Williams came to depend on his creativity as a painter to give his life meaning. Perhaps in his anxiety he painted too much, though there were fallow periods. Nevertheless, as a consequence, he also valued creativity highly in others, and was generous in his support of painters for whom he had respect. Peter Prendergast perhaps repaid him most fully and in the way he would have wanted – with commitment to work. I was briefly in college with Peter and, like him, would experience Kyffin's encouragement and support. Kyffin campaigned for years for a 'Welsh Room' at the National Museum of Wales. I know that he didn't see the necessity for the kind of reconception of the basis on which visual culture was exhibited that I favoured – for Kyffin, the Welsh Room would do the trick. In the event, we both of us failed to change anything, and gave up trying. I began to work on a project to develop an independent museum of Welsh painting, based on private collections. Kyffin knew about the project, and the difficulties it entailed. Eventually, I ran out of money. One day, the postman brought a letter from him. Kyffin's letters announced themselves clearly on the envelope by their flamboyant handwriting. Inside I found a brief note, the gist of which was 'carry on' – and a cheque for £5,000.

10

Courting

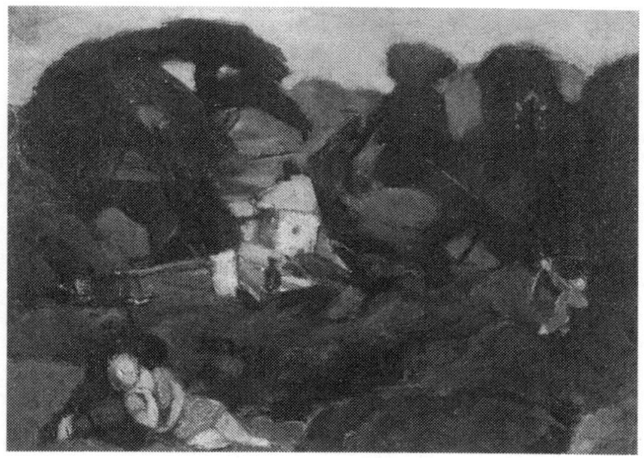

In 1998 I met Alexander Coombe-Tennant, a man whose mother had met Mark Twain – not to mention Henry James, Rudyard Kipling and Arnold Bennett. She had known the Pankhursts and worked with Millicent Fawcett. Then there was Cecil Rhodes, Lord Kitchener, Arthur Balfour and H.M. Stanley – 'Dr Livingstone I presume'. In fact, Stanley was Alex's uncle, though he never knew him, because that high Victorian had died a few years before he was born. He had been acquainted with Lloyd George though, and I think later on perhaps met Augustus John, though I didn't ask him about that. He certainly met several other Welsh painters of the early twentieth century, Cedric Morris, among them. But in particular he had known Evan Walters, which is why I sought out Alex in the first place. He owned a picture painted by Walters that I wanted to illustrate in the first volume of *The Visual Culture of Wales*, in which I wrote about the imaging of industrial society. I enquired if I might visit him at his home in Surrey to look at it. He agreed, and some weeks later he and Jenifer, his wife, welcomed me there. The house was full of pictures. There were family portraits from the nineteenth century, Russian icons, English engravings, and, most remarkably, whole collections of French and Welsh paintings from the first half of the twentieth century that culminated in early landscapes by Kyffin Williams and John Elwyn. They had all been collected by Alex's mother, Winifred Coombe Tennant, whose cool and refined portrait, painted by Evan Walters in 1920, hung in the dining room.

The collection came as a surprise to me, as did the archive of letters shown to me by Alex, that had been written to his mother by Walters and many other Welsh painters. The archive was more of a revelation than the dozen or so pictures that I had seen. The material greatly deepened my knowledge of art in Wales in the inter-war years and, most importantly, revealed the existence of a Welsh art world – a network of relationships between artists, intellectuals and establishment figures, comparable to that of the literati of the period. Painters known to me only through a few surviving works and skeletal biographies suddenly emerged in the letters with flesh on their bones and blood in their veins, meeting each other, discussing their work and their everyday lives. At the centre of the network was Winifred. Seán O'Casey wrote to her enquiring about the whereabouts of his old friend Evan Walters – of whom Cedric Morris had also written to her, though in patronising tones that revealed the social gulf between the two painters. William Grant Murray of the Glynn Vivian Art Gallery and Swansea School of Art alluded to the drink problems of

Archie Griffiths, who himself revealed the trouble he was having to track down another Swansea painter, George Martin, who Winifred was trying to contact. There was a letter from the young Mervyn Levy, soliciting her support, and dozens more. The revelation of this archive transformed the writing of the book, and the direction of my work for the subsequent decade.

Alex alluded to the existence of more pictures than were to be seen about the house which, for lack of wall-space, were stored in the attic. I was invited to return to inspect and photograph them, which I did, shortly afterwards, with my research assistant, Lindsay Clements. It was mid-summer and the attic was dirty, fly-blown and hot, directly under the slates, with no ceiling or insulation, but the contents were astonishing. Lindsay and I worked by the single small window in the gable end. Underneath it, there was a heavy oak chest to which we brought, one by one, the largest part of a Welsh collection that would eventually reveal over a hundred and thirty pictures. There were six early works each by Kyffin and John Elwyn, two Cedric Morrises, two fine Swansea landscapes by Grant Murray, and no less than nine watercolours by J.D. Innes.[111] Equally interesting – and, as it turned out, more important – were groups of pictures by painters of whom I had scarcely heard, including Archie Rees Griffiths and John Cyrlas Williams.

Late in the day, by which time we were both exhausted and numbed by the quantity and quality of the pictures under the slates, Lindsay pulled from a dark corner a long and grimy roll of wrapping paper. We laid it on the oak chest, and untied the string. As we began to unroll the paper, a brilliant red and black image emerged which, though I had never previously seen it, I recognised well before we reached the word 'Abertawe', printed across the bottom. It was the poster designed by Evan Walters for the National Eisteddfod at Swansea in 1926. 'The famous or notorious "celestial dragon"' had attracted the attention of the press at the time, though none of the newspapers had reproduced a picture of it, which was strange. George Clausen, one of the art competition judges, had intriguingly dismissed it with the observation that it had at any rate served its purpose – which was to attract attention. His use of the past tense about a new work had suggested why I had been unable to find a copy of the poster, or even a photograph. The whole print run had been pulped – except this one specimen, salvaged by Winifred. In pristine condition, a huge image of a young Welsh woman, identified by her national costume, emerged from the wrapping paper. She was depicted with her legs astride the thick and upward-thrusting neck of a dragon, her lascivious interest focussed on its erect tongue. Its iconoclasm reminded me that among Walters's friends had been Caradoc Evans.

In all, fifty or so of the pictures in Winifred's collection were painted by Evan Walters. There were landscapes, fluid water-colour still-lifes, portraits in oil and charcoal, and subject pictures – including *Courting*. Walters's letters to Winifred – and some of hers to him, preserved as copies – spanned a relationship that began in 1920 and ended only with his death in 1951. After dinner on the day of the exploration of the attic, I asked Alex if he remembered the painter. He did, though with the uncritical mind of the child that he was in the 1920s. He had liked him. Walters was a nice man – lively and energetic. He had brought Alex a goldfish that he won at the fair. Encouraged by his relaxed mood, and his glass of gin, I asked Alex an unpremeditated and impertinent question: Had his mother had an affair with Walters? 'No, no, nothing like that', he replied, quite unruffled, and the conversation moved on. In the light of things I know now, I wonder what Alex really thought about that question. His answer was quite accurate, but my enquiry had been curiously prescient with regard to another part of his mother's life, and might have stirred him more than he cared to show.

I did not know at the time – and Alex would never reveal – that in addition to writing thousands of letters, Winifred Coombe Tennant had, from shortly after her marriage, kept first a journal and then a detailed diary of her life. It extended from 1897 until 1955. Most of the volumes were small but densely written. They were kept locked in a safe in Alex's study. He may have perused them on the death of his mother in 1956, but after that time they remained unexamined. I learned later that, following my visit, it became Alex's habit every day to retire to his study, unlock the safe, and read the diary. In his 90s, he began to discover his mother as a woman and, I imagine, to try to make some sense of events and attitudes that must have seemed inexplicable to him when they had happened. However, his knowledge would never be complete, because in her will Winifred had placed under embargo for fifty years after her death six of the diaries and a considerable number of letters, that dealt with the most intense and crucial years of her life.

Winifred feared the finality of death – 'my mind always revolts against death', she wrote in 1898.[112] 'Is there any spring for human beings? Is there a beyond? Is there a loving father who knows and cares? Do we die like dogs and end *there*, in weakness and corruption?'[113] A lifetime's experience provided her with no answers to these questions: 'I can't understand life, or man, or God', she wrote in 1947. 'The deep loves of the heart, the helplessness of love in a world like this. The certainty of God's love & the pain of the world .. & the ceaseless flow of the generations of men .. How – Why – Whence – Whither – ?'[114] From her childhood she had experienced psychic phenomena, perhaps influenced by her father's account of an apparition that had appeared to him in his own youth. When she married Charles Coombe Tennant in 1895, she acquired as a brother-in-law Frederic Myers, the most prominent theorist of the Society for Psychical Research and, subsequently, its President. The Society sought to prove by scientific method that human existence did not end at bodily death. Through comparative study of their messages from 'the other side', the work of psychic mediums, tested against deception, might prove by correspondences of content that their sources were external and, therefore, emanated from the dead. Winifred came to feel the necessity of belief: 'Personal immortality, that is the only thing that can make life sublime, can give it meaning and dignify it into a rational responsible whole.'[115] Alex grew up in this context of belief, and with evidence of the involvement in the SPR of his mother and his deceased uncle Frederic about the house. What he did not know, and remarkably, did not discover until his mother's death, was that she herself had become one of the most closely studied and celebrated mediums of her generation. Winifred's psychic activity was hidden behind the pseudonym of 'Mrs Willett'. The diaries read by Alex described how she came to discover her remarkable power as a medium, following the death of her infant daughter, Daphne, in 1908 – but only the embargoed diaries contained the details of the strange consequences.

By 1908 both Myers and his colleague in psychical research, Edmund Gurney, were dead, and it was from these two that Winifred received most of her communications. In a trance state, she wrote their messages or directly voiced their words. When she returned to normal consciousness, she would have no memory of what had transpired. In late 1910, Winifred was told by Edmund Gurney of 'The Plan'. Gurney revealed that he was in love with her, 'in the full sense of the word', and wished her to conceive a child, which 'on its psychic side would effectively be his'.[116] The child would be a genius – a messiah, who would lead the world towards a new era of peace and social justice. These were issues that deeply concerned Winifred. She had always been fascinated by politics and international diplomacy. From the Ladies' Gallery she frequently viewed debates in a House of Commons from which she was excluded by her gender. 'I never go to the House without desiring intensely that I had been a man', she wrote in 1898.[117] Among those she observed from a distance at this time were Arthur Balfour, who would become Prime Minister in 1902, and his brother Gerald Balfour, at that time Secretary for Ireland. In their private lives the brothers were involved with research into psychical phenomena – indeed, both served as Presidents of the SPR. Shortly after receiving Gurney's astonishing communication of The Plan, in February 1911 Winifred met Gerald Balfour for the first time. He had invited her to his home so that he could sit with her in a séance. They became lovers. In the spring of 1913, Winifred gave birth to his child, Augustus Henry, referred to as 'The Wise One'. It was the initiation of The Plan. Alex was not told by his parents of his brother's paternity. On his visits to the family home, Cadoxton Lodge in the Neath Valley, Balfour was known as 'Godfather'.

During the evening after the exploration of the attic, Alex talked about the most ambitious of all the paintings commissioned from Evan Walters by his mother – the family group portrait called *Dominoes*. Winifred kneels on a pink carpet with Augustus – by this time known in the family by his second name, Henry. He is seven

Evan Walters, *Dominoes*, 1920
City and County of Swansea, Glynn Vivian Art Gallery

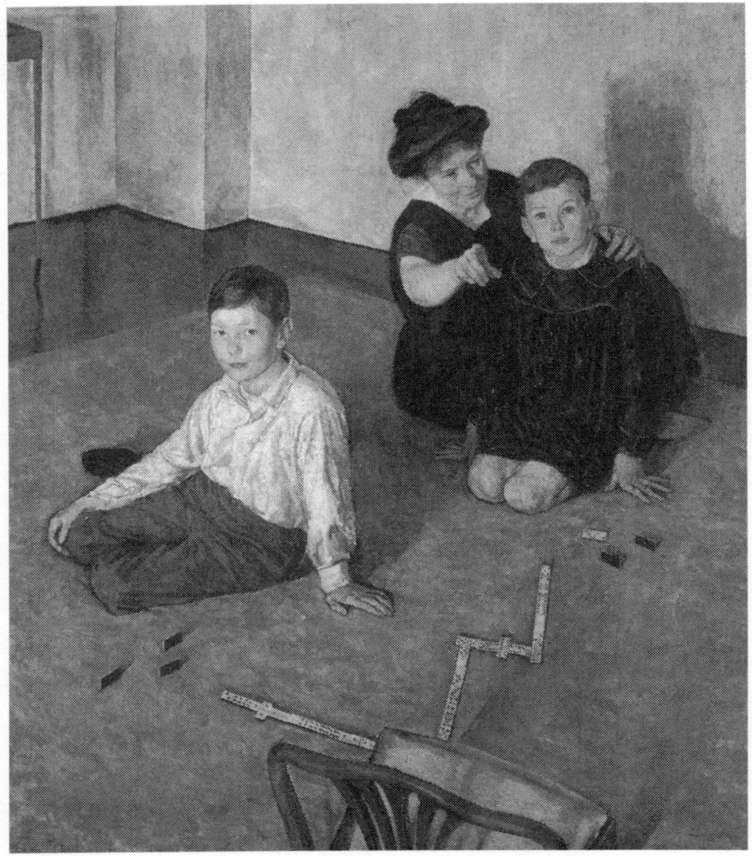

years old.[118] Winifred's whole attention is upon him – she smiles at him, one hand on his shoulder. With the other she points upward at the painter, and Henry's eyes follow the direction of her index finger. Alex sits at a distance from these two, his back towards them, separate and isolated, linked only by the pattern made by the chance association of the dominoes on the floor. It is the antithesis of a conversation piece, and Alex disliked it intensely. At the time, I could not understand why he had given away what seemed to me to be the outstanding picture in the collection (though, in fact, Winifred had willed it to the Glynn Vivian Art Gallery.) I was not alone in that opinion. During a visit to Winifred in 1924, the Keeper of Art at the National Museum had described it as 'a great masterpiece'. He had been 'amazed and excited over it'.[119] Alex explained to me that he couldn't abide the pink carpet. Fortunately, I had the sense not to pursue the matter. In his painting Walters had conveyed deep, and as far as Alex was concerned at the time, mysterious tensions in the relationships linking the three sitters. Years later, Jenifer would tell me that Alex had once said to her that he 'always knew there was something different about Henry'. During his childhood, the picture had hung in the music room at Cadoxton, between the portraits of Gerald Balfour and David Lloyd George, also painted by Walters. The portrait of Charles – Alex's father, to whom he was deeply attached – hung elsewhere.

It is possible that the structure of *Dominoes* was contrived by Walters on the basis of things he knew. He was certainly close to Winifred at this time, though he had yet to paint, at her request, his portrait of Balfour. Nevertheless, it is much more likely that the psychological power of the image that affected Alex so strongly sprang from the kind of intense perceptiveness that many years later would enable Kyffin Williams to reveal Jack Jones. Like Jones, Winifred recorded her feelings as she was painted, firstly as she sat for Walters's earlier, single portrait:

24 June 1920, Thursday
I in a black crepe de Chine teagown, sitting, three quarter face.
I sat from 10.45 to 1, and he works very rapidly, so that there

I am, all sketched in, beginning to breathe – a very happy likeness I think, very much me. Wonderful to watch him at work – creative genius – and most of us, bound up on the wheel of things, hardly lift our heads from our tasks, whilst this man moves among the stars and is of the company of the sons of God, who shout for joy.

I think genius is something shining through the individual from beyond him – it looks like something focussing a ray of God-light.

28 June, Monday
Sat morning and afternoon for Evan Walters. At one moment after lunch he lost the likeness – despair. I sat on and on, and finally all went well. The picture promises to be really good work, and very interesting. Long talk at night on painting – Renaissance man, Blake, to Cézanne and the modernists of Wyndham Lewis type.

13 July, Tuesday
Today Evan Walters began to work at my picture in a black mood – shooting intent and displeased glances at my face, and painting away in dead silence. At the rest, found the me I had got accustomed to in the picture had somehow changed. I was disconcerted – the eyes had changed. After my rest he worked away again, the cloud gradually lifting …

16 July, Friday
Sitting all morning and all afternoon, finishing touches. How much I have entered into this picture – a happy sitter. Certainly this young Welshman will go far. The things he does know about life and the things he doesn't equally interesting to watch! I feel

that [to be] the divine right of artists – somehow they form a separate category of human beings, and while one is a model one is lifted for a moment to the outer courts of their world. Often sorrowful in heart, they pour out things that give joy to others. Possessing nothing, they have all things. They pass us by, these kings, sometimes unguessed, and their name is a living flame in later generations.

Winifred sat to Walters over a much longer period than did Jack Jones to Kyffin. Her account is more objective than his, though it contains flashes of intensity, such as her reaction to Walters dramatically changing the background colour of the portrait from warm gold to cool blue-grey in a single sitting. Nevertheless, the underlying understanding of the process of making a picture was closely similar for Jack and Winifred. Both sitters believed in the ability of the artist to perceive things beyond the grasp of 'the ordinary being':

Evan Walters. What a wonderful thing genius is! It makes all my hum drum wrestling with things and people shrivel up into a handful of dust. I believe in genius we see man as God meant him to be. This young man has it, and it is wonderful to watch. He is highly nervous, vivid, quite unaffected. He functions on a different plane to the ordinary being – his reactions are other, other his joys and his sorrows. Through his eyes another world is open to him, and what he sees enters the crucible of his spirit and then he gives it back, lays it on canvas that all may see.[120]

Jack and Winifred attributed the artist's perceptiveness to the accessibility of a god in whom they both had deep faith. Since I do not share their faith, I find it difficult to understand how Winifred, in particular, was untroubled by a contradiction between the elitism inherent in a belief in the special nature of the artist, 'focussing a ray of God-light', and her otherwise egalitarian social instincts. Mervyn Levy manifested the same ability to divide art from the world, and to judge the artist and the artist's works by different standards to those of the politician or the plumber – the 'dross', the 'genetic waste', of whom, I regret to say, he wrote. Walters seems also to have suffered from a split personality where art was concerned. In 1926 he painted *Bydd Myrdd o Ryfeddodau*, his most socially engaged picture. It is indisputably both the product of and a comment upon its troubled time, and so makes no sense without an awareness of its philoso-phical and political context.[121] Yet later in the year he gave Winifred as a present Clive Bell's connoisseurial polemic, *Art*. Presumably, therefore, he approved of Bell's 'aesthetic hypothesis', that silly notion, undermined by the power of his own picture, that 'To appreciate a work of art we need bring nothing with us but a sense of form and colour and a knowledge of three dimensional space.'[122] Perhaps it is significant that Winifred had been puzzled by *Bydd Myrdd o Ryfeddodau*, for she too was delighted with the book. She excitedly underlined dozens of passages that appealed to her, especially those where Bell expounded his theory of 'significant form':

> The contemplation of pure form leads to a state of extraordinary exaltation and complete detachment from the concerns of life ... Be they artists or lovers of art, mystics or mathematicians, those who achieve ecstasy are those who have freed themselves from the arrogance of humanity.[123]

'C.B's mind a real joy', Winifred wrote on the fly leaf of his book – adding a quotation from Browning that underlines the Christian entanglement in her conflicted attitudes: 'Where Swells Enjoyment –

there is He.'[124] Without the concept of an accessible or interventionist god, the artist and his priesthood of aesthetes cannot set themselves apart from the common herd. Even if in Bell's case the belief in the special nature of the artist and the unique capacity of the *cognoscenti* to appreciate him (and it always is a him) was no more than a vanity indulged in order to sustain a grossly inflated ego, the wider influence of his writing and that of like-minded individuals since Vasari himself, has been pernicious – consistently deployed to legitimise temporal power through its specious spiritual authority. Winifred read *Art* while staying at Eton College, where Henry was by then a pupil. It was characteristic of the many unresolved conflicts in her thinking that Henry had been sent to Eton notwithstanding her frequent expressions of disgust – some of them published – at the ethos of public school education.

Winifred's prediction that Walters would go far proved correct. At the 1926 Eisteddfod in Swansea, in addition to embarrassing the organisers with the iconoclastic sexuality of his poster, he divided the judges of the art competitions. George Clausen awarded him nothing, but Augustus John gave him first place in every competition he had entered. The prizes were divided. More importantly, the following year John suggested he be given an exhibition at the Dorothy Warren Gallery in London, for which he himself had failed to produce the necessary work. Winifred lent two of her pictures. 'He will become famous now', she noted. 'In a sense I feel I am losing him – but he will not I think forget the help I gave him in his salad days.'[125] Winifred followed the story of his success in the newspapers:

The *Western Mail* and *South Wales News* have huge headlines proclaiming Evan Walters' great success – fame achieved at one

step. His 'one man show' has brought him in to the very front
rank among contemporary painters – as I foresaw it would. I
rejoice to think of my share in his career. He was a very raw timid
boy when I first met him and he came here to paint the portraits
of myself, CCT and our big group, living here most of the summer.
I was among his very earliest friends and he has always shown
gratitude and friendliness to me, and loves the Emperors. I have
little doubt he will go to the very top of the tree.

I feel like a hen who sees her swan breasting the waves
after years in which many people kept yelling abuse at me
for championing a one legged ugly duckling!

Magnum est Veritas et preva – I don't know the Latin, but thank
God in my life I know the truth of that Divine affirmation.[126]

'The truth is mighty and it shall prevail.' The Emperors were, of course,
Winifred's sons, Alexander and Augustus Henry. A month later, tired
after again visiting Henry at Eton, Winifred delayed her journey
home in order to meet Walters at his London studio for the first time:

Left Windsor 9.27 and on reaching Paddington <u>made</u> myself
go up to Hampstead to see Evan Walters' studio – by bus to
Tottenham Court Road then by tube to Hampstead station.
Found the studio easily and had a long talk, then looked at
pictures come from the Warren Gallery show which had not
been sold – only a few, but the two I most wanted were among
them, and I bought them for much less than the catalogue price
as E.W. had no commission to pay.

I bought *Llangyfelach* for £14 and *Courting* for £16 – the
former, a fine landscape, had been greatly admired by Augustus
John, and he had it photographed. *Courting* is an odd picture,

but something noble and big about it. Evan Walters wrapped them up and carried them by tube to Oxford Street, whence I taxied to Paddington – <u>just</u> caught my train, and so home.[127]

The following day Winifred unpacked the pictures and set them on her easel. 'Very joyful things they are', she observed. *Courting* sits on the same easel in front of me now, as I write, eighty four years later.

Winifred was not making the best of a bad job in celebrating her purchase of works that had failed to find buyers at the exhibition. Seen in the context of her other Welsh and French paintings, it is clear that they were very much the kind of pictures to which she was drawn – domestic in scale and, to her eye, modern in style. Both of the new works were landscapes of the north Gower, an area that she knew well and which was home to Walters. *Courting* was an 'odd picture' because it was a subject painting in addition to being a landscape. It was 'noble and big' because, like the very first painting by Walters that she had bought, *Mother and Babe* – 'the typical Madonna and Child of Industrial Wales' as she described it – the picture harmonised those paradoxical instincts within her to identify both with a common people in their particular place, and with the elitist traditions of trans-national high art. The landscape of *Courting* is dark and intense, and difficult immediately to read. Its apparent focus at the deep centre is a group of houses from which a flat-capped figure emerges, coming up the hill. However, this visual focus is framed under the arch of the subject focus – the right to left trajectory of an arrow, fired by Cupid at the hearts of a collier, unwashed from his day's work, and his lover, who lies in his arms.

Old pictures are like old people. Many things have happened to them. Their physiognomies bear the marks. On the recycled gilt frame of *Courting* (it must previously have held a portrait) a yellowing ticket with the number eight remains attached – its catalogue number in Walters's 1927 London exhibition. It is a part of the biography of the picture – the posh word is 'provenance'. Clive Bell sought to strip pictures of biography. Put into the common parlance of the believers, he asserted that pictures should 'speak for themselves'. This is to impoverish them, by locking them into the perception of the painter's mind in the now of the act of painting. It locks them inside a darkened room – and pictures, by their nature, demand light. The light that gives them their vicarious life, manifested in the imaginations of all those who see them, is the fluid light of history. In the biographies of pictures lie the clues to the evolution of their meanings. Sometimes these biographical clues are visual – the yellowing exhibition ticket on the frame, the collector's label on the back, the simple patina of age on an unrestored work, overpainting. The startling erect codpiece displayed by Christopher Vaughan of Tretower in his portrait of the mid-sixteenth century proved rather too much for one of his Victorian descendents, who had it skilfully painted out. Probably on the death of her husband in 1844, Hugh Hughes removed the frills and trims of his sister-in-law's bonnet, that adorned her youthful portrait. History is denied when changes like these are reversed in restoration. Perhaps Evan Walters's portrait of Caradoc Evans, slashed in 1938 by a patriot in defence of the Nonconformist nation, should not have been restored.[128]

Sometimes biographical clues can only be revealed by manuscript sources. When Winifred began to make her collections of Welsh and French pictures, her diary and letters make clear her intention that eventually they be donated to the National Museum of Wales. In the 1920s she felt that in two respects the Museum was not properly carrying out its responsibility to the public – firstly, by not collecting the work of young Welsh painters, and secondly by not providing those of them unable to travel, because of their economic circumstances, with examples of the best of contemporary painting from abroad to study and inspire. The gift of her collections would help to address both these failings. However, while her relationship flourished with William Grant Murray at the Glynn Vivian Art Gallery in Swansea, she developed a low opinion of Isaac Williams, the Keeper of Art at the Museum – 'Poor fellow, so kind and so utterly boring.'[129] Subsequent occupants of the post did not restore her confidence. In July 1947 John Steegman wrote to her in London 'questing after my French collection and other pictures'. The approach sent her to her tin boxes of papers relating to the works: 'Oh! what memories .. Paris & the days when CCT & I hunted for pictures, & met painters .. & at Rouen .. & then the Welsh ones taking me back to Cadoxton days with Evan Walters & young painters working in the Music Room & the children posing as models. A vanished world!'[130] Winifred had not seen her French pictures since the early 1930s, and some of the Welsh pictures, though mostly now with her at her London apartment, were still crated from their war time storage.

John Steegman was an unabashed high art snob, of the Clive Bell persuasion. Shortly after writing to Winifred, he participated in a debate on the wireless about the future of art in Wales. Since 'an artist is different from other people', he intoned, he did not believe that 'the community in England or Wales will ever be interested in art'.[131] Winifred agreed with the premise, but objected passionately to the conclusion he drew from it. In November Steegman paid her a visit to inspect the Welsh Collection. During the meeting there was 'much interesting talk', but Winifred did not respond to his effort to solicit *Courting*, the picture that he singled out from the collection, as a gift to the Museum.[132] Soon afterwards he lost interest, as the first bequest from the Davies sisters' collection reached the Museum.

After Winifred's death in 1956, the Welsh and French pictures were retrieved by Alex, and taken to Surrey. Some were hung, but *Courting* was among those that went into the attic. When Alex himself died, Jenifer Coombe-Tennant came to me to talk about the future of the Welsh Collection. Jenifer decided to exhibit the pictures and, since it seemed likely that the collection would afterwards be divided, she asked me to write an account of Winifred's patronage, and a catalogue raisonné. The exhibition, in 2007, marked the collection's belated arrival at the National Museum, if only for a stay of a few weeks. *Courting* was hung with the landscape *Llangyfelach*. Afterwards Jenifer and her family were kind enough to allow me to acquire it.

In its present life, *Courting* usually hangs next to a picture by Archie Griffiths called *Miners Returning from Work*. Though they were painted close together in time – the one in 1926 and the other in 1928 – their physical proximity is not a matter of chronological tidiness but of deeper biography. In September 1928 Winifred had invited Griffiths, then newly graduated from the Royal College of Art, to stay at Cadoxton. He was the most memorable of the 'young painters working in the Music Room' that she would reflect upon in her diary, twenty years later. His career as a painter by then effectively at an end, Griffiths might have remembered the occasion with less affection. The experience of working under Winifred's scrutiny had initially been too much for the 'gentle and sensitive young man' that she perceived him to be, and the work he produced was poor. Then Walters came to visit:

Dear Evan arrived at 3. We talked tête à tête for an hour, had tea, then he saw Archie Griffiths' things. Told me privately they were 'rather bad' but that what he most needed was to 'slap on paint freely caring nothing for detail but putting down the strong facts of anything seen without a care of what the result was.' To learn to handle paint freely – that was the aim …[133]

Walters's advice and the opportunity to study his pictures in the house had a liberating effect. Griffiths produced an imaginative study, *Miners Underground*, that was significantly close in colour, tonality and handling to *Courting*. In addition, Winifred offered two guides of her own to the direction of Griffiths's work. Firstly, she lent him her copy of *Art*. Fortunately, if he read it at all, it left little impression on his work. Secondly, she seems to have shown him a reproduction of *The Way of Rest*, a painting by Laermans. Immediately after leaving Cadoxton, Griffiths painted *Miners Returning from Work*, which, clearly, derives its structure from the work of the Belgian painter. Winifred would soon buy Griffiths's new picture:[134]

I feel greatly encouraged that 'Miners Returning from Work' is to be included in your collection of paintings. I feel convinced that this painting is the best among my mining subjects – whilst painting it I just let myself go – and I feel that my impression has been conveyed more truly than in any of my previous work. It was painted the week following my stay at 'Cadoxton' and certainly the results of our talks.[135]

Courting and *Miners Returning from Work*, now hanging together in this house, evoke the tangled trace of biography that, from their own time and into mine, leads through the extraordinary mind of Winifred Coombe Tennant. It seems strange now, 14 years after I met

Alex and first listened to what seemed to be his authoritative voice, that I should, in some ways, know more of her than did he. Why did Winifred conspire to grant to the world knowledge that she denied her son? She certainly wished the six diaries of the most important years of her life to be read by others, because she left them for public access at Harvard University in the United States – but only at the expiry of the fifty year embargo that she placed upon them. Alex died in 2003, before those fifty years expired, as she surely anticipated he would, and he never read them. It seems that his mother's intention was that he would die still her child. She would not trust him with the privilege of adulthood, to know his mother fully as a woman.

After I die the biography of *Courting* will continue to evolve. I have glued my collection label on the back of the picture for the interest of its next guardian. Perhaps it is the certainty of their perpetual evolution that makes being surrounded by pictures so important to me, in contrast to the finality of my approaching demise. Unlike Winifred, I have no doubt that the notion of continuity of human life after death is nothing but a desperate delusion.

On the Coal Tips

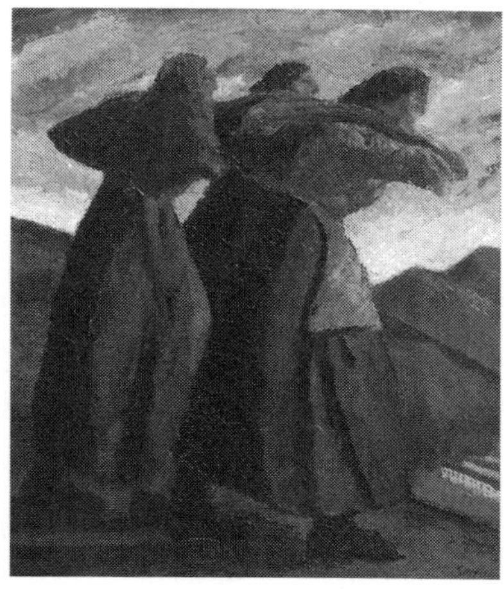

Crossing a busy street with Luned Emyr has a calming effect on the traffic. Luned is a most beautiful woman, who it is impossible not to notice. On a dull day in Gorseinon in 2006 she was particularly conspicuous, wearing a skimpy, grass-green dress and matching shoes. Luned and I were working with the director Geraint Ellis on a film about Archie Rees Griffiths, a painter whose forgotten life and work we hoped to resurrect. The traffic duly slowed for Luned to cross the main street, and at the other side we walked on a little for an establishing shot. Blocking most of the pavement with the para-phernalia of television, Luned then prepared for a piece to camera. There was a loud interjection from behind us, emanating from a lady of a certain age with a shopping bag. *'Be chi'n wneud te?'* Geraint turned to her and began an apologetic explanation about making a film for S4C concerning a painter who had grown up in Gorseinon in the 1920s but whose work had been forgotten and … *'Oh, Wncl Archie chi'n feddwl?'* Apparently Archie Griffiths was not entirely forgotten, at least, not by his own people. [136]

The shopper's memory of Uncle Archie proved to be no more than a fragment, but it was a revealing one. For those of us making the film, the story of Archie Griffiths was a tragedy – it was a narrative of failure. Apparently, the folk memory was of success. Archie, who had begun his working life underground at the local colliery, had gone to London, to the Royal College of Art. He had done well, even though what happened afterwards, apparently, was unknown.

Ten years before making the film, my colleague, Paul Harris, had conducted a trawl through the south Wales newspapers, noting references to visual culture. The story of Archie Griffiths had been among the most surprising that he found. I had never heard of Griffiths, but he proved to be well documented throughout the 1920s. His progress was reported in most detail in the *Cambria Daily Leader*. Before the war, the young *Leader* reporter, John Davies Williams, had been the first person to notice the work of Evan Walters. After the war he became editor of the paper and used his position to promote other young, working-class painters. He first reported Griffiths following his success in an Eisteddfod art competition, then noted his development through Swansea School of Art and the Royal College. In 1926, the year in which the painter graduated, he commissioned a series of drawings for publication. These drawings, along with photographs of Griffiths's Prix de Rome competition painting and a mural commissioned for the Camden Town Working Men's College,

Archie Rees Griffiths,
Della Salute, Venice, 1928

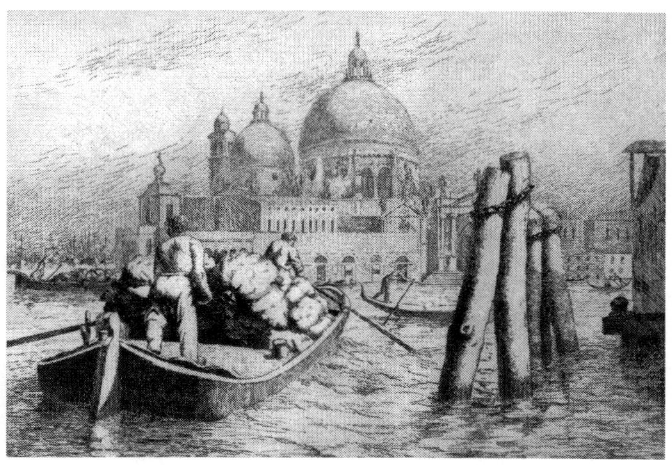

were the first of his pictures to come to light. Many of them depicted the lives of working people in the mining community, though not only in the documentary tradition. The Prix de Rome painting and the mural were allegorical works, and important because, at the time, no other painter is known to have attempted such things with this subject matter. The catalogue of an exhibition of the painter's work at the Glynn Vivian Art Gallery, Swansea, in 1928 suggested that there had been many such subject paintings, but enquiries to public collections revealed just a few etchings and drawings. Most surprisingly, there was no record at all of the mural at Camden Town. It seemed that only three oil paintings had survived – two in the Glynn Vivian collection and one at the National Library of Wales. However, the Glynn Vivian's *Lighting a Miner's Lamp* and the National Library's *Miners Returning from Work* were impressive, and confirmed that the story of Archie Griffiths was worth pursuing.

By the summer of 1996 we had obtained Griffiths's death certificate, which revealed that he had died in London in 1971. Two other sources of information had also come to light. Paul Harris had located a relative of Griffiths's second wife, Edith. She was still alive, but resident in a nursing home and suffering from dementia. We could not see her. Our informant was cautious, especially on matters related to other family members. However, it did emerge that hanging at the head of Edith's bed was a large painting of a collier, and that there was a scrapbook. Much later we had sight of the scrapbook, but most of the material it contained had already been noted by Paul. In the meantime, a substantial essay written by Geraint Goodwin, published in the *Welsh Outlook* in 1932, revealed that Griffiths had been a close friend of the author. He had made a portrait of him. I wrote to Goodwin's biographer, Sam Adams. Unfortunately, his main informant, Goodwin's widow, Rhoda, had died. There was a daughter, Myfanwy, but Sam had no address or married name for her. He had not seen the portrait – though he was aware that Goodwin had been drawn also by Evan Walters, which suggested that the two painters might have known each other.

By the spring of 1997 we had traced the doctor who attended Griffiths during his last illness. I arranged to meet him in north London. Dr Sanders had bought three pictures from Griffiths in the 1960s for a very small sum of money. The pictures confused matters further. Two of them were nothing like his earlier works and, indeed, were remarkably crude, showing no sign of a high-level art training. The third picture was equally difficult to interpret, though in a different way. It depicted an old man, walking with bowed head along a road. I called it *Tramping*, and in the context of what the doctor told me about the painter, I concluded – wrongly, it would transpire – that, like the others, it was the product of Griffiths's old age.[137] It was a deeply sad picture, that I perceived as a kind of self-portrait. Dr Sanders had told me that at the end of his life Griffiths was 'depressed, crumpled and monosyllabic'.

Through an informant in New Zealand, originally from Gorseinon, I learned that Archie Griffiths had a younger brother, who was still living in the town. In June 1997 I interviewed Winston Griffiths in his terraced house. It quickly became clear that his memories of his brother were heavily shaded by moral condemnation. There had been four brothers and a sister in the family, and in his mind Winston had them divided clearly into two groups – those who stayed, and those who left. Those who left – in particular Archie – had abandoned the language and religion of home. Winston had remained firmly embedded in the Welsh-speaking chapel-going community in Gorseinon. Archie associated with London bohemians. It was 'contrary to the way he had been brought up'. Apparently, Winston was unaware of the fact that the bohemians had included Geraint Goodwin and Evan Walters. His condemnation of his brother extended to casting doubt on whether he had, in fact, ever worked underground in the colliery. He alleged that Archie 'never spent more than a day down the mines'. Among the few memories untainted by Winston's judgemental attitude was that of a visit to London with another brother to see an exhibition of Archie's work. This would have been in 1932 – it was Archie's only London show, held at the Young Wales Association. Winston's memories of the occasion were sketchy, though he conceded that it had been a success. However, within a few years Archie had left his wife, Bobby, and his two children, though Winston stayed in touch with them. Winston's father had died in 1940, but Archie didn't attend the funeral. When the London Blitz began he had come home for three months, but in the evening he would go to the pub. Winston would go to chapel meetings. 'Drink was his downfall,' he said. His 'talent was wasted'. Archie had returned to London. In about 1947 he briefly called to see Winston, bringing Edith. They had visited someone in Porthcawl. Winston never saw or heard of his brother again. 'It's been very difficult over the years', he said. 'He was so respected and popular in our town, people always wanted to know how and where he was; we didn't know whether he was alive or dead.'

Clearly, Winston felt Archie's disappearance reflected badly on the family. During the interview, he did not speculate on why his brother might have behaved in the way that he did. He revealed no curiosity about the cause of Archie's alcoholism or his depression – if, indeed, he was aware of it. At the time of an interview such as this, one seldom knows enough of the story to ask the right questions, since the interview is a part of the process of discovering what those questions might be. By the time one does know, often it is too late. I would like the chance to go back now, and ask the right questions of Winston Griffiths – not that he would be obliged to answer them. The questions would undoubtedly be intrusive.

Winston owned no pictures by his brother, and neither did members of Archie's family by his first wife, who I was now able to contact. Archie's son had become a successful playwright under the name Rhys Adrian, but had died in 1990.[138] Diana, Archie's daughter, was living near London. I corresponded first with Diana's son, who had taken an interest in his grandfather's life but knew little more than what he had been told by Winston. Diana had been very young when her father left home, and apparently could remember almost nothing of him.

It was now two years since the story of Archie Griffiths had begun to emerge. The only pictures that had come to light were those bought by Dr Sanders, and documentary research had arrived at a dead end. Since I do not believe in a provider, I cannot believe in providence – but, occasionally, events do unfold in a way that gives pause for thought. When I visited Alex and Jenifer Coombe-Tennant in Surrey for the first time in March 1998, in pursuit of Evan Walters, I made no connection between Winifred Coombe Tennant and Archie Griffiths. Had I been paying attention to the details of what I had been told, I would have done, because during our interview, Winston Griffiths mentioned that Archie had worked for 'wealthy local families', the Coombe Tennants among them. However, at the time, their name meant little to me. On my second visit to Surrey, in September, the now celebrated attic yielded six pictures by Griffiths, thereby doubling the number of known and extant works. Furthermore, Winifred's written archive contained a series of letters from and about Archie that revealed a different life from that presented by his brother. Along with his former teacher, William Grant Murray, and the *Cambria Daily Leader* editor John Davies Williams, between 1926 and 1932 Winifred had been closely involved with encouraging Archie in his career.

Then Sam Adams telephoned. He had heard that Myfanwy Goodwin was living in Montgomery. I made contact with Myfanwy and her husband, the print maker Alan Lumsden. There were pictures by Griffiths in the house, and though she had no knowledge of a Griffiths portrait of her father, she did have the Walters portrait. I arranged to visit, and the story of Archie's relationship with Goodwin emerged, as told to Myfanwy by her mother. After the successful 1932 exhibition in London, to coincide with which Goodwin had written his essay for *Welsh Outlook*, Archie's life once again began to spiral downwards. There was little money, and much of what there was went on drink. The family moved from one set of rooms to another as Archie failed to pay the rent. Myfanwy remembered being told how her father helped him to load their belongings onto a handcart and wheel them through the streets to the next lodgings. The Goodwins left London to rent a farmhouse at Dagnell in Essex. Archie came to stay, bringing his pictures. It was there that he painted the landscapes and still life studies that now hung on Myfanwy's wall. However, in about 1937, without warning Archie departed, and never again contacted Goodwin. They concluded that he had died during the Blitz. Myfanwy believed that Archie had left many of his pictures at the farm, and that when the family returned to Wales to live, her mother had disposed of them.

This brought the conversation back to Archie's mining subjects. Rather apologetically, Alan revealed that there was another Griffiths picture upstairs. He fetched it, and set it down on the floor, observing that it was a 'student work' and of no interest. That was not my perception. Unlike the pictures hanging on the walls, it was in poor condition. It was also a different kind of work to the others in the house – it was large and clearly belonged with the subject pictures in the Coombe Tennant collection, the National Library and the Glynn Vivian Art Gallery. Furthermore, it had a particularly beautiful art deco frame – far too expensive for Archie. I remembered that in a letter to Winifred he had thanked his patron for her gift of frames, made to enable him to show his work properly to potential clients. The subject was three women carrying sacks of small coal from a tip – an image with a long art historical pedigree. The sky was stormy and threatening, the women were moving homeward to the rows of terraced houses shown far below. It was difficult to conceal my bewilderment at Alan's low opinion of the picture. However, in retrospect, I can see that his sense of it had nothing to do with any failure of critical faculties on his part, but was the consequence of the family narrative of the picture. Contrary to the mythology of mainstream art history ('let the picture speak for itself!'), narrative context affects profoundly our perception of an image, the power of which can only emerge when its significance is understood. The narrative available to Alan was that of Rhoda, Myfanwy's mother – the story of a sad man who came to stay and then disappeared, leaving some nice but unremarkable landscapes and still life studies behind. The reason that *On the Coal Tips* had survived among them did not emerge until later. The catalogue for the 1932 London exhibition revealed that the picture had been loaned on that occasion by Geraint Goodwin. *On the Coal Tips* had belonged already to Myfanwy's father when Griffiths arrived, homeless, at Dagnell.

The outline of Griffiths's career to the late 1930s was now clear. What happened subsequently, less so. It was some years before I was

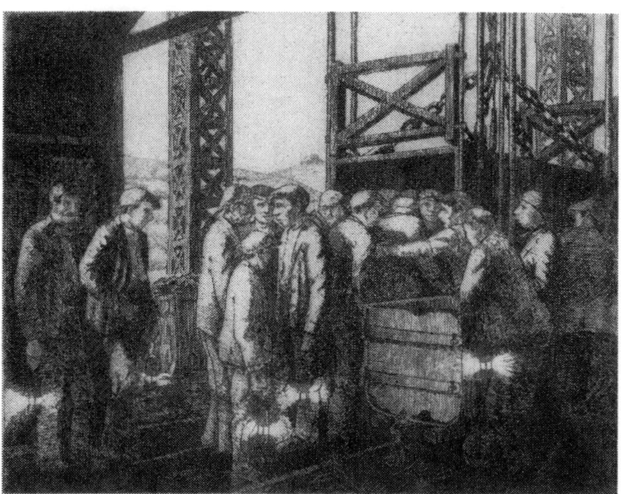

Archie Rees Griffiths,
Miners Descending, 1925

able to contact Yvonne Spinks, the painter's niece by his second marriage, and cousin to our reluctant early informant. Edith had died, and the machinations of wills and property had been resolved. In January 2003 I visited Yvonne at her home in north London. From Edith, for whom she had done what she could in her last years in the nursing home, she had inherited the remains of Archie's work. There were some twenty pictures, mostly crude landscapes and seascapes, painted when he and Edith lived on the south coast of England. From among Edith's more personal belongings, Yvonne had salvaged ten dog-eared photographs, Archie's Eisteddfod certificates, his graduation photograph from the Royal College of Art (still rolled in its maroon tube with the royal crest), and a torn identity card. Archie had narrowly failed to win the Prix de Rome in 1927, but had been awarded a travelling scholarship that briefly took him, the following year, to France and Italy. The torn identity card was the only surviving evidence of his experience as a student at the British School in Rome. However, there was also the large picture which had hung at the head of Edith's bed in the nursing home, painted in the early 1930s. The subject was a miner underground, kneeling at rest, his face illuminated by his lamp – but on the back of the canvas, partly obscured by the stretcher and by dirt and damage, was another picture, quite different in style. It was a narrative, depicting a sequence of events from an accident underground to a funeral. The story was revealed in vignettes, painted as sections through the earth, looking into the mine. This was the approach that he was to have used in the Camden Town mural.[139] My impression was that Griffiths had abandoned the picture and, because of his poverty, turned the canvas and re-used it. He had also re-used the stretcher, because inscribed on it was the name of a lost picture called *Tro yn yr Yrfa*, that had attracted much praise from the critics when it was exhibited in 1928. He had given the drawing for that picture to Winifred Coombe Tennant in thanks for her support. In a contemporary letter to her, Griffiths, then 26 years old, acknowledged the steepness of the 'idealistic hill' that he had set himself to climb as an artist. Eighty years later, the surviving material fragments of the life that followed seemed deeply pathetic. As I left Yvonne's house, she returned to the table where we had spread the photographs and certificates. She collected them together and gave them to me.

Three years later, when I was working with Luned Emyr and Geraint Ellis on the film about Griffiths, we revisited Yvonne. We filmed *Miner Resting* and *Turnings in the Journey of Life*, which subsequently I discovered was the title of the painting on the back of the canvas. It had not been abandoned, but completed in 1928 and – like most of his other pictures – it had not found a buyer. We travelled on to interview Diana, Archie's daughter. It would be my first meeting with her. I knew that she owned nothing of her father's – no personal items, no letters, no pictures – and so I had photocopied Archie's correspondence with Winifred Coombe Tennant to give to her. There was to be one other surprise. Among the paintings of his that had emerged eight years earlier from the attic that held the Coombe Tennant collection had been a gentle, yellow-lit portrait of a baby in a cradle, called *Child Sleeping*. The picture had been shown at the 1932 London exhibition. Reconsidering the surviving pictures while researching the television script, I realised it must have been painted shortly before the exhibition, because it was signed 'Rhys Griffiths' – the name with which Archie had been rebranded by the London Welsh intelligentsia who were promoting the show. The child in the cradle was Diana.

Geraint decided that he would film Diana sitting in her garden, with the camera placed as discreetly as possible. She had been excited at the prospect of being involved in the film, but the atmosphere changed as the camera and sound equipment were put in place, and the focus shifted entirely towards her. She became introspective, and her tension spread through us all. The garden seemed to become unnaturally quiet, and the greenness of the grass and the plants all around, and of Luned's dress, became saturated. The colour and the silence framed Diana's voice as she began to tell us the few sad things she remembered about her father. She remembered a Christmas, perhaps in 1936 or 1937. Archie had gone out early to drink, but he took with him the key to the bedroom where the presents for her and her brother had been hidden. He did not return, and so there were no presents that Christmas Day. She didn't remember any rows, but Archie must have left home for good soon afterwards, and she didn't know where he'd gone. After the war, he re-emerged in rented rooms in Kilburn. On Sundays, Diana's mother would cook his dinner, and Diana or her brother would take turns, alternate weekends, to carry it to him on the bus. Her mother must have cared a great deal for him, but after he took up with Edith, there was no further contact. 'You never saw him again?' I suggested. She had not. There was a pause, and Diana reconsidered her answer. Yes, she had seen him once more. It was in about 1954, when she and her husband were living in Paddington. One day they were walking in the Bayswater Road, where painters exhibited their work, spread on the pavement and hanging on the railings. Archie was among them. He packed up his pictures, and they went for a cup of tea in a café. Diana did not reveal what was said, but after they parted that day, she never again saw him or heard from him.

The spontaneous emergence of long-suppressed distress brought the interview to an end in tears. As we prepared to leave, I offered Diana the copies that I had made of her father's letters. She did not want to look at them.

A few days later Diana wrote to me. Her mood had lightened, and she briefly and calmly reviewed some of the things she had told us in the interview:

I don't think Archie or I come out of this too well. Why didn't I resume contact with him and give a helping hand when I grew up, and why did he not seek out me or Rhys? Did he never wonder how we were or how we were being fed or clothed? He obviously wasn't interested enough …

Oh well, it's too late now, and I'm sure we've all got an If Only list.

I would really like to see *Child Sleeping*. It's uncanny, I have the strangest feeling I've seen it, and yet how could I when Winifred Coombe Tennant bought it in 1932?[140]

The tiny archive of material fragments of Archie's life, given me by Yvonne, remains in my care, and to it I have been able to add nine of his pictures. Among them are *On the Coal Tips* and his reinvention of that oil painting as a print. They are his most powerful achievement as the serious artist that, as a young man, he aspired to be. For the print, he worked in the simplest of media – black and white lino-cut – which further intensified the power of the painting. It stimulated the last newspaper review of Archie's work, written in 1935. The reviewer was John Davies Williams:

The Gorseinon artist has done much work of urgent poignancy, but this, which he calls 'On the Coal Tips,' is the height of his feeling from the pathos of life. Three old women, bourne down by heavy burdens – that is all. But somehow its drawing, the arrangement of its blacks, the strength of its lines, suggest the unbearable sorrows of the poor.[141]

John Davies Williams was not indulging in vacuous rhetoric. He responded passionately to the pictures of Archie Griffiths, and it is likely that his feelings were intensified by his awareness of something of the troubled personal life of the painter. Griffiths had expressed his own weakness in his observation of the vulnerability of those he painted – 'the unbearable sorrows of the poor'. Like Williams, I find myself also writing repeatedly about Griffiths and the relationship between his personal difficulties and the traumas of the times through which he lived. In the exploration of his world, I also explore my own, of course. 'Great artists' do not interest me much. I write mostly about artisans and about trained painters marginalised by the mainstream of art historians. This does not reflect in me a perverse interest in failure, but rather an acknowledgement of the fundamental vulnerability of us all that is most clearly expressed in the lives of those whose struggles have not resulted in celebrity or financial success. By painting pictures, for a time, Archie Griffiths attempted to defy the chaos of his life and the finality of death – attempted to make sense of the absurdity of it all. Writing about him and keeping his pictures is an expression of respect for that attempt, and an acknowledgement that in this way his life stands for all our lives. He was relentlessly driven by the same unknown force that drives us all towards nothingness. His relics are pathetically few and fragmented, but in writing his story, oblivion is denied, even at the last moment.

12

Breton Woman

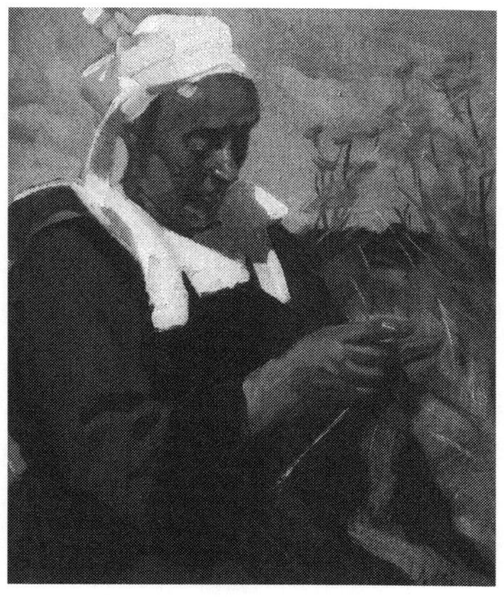

In this house there are many paintings by John Cyrlas Williams. Sometimes conveyed through an apparently random informality, sometimes through a sensitivity to particular light, they have an immediacy that makes the best of them unusually attractive. They have a characteristic quality that sets them apart from the pictures around them. Though they exude the 1920s, it has little to do with period, because they are as unlike the contemporary pictures of Evan Walters and Archie Griffiths as they are those of William Roos and Hugh Hughes, painted in the preceding century. All of the pictures were painted before Williams reached the age of thirty, but they convey an unsettling urgency, that runs deeper than youthful impatience. There is something wrong.

Cyrlas Williams was unknown to the public until 2007, and the pictures survive as the consequence of a chain of events that began in that year with the exhibition of Winifred Coombe Tennant's collection of pictures. Winifred had bought six of them from Williams in the 1920s and came to know him a little. At the time of the exhibition, the only information available about his life was contained in her diary and in a few letters written to her by Williams and his mother, Gwladys, that Winifred had preserved. During the exhibition, Williams's pictures – the first examples of his work to be seen for seventy years – attracted the attention of many visitors. Among them was the painter Mike Jones. Eighteen months later, in April 2009, Mike visited his local saleroom in Clydach, where, from time to time, he had found interesting pictures to buy. On this occasion, he was astonished to find well over a hundred works by a single unidentified painter, bundled into lots of four or five. The style seemed familiar, and a closer examination revealed the signature of John Cyrlas Williams on just a few canvasses. Mike immediately alerted the auctioneer to the historical interest of the collection, and they were withdrawn from the sale. He telephoned me, and a week later we met in a small room at the auctioneer's office and began to photograph and catalogue them. They surrounded us, stacked five and six deep against the walls, some battered and almost all unframed. They were very dirty, but a wipe over the surface with white spirit revealed their original vivacity – and why Winifred Coombe Tennant had been as excited all those years before as we were now by the work of the unknown and elusive young man. Among the pictures we found was the sketch for *Ogmore Castle*, a 'delicious picture' which, in 1926, had been the first of his that she bought.

The pictures had been found in the attic of a house in Porthcawl. The owner came across them when clearing the property. They were destined for a bonfire with the rest of the rubbish but the auctioneer told him that they would probably fetch a few pounds each, so they were sent for sale with the furniture and bric-a-brac. Unfortunately, the revelation of their historical interest suggested to the owner that he had stumbled on a financial fortune. This is the *'Antiques Roadshow* effect'. Attempts to persuade him to sell the collection as a whole, so as to keep the pictures together for an exhibition, failed. When eventually they did come under the hammer in Cardiff, they attracted the interest of half a dozen private collectors, most of whom had also become aware of Cyrlas Williams through the Coombe Tennant exhibition. There were no institutional buyers. Mike and I were able to acquire some sixty of the pictures between us. I decided to have a few of them cleaned immediately. The conservator Hoss Macro collected them from Aberystwyth, and set off home. Three hours later the telephone rang with the news that he had removed the first canvas from its stretcher and found underneath a second finished painting. It was a good picture, and had not been covered up as a reject. It belonged to a series painted at Martigues, in the south of France, of which Winifred had acquired two examples in 1928. Subsequently, some twenty additional pictures were revealed in this way.

John Williams is a common name. It took a year, assisted by Edna Dale-Jones, an expert on family history research, to find the painter in census and other records. The distinguishing 'Cyrlas' was misleading, since it proved not to be a baptismal name, but one adopted much later – and, in any case, he was always known as

Jack. Eventually it emerged that John Alured Williams had been born in 1902, and into rather different circumstances from those in which he would grow up. At the time, his newly married parents were living in a small terraced house in the mining village of Pontyrhyl in the Garw Valley, north of Bridgend. Both his father and his grandfather, whose house it was, were colliers, though well travelled ones. In the mid-nineteenth century, grandfather, who left school at the age of nine, had emigrated from the valley to Thomastown, a Welsh mining community in Ohio. He attended the Independent Welsh-speaking chapel there, and was the original John Cyrlas Williams – the middle name being that of the family farm. His son, William, father of the painter, was born at Thomastown in 1872, but a year later the family returned to Pontyrhyl. The decision to come home proved a wise one. By 1911 William's status had changed from that of collier to colliery proprietor, the owner of the Braich y Cymmer level. The demand for coal was near its high point, the business prospered, and the family rose. In 1916 they confirmed their ascent into the middle class with the purchase of the Porthcawl town house, where the pictures had been found. Far from going down the pit like his father and grandfather, Richard, the younger brother of Cyrlas Williams, would be educated at Christ's College, Brecon, and Peterhouse, Cambridge.

Cyrlas Williams's mother – 'a little woman with a big voice' – was born Gwladys Davies, the daughter of a tinplate worker at Llanelli. Her own mother, Hannah, was a most unusual woman. Back in 1871, at the age of only 21, she had given her occupation to a census taker as 'poetess'. Later, she would acquire the bardic name of 'Brynferch', and would become known also as a preacher, I presume during the 1904 revival. Early in her married life she moved to Mold in the north east Wales coalfield but, with several of her children, as a widow she returned south to live at Merthyr. On census day in 1911 her grandson, Cyrlas Williams, was staying at the house, along with assorted aunts and uncles. Their names – Arthur Taliesin, Idris Garmon, John Alun, Myfanwy Eurgain – indicate the literary interests of their mother.

It was a cold day when I visited Porthcawl for the first time. I looked over the grey channel towards Devon, where I had grown up. A large sign painted by the steps leading to the beach warned 'Bathing Dangerous', which did not seem the most auspicious introduction to a seaside resort. The buildings appeared run down but the massive Sea Bank Hotel, dominating the end of the esplanade, indicated that the town once had aspirations to become a resort of choice for the well-off. Winifred Coombe Tennant had been one of many who regularly took a suite at the Sea Bank in the first quarter of the twentieth century. Her first visit had been in 1916: '17 January, Monday. Porthcawl, Sea Bank Hotel – pouring with rain.' Perhaps Cyrlas Williams, four days after his 14th birthday, had been looking at the same rain from the window of his new home a few hundred yards away. 'Sandringham' is a substantial three-storeyed terraced house in the middle of town. He painted his first picture – a small landscape of a field of ripe corn – two years later. At the end of 1918 came his first portrait. The information is recorded on the canvas stretchers. The pictures reveal unusual skill for a sixteen year old, and before long he began to train as a painter. A portrait of his younger sister Lynne, seated at table, probably inside Sandringham, records his progress. She is surrounded by the dark oak accoutrements of the twenties bourgeoisie, but her brother had probably already left these behind him. By 1922 he had been able to study painting in the lighter atmospheres of both Newlyn and Paris.

It seems likely that Cyrlas Williams went first to Newlyn. Stanhope Forbes, at work in Cornwall since 1884, had opened his art school there in the last year of the old century. On the strength of his own reputation, and the influential experience in Cornwall of a younger generation of by then well known painters that included Alfred Munnings and Laura Knight, the art school attracted a steady flow of students. Before the war, Carey Morris had been among them, a contemporary of the English painters Ernest and Dod Proctor. Morris moved on, first to London and eventually back to Wales, but the Proctors stayed. They were in residence and at the height of their careers when Cyrlas Williams joined the community after the war. He took lodgings in Penzance, and helped to finance his training by working at a sawmill. From Penzance, he would have walked or bicycled to Newlyn, just over a mile away, where the celebrated school consisted of three wooden huts, 'one of them a large and elaborate structure with a basement':

> They stood in what was known as The Meadow, though it was really an orchard in a green wilderness. In the cast-room, the smallest of the huts, were the beginners, drawing with bits of charcoal and lumps of crumbling bread. In the head-room, the largest of the huts, people painted or drew from the living model. In the life-room … a medium sized hut, were the students of the nude.

Among the most attractive of Williams's pictures is a study of fellow students at work in the life hut. Two young women in pinafores paint with 'an air of intense concentration', just as described by Colwyn E. Vulliamy, another young Welsh student who had been in attendance shortly before the war.[142] Williams also painted an

John Cyrlas Williams,
The Life Studio, Newlyn, c.1920–22

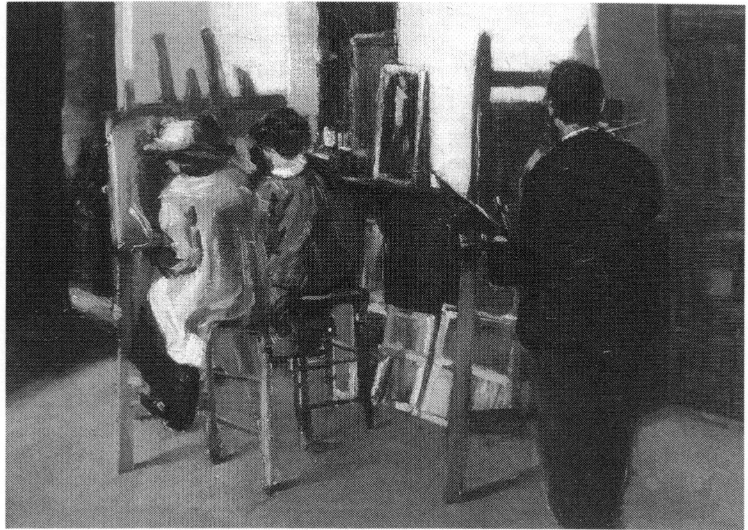

interior of Forbes's own studio, apparently depicting the great man installed at the centre in his wicker chair. Both pictures share the dark tones of his sister's early portrait, and so reflect many of Forbes's own interiors. However, the practice promoted at Newlyn was two-fold. Alongside study of the figure in the studio, the students worked from nature in the open air. Williams followed this pattern, painting in sunlit colours at some of the most frequented outdoor locations – the boatyards at Newlyn itself, the cove at Lamorna, St Ives and Mousehole. His style became fresh and direct. Probably after this initial training at Newlyn, he followed the well-trodden artistic path to the *ateliers* of Paris. He may already have been familiar with the city. The comfortable circumstances of his parents enabled the family every year to travel on the continent. No details of his first working trip to France survive, so it is not clear whether undated pictures such as a townscape of *Chartres Cathedral from the Rue du Bourg* were painted then or on a later visit. One of several seascapes is dated March 1922, and indicates that Cyrlas Williams had returned home, because it almost certainly portrays the Glamorgan coast. The format and small size of these simple pictures suggest that the painter may have become aware of works made by J.D. Innes and Augustus John in Wales and France just before the war. However, later in 1922 or early in 1923 Williams's development was interrupted. There would be no pictures for four years. It was not until the summer of 1926 that Williams began to work again, and came into contact with Winifred Coombe Tennant. He submitted three pictures to the National Eisteddfod art competitions in Swansea. Winifred probably saw *Ogmore Castle* as she ferried one of the judges, George Clausen (who was staying with her), to and from the Patti Pavilion, where the competition work was shown. By the time the exhibition was open to the public, she had bought it:

> 29 July, Thursday. Much shopping and then to Arts and Crafts show. I like my little oil of Ogmore Castle more than ever and am interested to find it is by a young man living at Porthcawl who has studied in Paris, then had a nervous breakdown and been ill for four years through overwork and has just begun to paint again.[143]

The source of this information had been Gwladys Williams though, for reasons that would not become apparent until much later, she had not elaborated on the cause of her son's breakdown.

Winifred now adopted Cyrlas Williams as she had done Evan Walters, who had 'greatly admired' his *Ogmore Castle*. She was experienced at mobilising the support of newspapers for her *protégés*, and it was perhaps at her instigation that the *South Wales News* published a small piece about him, with a photograph, before the end of the Eisteddfod. Furthermore, she had the ear of William Grant Murray at the Glynn Vivian Art Gallery, and so was in a position to launch Williams's career. She wrote to the painter and received a brief courteous reply, but perhaps it is significant, in view of subsequent events, that it was Gwladys Williams who, in the main, took up the correspondence with Winifred on behalf of her 24-year-old son. In November Gwladys reported that Jack was again in Paris, painting, as she said, 'at the Grande Chaumière'. Since the 1870s the Rue de la Grande Chaumière had been the location of the celebrated *atelier* founded by the Italian Filippo Colarossi as a radical alternative to the École des Beaux Arts. Among Williams'

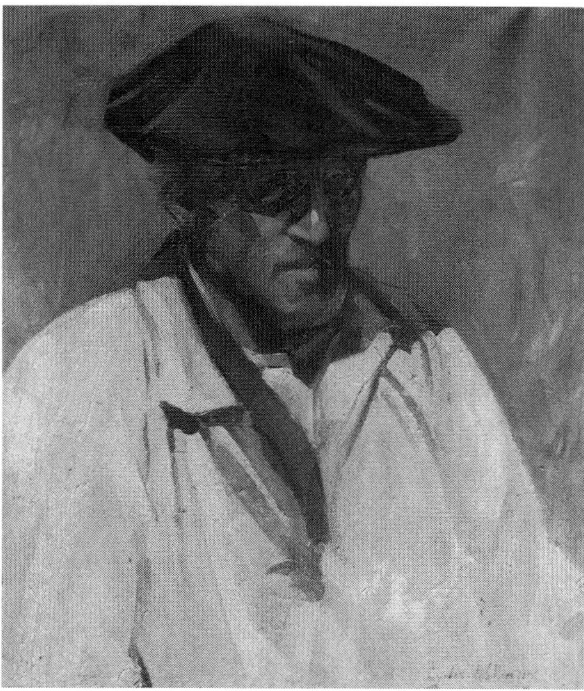

John Cyrlas Williams, *Breton Man*, c.1927

predecessors there had been Dod Procter, Sidney Curnow Vosper and Cedric Morris. They had been enrolled students, but Williams is more likely to have attended on a casual basis. He painted from both nude and clothed life models. Although many of the *atelier* canvasses present only rapid impressions – probably the work of a single session – the drawing and the use of colour reveal increasing self confidence and an exceptional level of talent. On several occasions Williams worked at the back of the class, painting the other students studying the model and producing pictures that exude the atmosphere of the period. Prominent is a dark haired model – his Jewish girlfriend, Ruth.

In December 1926 Williams was joined in Paris by his parents, his brother and sister. As yet he had failed to find his own studio, and he may never have done so. By the summer of 1927 he was working at Concarneau in Brittany, where he made landscapes and portraits of local people in the tradition of visiting painters since Gaugin. Again, his mother was with him, combining her visit with attendance at the Gorsedd ceremonies. There, for the first time, she met Winifred Coombe Tennant, who had travelled to Pont-Aven with the Welsh Gorsedd delegation. Winifred gained a favourable impression of Gwladys, later reporting to a friend that she regarded her as 'an example of the very best type of cultured Welsh woman'. The attraction was not surprising. Notwithstanding her social rise, Gwladys Williams retained the Labour politics of her youth and – like Winifred – held radical views on women's rights. However, although he was working nearby, at this time Winifred still did not meet Cyrlas Williams. By the autumn he seems to have travelled to the south to the coastal town of Martigues, near Marseilles. He may well have done so at the behest of his ambitious mother. She would have known that Augustus John worked there often, living at the Villa Ste-Anne. For John the place was 'like some rustic mistress one is always on the point of leaving but who looks so lovely at the last moment that one falls back into her arms.'[144] He had worked there since 1910, but in April 1927 he finally broke off the liason, and left the villa. Williams was six months too late. Nevertheless, at Martigues he produced what would prove to be his most developed and assured paintings. The canals of the town led visitors to liken it to Venice, and Williams painted many studies of moored boats, becoming interested in the complicated interplay of their lines, masts and rigging, and producing canvasses that began to depart from the impressionistic realism of his earlier work.

Back in Porthcawl, Gwladys continued to lobby Winifred on her son's behalf. She felt that he should paint under another name, Williams being too common in Wales. This was not an eccentric perception. In the mid-nineteenth century the painter Benjamin Williams had adopted his mother's name for the same reason, and become famous as Benjamin Williams Leader. Gwladys observed 'that Mr Augustus John's help and patronage has been of great benefit to Mr Walters, especially in Wales, where the people are not artistic and require to be told what is right in art by a man of weight in the profession.'[145] She was clearly well informed about Welsh painters, noting also that Margaret Lindsay Williams had been assisted by Sargent, and suggesting that her son would benefit from the influence of Orpen. Winifred did not know Orpen and, at this time had yet to meet John, but in the following spring once again she did her best to encourage Williams, who had now returned to Wales. On 15 April she 'Motored … to Porthcawl to see John Williams, the young painter who painted the castle I bought at the National Eisteddfod exhibition two years ago':

He had a number of canvasses with him, and I bought three and a small sketch. He shows great promise I think, painting in a direct, vivid style. I have commissioned him to do a head of Wise One [Henry], an oil sketch, at the end of the month. The pictures I bought are two of boats, and one of figures in an *atelier*.

Among the pictures acquired by Winifred was *The Dark Boats*, the most radical in style of the Martigues works. The following day she took it and the two others to Grant Murray at the Glynn Vivian:

He was *very* appreciative of them, praised them warmly, invited John Williams to send in six oil paintings to the South Wales Art Society's show next month, and promised to give him a one man show next year. He said "This boy will go far". I am delighted with this and delighted to be able to send John Williams good news.

Williams carried out his portrait commission while staying with Winifred at Cadoxton Lodge. The picture was shown at an exhibition of the Swansea Art Society and a complimentary notice appeared in the *Cambria Daily Leader*, but from that point things began to go wrong. At the end of the summer an expectant Winifred travelled to Porthcawl to inspect Williams's latest work:

Disgusted to find he has done *no* work all these months since he painted Henry – he has great talent but he evidently is no worker. Urged him to work hard for six weeks and go up to London at the end of October to see Evan Walters and Cedric Morris.

Winifred made the arrangements, and the meetings took place in September. Morris 'did not find him an arresting personality like Evan[Walters] for example', she noted, but 'liked and found him intelligent'. However, little seems to have come of this introduction, and the promised one man show at the Glynn Vivian did not take place.[146] It was the 1928 exhibition of the work of Archie Griffiths, whom Evan Walters had thought less promising than Williams, that attracted the attention of the press and the public at the gallery.

Winifred reported seeing good pictures by Williams in June 1929 at the Swansea Art Society show, but despite his participation in a further group exhibition, in May 1931 Grant Murray wrote to Winifred that he remained reluctant to buy the painter's pictures – clearly now unsure about Williams's ability to work steadily and develop. Murray's doubts were well founded, because Williams would soon cease to paint altogether. Nothing more would be heard of him in Welsh art circles until February 1952, when an article about the collection of Winifred Coombe Tennant appeared in the *News Chronicle*. In the course of the interview that Winifred gave the newspaper, she mentioned the promise shown by Williams when a young man. An unidentified member of his family read the article and contacted her. Gwladys Williams wrote to her soon after. In May, Cyrlas Williams took tea with Winifred at her London flat:

> Cyrlas Williams, the artist, came. I showed him his five pictures bought in the twenties. He was amazed. I think he is in some state of mental confusion, and I ask myself, will he ever paint again? I doubt it. He is on the Board of Trade, been living in London all this time … I felt an ailing mind. He was surprised at the warmth of my welcome. He had it in him to be a very considerable painter …

There was no further contact between the two, and so, until I resumed research following the discovery of the cache of pictures at Porthcawl, the subsequent history of John Cyrlas Williams remained obscure.

I discovered that Williams had been buried at Porthcawl. I visited his grave, which was shared with his mother. Apparently, he had not married and had no children. However, his sister Lynne had married and there was a son. He grew up in Birmingham and became a doctor, eventually making his career in Swansea. Dr Beverley Littlepage became a prominent figure in Unitarian circles but through the church I discovered that, unfortunately, he had recently died. However, his widow, Marian, was living in Pontardawe – and in the strange way of these things, it turned out that her house was less than half a mile from that of Mike Jones, who had discovered her uncle's paintings down the road at Clydach. Marian had known Cyrlas Williams in his later years, and both from her personal acquaintance with him and through her memories of her husband's conversation, she was able to throw some light on the 'nervous breakdown'. There had been rather more to it than that. Cyrlas Williams had told her that, at the time, he had a serious problem of alcohol addiction. Furthermore, his girlfriend, Peggie Mills, was pregnant with his child. The family and, it seems, in particular his sister, Lynne, had opposed their desire to marry. He was despatched to Australia to remove him from the scene while his daughter, Sharon, was born. Sharon was about three years old when her father returned from Australia. He would not stay long in Porthcawl and would come to know her only slightly. Peggie brought up his daughter alone, with the financial assistance of his father.

Marian was able to complete the story, in so far as we have it. Like his younger brother, Roy, who would be killed in north Africa, Cyrlas Williams joined the army early in the war. Afterwards, he returned to London to his work as a clerk at the Board of Trade. He lodged in a house near Hampstead Heath, owned by two sisters. The conventionality of his weekday life was broken at weekends. On Friday nights and through Saturdays he drank heavily. Sundays were spent recovering, before he returned to his desk on Monday mornings. He remained in contact with his family in Porthcawl, and was with his mother when she died there, in 1958. On his retirement he moved to a cottage at nearby Newton, bringing his London landladies with him. The arrangement failed, and he moved back to Sandringham, where he lived with his sister, now divorced. He died there, following a heart attack, on 3 August 1965.

Lynne took in lodgers. Among them was a young man called Kevin Sinnott, from Sarn, a few miles south of Pontyrhyl, where Cyrlas Williams had been born. He was yet to become a painter, but the pictures he saw on the walls of Sandringham made a strong impression on him. Forty-five years later, his description from memory of the Williams portrait of a Breton Woman was easy to identify among the cache so nearly burned at Porthcawl. Shortly after Kevin's stay at Sandringham, Lynne sold the house. She bundled all her brother's pictures into a cupboard, and left them.

The question remains as to why John Cyrlas Williams failed to fulfil what his contemporaries believed was exceptional promise as a painter. Winifred Coombe Tennant's conclusion, that he was 'no worker', drawn in 1928 following a few months of inactivity, was certainly incorrect. Nearly two hundred pictures survive, painted between 1918 and 1930. For four of those years Williams certainly did not paint at all, and the observations of Winifred and William Grant Murray indicate further sterile months. It follows that in between the spells of inactivity Williams was highly productive, an impression reinforced by the urgent style of many of the pictures.

Again, the letters of Gwladys Williams and her presence in France at the side of a son who was in his mid-twenties suggest an exaggerated concern for his well being. It seems unlikely to have been simply a matter of alcohol addiction. Williams's niece remembers him, in old age, as 'a charming man, but directionless'. She feels 'he lived with lots of regrets'. Taken together with Winifred's sense of his 'ailing mind', the evidence is consistent with Williams suffering from some form of personality disorder, resulting in cycles of intense activity and sterile depressions. Something was wrong.

The talent of Cyrlas Williams cannot be in doubt – he could paint. Furthermore, his comfortable financial circumstances enabled him, at an early age, to experience what was then widely considered modern painting in England and France – a conservative-minded evolution of the Impressionism of the 1880s. At the same time, Winifred was making regular visits to Paris to buy the work of young French painters, bringing the pictures back as exemplars for their working-class Welsh contemporaries, who did not have the means to travel. Her French collection and the paintings of Cyrlas Williams clearly emerge from a single tradition. Like Harry Hughes Williams, painting landscape in Anglesey in the same period, if Cyrlas Williams was aware of the Paris *avant-garde* of the 1920s, his work was not influenced by it. Closer to home, a comparison with the story of his exact contemporary Archie Griffiths is instructive. Both Williams and Griffiths were the children of colliers in the south Wales coalfield. Griffiths began painting a couple of years after Williams and worked seriously for a little longer, but essentially their short careers over-lapped. Nevertheless, the product of the two painters could scarcely be more different. Certainly setting out with less natural facility to draw, Griffiths produced a small body of narrative pictures that

John Cyrlas Williams,
Self-portrait, c.1927

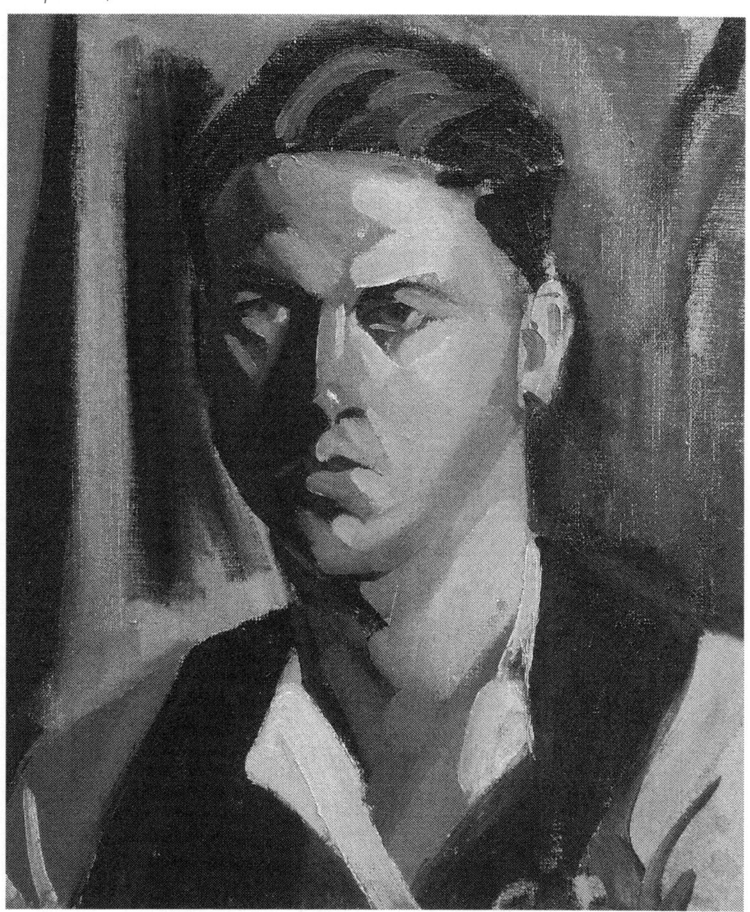

were rooted in, and powerfully expressed, the social trauma of
the coalfield during the Depression. As far as is known, Williams
produced no narrative pictures. The much larger body of work
that he left certainly reflects the world in which he moved, but it
was not a world of intellectual critique or of imagination. Rooted
in Porthcawl, it was a world insulated from the social trauma to

which Griffiths was exposed and, indeed, also from the professional marginalisation that might have accompanied a more radical choice of aesthetic direction. The body of work that remains is redolent of its period and its place, but that place is not the one that tradition generally presents south Wales to have been in the 1920s. Yet, at the level of the individual at least, the middle-class experience must surely be as legitimate a subject for painting as that of the working class. The question that arises is whether Williams's attitudes, from which social, philosophical and aesthetic critique seem to have been absent, diminish his paintings? Perhaps the psychological make up that exploits technical facility, whether to create expressions of inner emotional experience or considered statements about the condition of society, was inhibited by the personality disorder that seems to have afflicted him. His was a brief flowering – though, for Winifred Coombe Tennant at least, as she expressed it in a letter to William Grant Murray in 1928, it was none the less a flowering of 'the real thing'.

13

Edward Owen of Penrhos

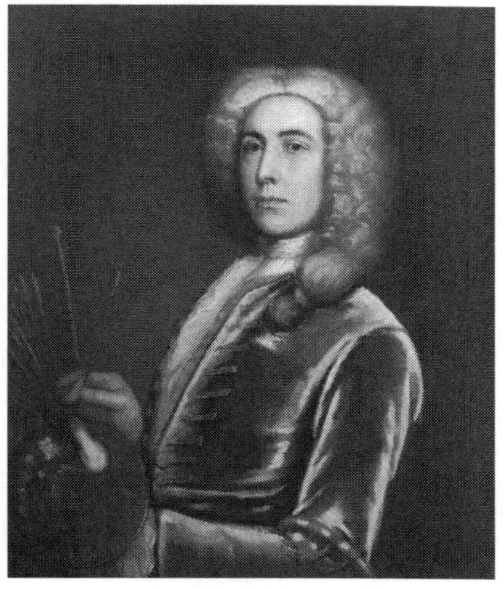

At the National Museum, among the most interesting relics of the early days of research in Welsh visual culture is a copy of the Rev T. Mardy Rees's pioneering volume, *Welsh Painters, Engravers, Sculptors*. It was published just before the Great War, when the hopes of the generation of Cymry Fydd were still high, at least in so far as cultural revival was concerned. T. Gwynn Jones was at the peak of his creativity as a poet, J.E. Lloyd published his *History of Wales to the Edwardian Conquest*, and Christopher Williams painted his allegory of national renaissance, *Wales Awakening*. Mardy Rees's work on Welsh artists appeared in 1912, the year after Williams's massive picture. It drew heavily on the enquiries made by a wider group of enthusiasts, the most important of whom was T.H. Thomas, a prominent campaigner for the establishment of the National Museum. In his will, Thomas left the nation a large archive of his papers and art work, amongst which was his own copy of Mardy Rees's book. He had annotated it with additional information, a process that was continued after his death by the first Keeper of Art at the Museum, Isaac Williams. The volume became a sort of hagiography of the field.

Some twenty-five years ago, examining Williams's elaborations on the text, I found a particularly interesting note made in November 1926. The Keeper of Art had returned from a tour of gentry houses in Anglesey, where he was searching for pictures to show the following year in an exhibition at the National Eisteddfod at Holyhead. In the north of the island, at Penrhos, home of the Stanley family, he struck lucky.

> I discovered hanging on the wall of the bed-room corridor,
> in the old part of the house, the portrait of a man, showing a
> painter, with a palette in his hand. On the back of the canvas
> is the following inscription: Self portrait, Edward Owen. Born
> 1707. Died 1748. Portrait painted at Penrhos, 1732.

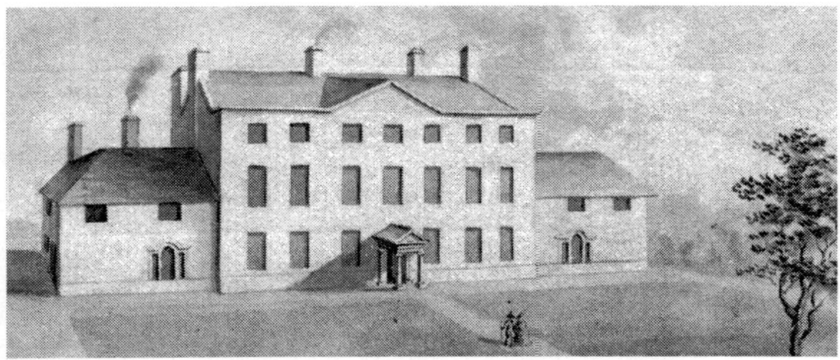

T. Boydell, *Penrhos House*, c.1769
Archives and Special Collections, Bangor University

I was as surprised to find this note as Williams had been to find the picture, seventy years earlier. The date of the painting, if correct, would have made it the earliest surviving portrait of a Welsh artist shown with the tools of his trade, as a painter. Indeed, it would be rather an early example of the genre in the wider British context also. I knew of no published record of Edward Owen's work, other than a newspaper review of the Holyhead exhibition written by Williams himself, so I contacted the Stanley family, descendents of the Owens of Penrhos, who still lived in Anglesey. The news was bad. The family had disposed of Penrhos and much of its contents, including the picture, at the beginning of the Second World War, and it had been taken over by the army. The only surviving portrait by Edward Owen was hanging in Lord Stanley's present house, and it depicted Ann Owen, the mother of the painter. According to its inscription, it had been painted in the same year as the missing self-portrait. Next, I contacted a relative of Lord Stanley's, Victoria Woods, who was living in Canada. She revealed that, in fact, another Owen picture had survived and was in her possession – a portrait of the painter's younger brother, Hugh, through whom the Stanleys descended. Furthermore, Victoria could recall seeing the lost self-portrait at Penrhos before the war. However, she wrote to me that it was 'not particularly esteemed at that time of being either of artistic or of historical merit' and so it had disappeared with the furniture and assorted bric-a-brac when the army requisitioned the house in 1939.

I learned that there were family documents surviving from the first half of the eighteenth century in a very large manuscript archive, mainly held at Bangor University. I visited Bangor and discovered that, remarkably, the archive included many letters written to and by Edward Owen.[147] In his own letters he revealed to his mother, his uncle and his brother details of his life as an apprentice painter in the radical atmosphere of London in the 1720s. Little enough is known first-hand of the formative experiences even of those who reached the top of the greasy pole of art world success in the early eighteenth century. The survival of the observations of one of the dozens of obscure apprentice painters who thronged Covent Garden in the period was an unusual piece of good fortune.

Edward Owen showed an interest in art as a child at Ross-on-Wye. He had been sent there to be educated under the supervision of his mother's uncle, the cleric and scholar Dr Robert Morgan.[148] At the age of about sixteen he wrote home to his mother that 'I draw picktures very much'. Morgan thought it 'a pretty exercise enough' and encouraged him. Edward appealed to his mother to 'alow somewhat to buy books to draw and engrediens to paint', but she was on a tight budget – the estate was impoverished, embroiled in law suits, and Edward had not one but five living brothers. Only his uncle was flourishing. Edward Wynn, his mother's brother, had progressed in the church to become Chancellor of the Diocese of Hereford, where he lived when not at his family home, Bodewryd, in Anglesey. As his education drew to a close, Edward turned to his uncle for career advice but was forced to reveal that the church did not appeal: 'I like a limner best', he protested, pointing out optimistically that it was also likely to be 'more beneficial than a parson'. In response, Chancellor Wynn wrote to Edward's mother:

Dear Sister

I ordered Nedy to write his mind him self, since he has discovered it to ye Dr and me As his inclination tend that way, so it is best to let him follow it, and no doubt but with Gods Grace he may make a competent Honest lively Hood No time ought to be Lost in placing him out, I have this post writ a Letter to Dr Foulks under Cover to Sr Thomas Sebright to desire his advice and assistance because I think he Knows some professors of that art … no stone must be left unturned to endeavr to settle him …[149]

It was presumably Sebright, whose foppish appearance is known from a delightful group portrait painted by Benjamin Ferrers, who recommended the family come to terms with the portrait painter Thomas Gibson in Charles Street, Covent Garden. Gibson was an ambitious choice, since his reputation stood high. In January 1725, Ned set off for the metropolis:

I safly arriv'd at London last Thursday night and came to my aunt Lloyd's here I am at present. And [there] may [stay] till I go to Mr Gibson he being the first drawer in all England and a civil good humour'd man, as all giv's him the Character, as for my part I havnt seen him yet but shall a Munday it please God go upon triall, and when I am little settled with him I'l write agan to you.

Apprenticeship agreement between Thomas Gibson and Edward Owen, 1725 Archives and Special Collections, Bangor University

Terms were agreed with Gibson, who received the substantial sum of 120 guineas and was careful to ensure that he would not be responsible for any incidental expenses. His apprentice was to buy his own materials – 'Chalks Leaden pencills pens & paper', not to mention paying for his washing, and

> Item In Case of Sickness the Expense of Physick as also the necessary attendance as Doctor Apothecary Surgeon Nurse shall be defrayed by him …

Ned duly settled in, but among his first requests to his mother was for more money to buy clothes:

> I received yours of Mr Buller Tuesday last and he took my measure for a Cloake and being persuaded by my Aunt Lloyd and Mr Buller that every body now [wore ruffles] in London that was any thing genteel, and not one face painter Prentice but what did, especially my Master being one of the greatest I should go litle tydy and clean, I bespoke for some of Mrs Buller. My business is very changeable and will be this two year while I draw …

Ned's appeal to his mother for more money would be repeated at intervals for the next seven years. However, his insistence on improving his appearance with ruffles for his shirts reflected not simply personal vanity but a fundamental change in the nature of metropolitan painting practice in the period. It is significant that Ned arrived in London in the year of the publication of the second and enlarged edition of Jonathan Richardson's *Essay on the Theory of Painting.*, which was intended to raise the status of the painter from that of artisan (or 'Mechanick') to that of professor of a liberal art. The expectation of the Owen family had been that Ned would establish himself in 'a Sertainty by a Good Honest Trade'. Not belonging to the upper echelons of the Welsh gentry, their experience of painting would have been gained in the conservative traditions of generalist artisans at work in Wales, the English border towns and Dublin. The gentrification of painters in London took them by surprise though Ned, finding himself at the very centre of their world, was quick to revise his preconceptions. He also found himself close to the creation of the new professional institutions that would underpin upward mobility among art painters. In 1711 his own master had been a founding director of St Luke's Academy, and Thornhill's Academy was newly opened on his doorstep in Covent Garden.

Having settled as Gibson's apprentice, in March 1725 Ned wrote to his mother with a fuller account of his daily life:

I hope you'll excuse my silence since it was not out of neglect or lasiness, but being a little at present taken up with geometry, perspective, accounts and my business. I have but a very few leisure hours and those I mostly spend in reading over my school books. There died about 4 months ago a famous History Painter whose paintings and drawings were last week sold by Auction and my master bought me some of his academy figures which were reckned the best that ever were drawn, which I now draw after. Mrs Lloyd's Landlord married this painters maid who proved a good fortune to him left her by her master which was about 1500 pound and as people say for standing naked for him to paint after, and for other favours. I find my business vastly expensive to what I thought it would be when I was first bound, theres not a week passes but it costs me above eighteen pence only in pens pencils chalks blew brown and white paper, besides what it costs me in things to coppy after as drawings prints and plaister figures. My Master tells me it will yearly cost me 10 pound in my business, it is not meerly coppying makes a painter but seeing and buying great masters performances, and minding where in one excell'd, here in another. Tho' master is the best Drawer in England, as allow'd by every one, yet he lays out above 40 or 50 pound a year in drawings.

The studio auction was probably that of Godfrey Kneller. Following the hierarchies of the day, Ned identified him as a history painter, rather than as a painter of portraits.[150]

During his first winter in London Ned fell ill. He recovered through 'being my own doctor by taking opium and burnt wine every night', but in May 1726 he reported to his mother the ominous news of 'a terrible cold attended with an headack so that for two or three mornings I spate blood with caffing.' Nevertheless, he pursued his studies with diligence and over a range of subjects that underlined the necessity for social accomplishments in his calling. His Latin was adequate to translate Dryden on the art of painting for his mother's benefit. He proposed to dispense with his writing teacher, and had become 'Master of all arithmetick whatsoever both vulgar and decimal.' He hoped that soon he would 'have learnt Geometry suffitient either for my business or to proced without a master.' However, the cost of professional gentrification continued a cause of concern, in addition to his materials expenses:

It realy troubles me to think how money runs away I have very often made resolutions to be saving of my money and then as after one thing or another does happen that I am obliged to pay it out it has cost me 50 shilling for my French already and

> I suppose it will cost me 30 shill more before I shall give over.
> I must in a bout a weeks time buy a French Dictionary and that
> will cost me 10 shill. My Business has cost me a great deal of
> money for colours oils pencils cloths et[c] the cloths cost me 21
> pence and I use two a week of them to paint upon, besides what
> it costs me in other necessaries for myself as washing, shaving,
> shoes, stockings, wigs, hats, gloves, handkerchiefs etc all which
> run away with my money …

The only supplement that Ned was able to provide to his allowance
in 1727 seems to have been the two guineas commission that he
received for introducing his master to his uncle, who bespoke a
portrait, in which he was presented in the splendid red robes of
his office, and full wig. Ned was getting itchy feet. He recalled to
the Chancellor that when he first went to Gibson 'it was absolutely
necessary for his correcting my drawing 2 or 3 times a day', but he
now felt confident that 'once a fortnight or once a month it would be
as often as I should have occasion for him':

> I improve now by my own observation and industry with a little
> instruction, and not by the perpetual inspection and correction
> of a master as it used to be when I first came to draw … What
> would most improve me in Painting woud be to coppy good
> pictures and draw sometimes Pictures from the life …

but life drawing was difficult because of the dirtiness of his rooms at
the King and Pearl tavern on Tavistock Street:

> Were I parted with my master, I would borrow some of
> Richerdson's and Vanderbank's painting to coppy, and thereby
> get as near as I could to their manner of Painting but whilst I

continue with my mastor I know he would take it ill if I were
to coppy any Paintors works but his own.

Ned's observation reflected the developing hierarchy of portrait painters, that was leaving his master somewhat behind. Furthermore, at this point Gibson fell ill, which further checked his career and affected Ned's own confidence in his ability eventually to earn a living. Clearly, he sensed that Richardson and Vanderbank had surpassed his master in reputation, and that the value that might accrue when, in due course, he would 'Come to his buisness by his recomandation' (as his mother expressed it), was much diminished. He speculated on the advantages of buying a gentleman usher's place at court, and wrote to his uncle, Chancellor Wynn, to solicit his financial assistance, offering a list of excuses for buying himself out of his apprenticeship:

Another reason why my parting with Mr Gibson would be no prejudice to me is this. He has been so ill ever since you left the Town that he has painted but one picture all the time, nor has been capable of giving me the least instruction imaginable since his being taken ill he comes indeed about once a week into my Chambor but as soon as he looks upon my work he is immediately seized with a giddiness in his head in such a manner that he can't shew me my faults and realy I see no liklyhood of his recovery

Mr Gibson I believe woud be glad to part with me for I am of no manner of service to him since his being ill for he wont take business in and therefore has no coppying work for me – If I parted with Mr Gibson it would be but reasonable for me to make him ammends of some Present tho at the same time my stay woud be on no manner of service to him.

Letter from Edward Owen to his brother Hugh, requesting supplies
of paint, 1737. Archives and Special Collections, Bangor University

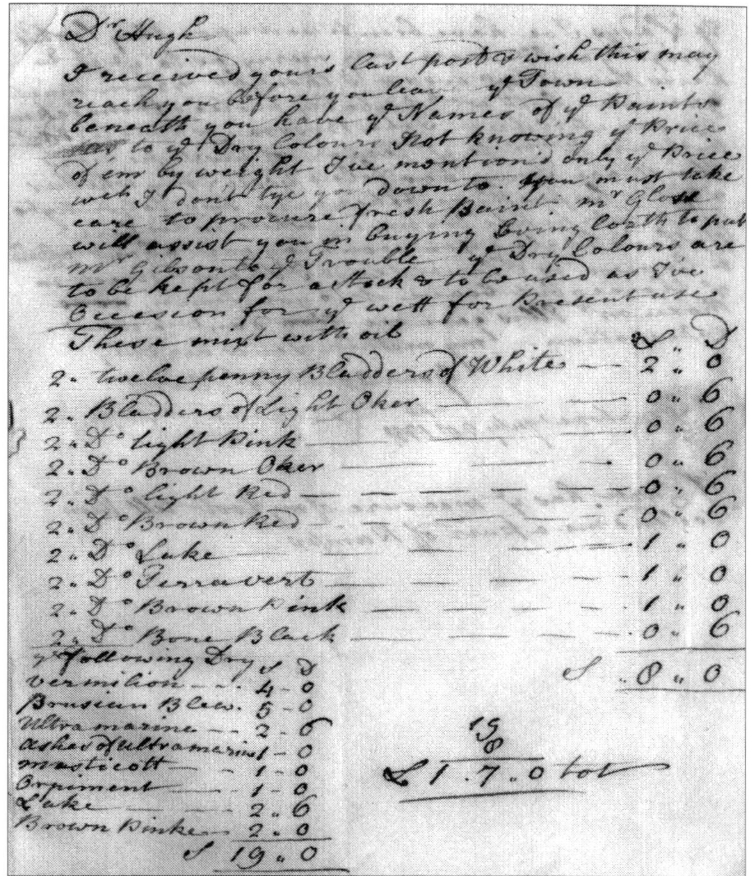

D: Hugh

I received yours last post & wish this may
reach you before you leav y: Town —
beneath you have y: Names of y: Paints
next to y: Dry Colours Not knowing y: Prices
of em by weight I've mention'd only y: Prices
w:ch I don't tye you down to. you must take
care to procure fresh Paint. M:r Gloss
will assist you in buying being loath to put
m:r Gibson to y: Trouble y: Dry Colours are
to be kept for a Stock & to be used as I've
occasion for, y: wett for Present uses
These mixt with oil

		£	s	d
2..	Twelve penny Bladders of White		2	0
2..	Bladders of Light Oker		0	6
2..	D° light Pink		0	6
2..	D° Brown Oker		0	6
2..	D° light Red		0	6
2..	D° Brown Red		0	6
2..	D° Lake		1	0
2..	D° Terra vert		1	0
2..	D° Brown Pink		1	0
2..	D° Bone Black		0	6
		s	8	0

y: following Dry
	£	s	d
Vermilion		4	0
Prusian Blew		5	0
Ultramarine		2	6
ashes of ultramarine		1	0
masticott		1	0
Orpiment		1	0
Lake		2	6
Brown Pinke		2	0
	s	19	0

£1.7.0 tot

The place would cost £600, and Ned sought £150 in subsidy from
Chancellor Wynn, to which his uncle was understandably reluctant
to agree. Furthermore, his mother remained keen for him to persist
with his original intention and do nothing rash, 'for in gods name my
Dear why [do] you dispare of Making a living by that Employment

more than others?' He was dissuaded, and settled to work again. In January 1731, temporarily at Penrhos, he received an intriguing letter from Gibson's servant, Stephen Watkin. Ned had requested he buy for him a large selection of paints and other materials. They were costly, especially the bladder of ultramarine and the chalks, 'for the French woman has very Extravagant Priceses'. Ned also ordered a number of engravings, including *The Lord's Supper* after Rubens, and a massive canvas of 15ft x 9ft:

> My master gives his Service to you, and says you have undertook
> a large piece of work, so he would advise you to send for Mr.
> Savaker to help you out, or for Mr. Reason, he will not Paint
> a great Deal, but he will Drink a great deal of your best Beer.

It would appear that Ned had ambitions to paint a large religious subject, perhaps for the church at Holyhead.[151]

Ned had frustratingly little to say of his contemporaries amongst the art community. A later letter from Anthony Lee, a young Irishman, by this time pursuing his career as a portrait painter in Dublin, suggests strongly that the two were apprentices together, but there is no mention of his Welsh contemporary, John Dyer, training in the 1720s under Thomas Gibson's most successful rival in London, Jonathan Richardson. Dyer painted a *Last Supper* at about the same time as Ned appears to have contemplated his own religious subject and, again at about the same time, they both painted their own portraits. Dyer's master was something of a compulsive self-portraitist, and his student's image strongly reflects Richardson's approach, with its emphasis on psychological concentration at the expense of the depiction of the tools of the trade which, according to Isaac Williams's description, had adorned Ned's picture.

By 1732, the last year of Ned's apprenticeship, his master had recovered his health and was doing very well at Oxford, where for a period he seems to have cornered the market in portraits of university worthies and divines: 'Mr & Mrs Gibson are at Oxford he is perfectly recovered & has a vast deal of Business I hear he's not to return to London these two months …' Ned established himself in new lodgings with a jeweller in Tavistock Street that he shared with his brother Hugh, now training as a barrister. It was a tight squeeze – they lay together in the single bedroom, the closet became Hugh's study, and the dining room became the studio, where Ned received his first paying customer, Mr Williams of Pwllycrochan, in early December. However, shortly afterwards, Ned was overtaken by disaster, when he fell victim to a vicious attack in Covent Garden:

The night this happen'd I went to see my Brother Wm. My sister being engaged in a party at Quadrille with some ladys who were in the house desired I would keep my Brother company till her company broke up which was at twelve, and then took my leave and wak'd home, but in Bedford Street Covt Garden (which is not an hundred yds from our lodgings) I was attacked by four street robbers who threatn'd to shoot me thr' the head if I made the least resistance or spoke a word, as for making any resistance I could not for two of them held my hands behind me the third held a B[l]udgeon which is a thick short stick leaded at top over my head whilst the fourth riffled my pockets where he found two guineas, a seal, a penknife, and the little gold wire ring you gave me; the fellow that riffled me using me a little roughly. I told him there was no necessity for it since I did not offer to interrupt him in his search. He reply'd very cras – damn you for a Rascal we

will use you as we please. When he had done they gave me a
shove from them, that the Gentleman who was to chastise me
might have his full stroke at my head, what became of them
afterwards I can't tell for I was so stunnd I could neither see nor
hear. I did not fall quite to the ground tho near it and shoud I
believe if I had not got hold of a post by which I supported my
self for about a minute as I guess. I call'd upon the Watch to come
to my assistance but whether twas before I Receiv'd the Blow or
after I cant really say. The Watch came upon my calling but not
time enough to take the rogues They found me leaning upon my
post by this time I had pretty well recoverd my self and after some
talk with em I walked home or rather reeled. I sent immediately
for Mr Nanney a surgeon who has now Cured me I was a month
under his care a fortnight of which I kept my rooms. My eyes
were very painfull to me for about 9 days. My head likewise was
sore and my face much swell'd not so much about the wound
as in the lower part of my throat. The Scare lies within the
thickness of a shilling to my eye …

The severe blow received by Ned may have resulted in
permanent damage and perhaps contributed to his decision not to
pursue his career in London, though another important factor was
certainly the death of his elder brother, William, in the following
year. Ned returned home as squire, probably at the end of 1733,
though he continued to paint, since his letters to Hugh, still in the
city, include requests to send supplies of pigment. In Anglesey, he
pursued interests in gardening and in music. He wrote to Hugh of
how the church choir of 40 scholars at Holyhead – 'côr Cybi' –
was going on pretty well: 'We have learn'd two or three psalm's, ye

magnificat, & an anthem out of ye Litany since your Departure the Bass improve prodigiously ...' In May 1737 he requested Thomas Gibson to organise a supply of pigments from Thomas King, colourman in Long Acre. His master, still engaged at Oxford, was pleased that the country suited him, but afraid that 'if you don't see these parts soon you will forgitt yor English.' However, tuberculosis, the first signs of which he had reported in 1726, took hold of him. In 1740 he wrote to his mother that 'no preservations can be of service to me, I shall send for no Doctors but use kitchin physick as my appetite is quite gone I'm oblig'd to confine dait to what I can eat without requiring its being hurtfull or Otherwise.' In March, a neighbour reported that he had been overtaken by 'a kind of galloping consumption, [and] in all probability can't live not above two or three days.' He did not, and was duly buried at Holyhead. 'That's how the world goes on.'[152]

The understanding of Edward Owen's slightly younger contemporary, Richard Wilson, the most celebrated and prolific Welsh painter of the eighteenth century, has always been limited by the near absence of personal documentation of his life. The situation was reversed in the case of Owen, with many surviving letters but only a handful of sitters noted and just two of their portraits identified. The loss of the self-portrait was particularly frustrating, and by the year 2000, my efforts to find it had reached the end of the road. I wrote to Lord Stanley: 'I should think the chances of the self-portrait turning up now are pretty remote ...' I could do no more than cast bread upon the waters in the form of a brief footnote about the picture in my book *Imaging the Nation*. Eleven years later, the tide returned. I received an email from Piers Davies, an art advisor in New York. Engaged to disperse a collection of colonial period American paintings and furniture in Massachusetts, Piers had found the portrait of a young painter, with palette and brushes, identified by an inscription as Edward Owen of Penrhos. Piers's grandfather had farmed in Wales and despite the context of the collection to which it belonged, he suspected that the picture might not, in fact, be American. This was not as obvious a suspicion as it might seem, since many eighteenth-century immigrants to America retained their Welsh names and called their houses and settlements in the new world after their places of family origin in the old. Piers consulted *Imaging the Nation*, found the relevant footnote, and sent me a photograph.

Despite the depth of contemporary information surrounding it, the portrait retains an air of mystery. Few details of Ned Owen's movements for the last seventy years have emerged. It is not clear if the picture left Wales at the beginning of the Second World War or later, perhaps through an English dealer. Unusually for American collectors, his previous custodians have proved uncommunicative. Only one firm piece of evidence has come to light. When the picture was lifted from its stretcher to begin the cleaning process, the business card of Howard and Priscilla Richmond of Southbury, Connecticut, fell out. In the 1960s and 70s, the Richmonds were prominent figures in the rapid expansion of market interest in Americana. They dealt in valuable pictures and furniture in the tradition as it was reaching the unchallenged height of its development at the hands of Jean Lipman, Mary Black, and wealthy antiquarians such as Nina Fletcher Little. Her portrait collection, begun in the early 1940s, provides the context and suggests the raison d'être for the export of Ned's self-portrait. Little's collection would come to include works by many masters of the new American hierarchy – Ralph Earl, Rufus Hathaway, Ammi Phillips, William Matthew Prior and Zedekiah Belknap. In her understanding of the tradition, the validating historical precedent for the masterpieces of the nineteenth century was provided by colonial period portraits from the eighteenth, a group of which she owned. The earliest among them was a portrait of Mary (Fitch) Cabot, of Salem, Massachusetts, attributed to John Greenwood and painted in about 1748. In her autobiography, Little described the picture:

> Characteristic of Greenwood's manner is the stiffness of the figure and his obvious ineptitude in attaching the head to the body. But the conventional pose and gracefully painted hands bespeak New England pre-Revolutionary portraiture that was firmly rooted in English academic style.[153]

Comparison of Little's origins portrait by Greenwood and the Edward Owen self-portrait reveals unsurprising similarities of compositional convention and colour, of technical competence, and even of presentation. The Owen self-portrait retains its elaborately carved oak frame, partly gilt, partly blackened, which may well have been made in Wales, rather than London. Period frames were an important consideration in the taste for these pictures, since they were shown as part of a continuum with furniture, textiles and ceramics, characteristically expressed in the range of the Little collection. It was in the art historical context of collections of this sort that the self-portrait of the obscure Welsh apprentice found a home, almost certainly masquerading as an American colonial work, in which it was accorded a high status that contrasted dramatically with its low standing in its country of origin.

We are a small nation, and losses such as these are disproportionately important when compared with the export of English, Italian or French works. The loss, in 1971, of the two magnificent landscapes of Castell Dinas Bran painted by Wilson for Sir Watkin

Williams Wynn, remains perhaps the saddest example – and that loss is irredeemable, since the pictures are now part of an institutional collection, and so will not return to the market. The opportunity to retrieve other pictures, sold into private collections may arise. Hugh Hughes's early group portrait, *The Gentlemen's Society Meeting*, was sold to a private collection at Greenwich, Connecticut, initially through Sotheby's hands, in 1996. A delightful portrait of one of the Stepney children, painted in Carmarthenshire in about 1745 by John Lewis, went to America from the Derwydd estate sale two years later, also through Sotheby's. However, the prices demanded in the American market for such works seem likely to be well beyond those that most private buyers in Wales are prepared to pay for anything other than pictures by Kyffin Williams, that mysterious and unique market phenomenon. We have yet to acquire the self-confidence needed to repatriate or even to retain pictures painted by any other painter.

The Edward Owen self-portrait has now returned to Wales – one of three Welsh pictures in this house that have made the round trip to the United States and back. Sadly, only a few months before its rediscovery, Ned's portrait of his brother Hugh passed in the other direction, through a New York dealership.

Their Burden

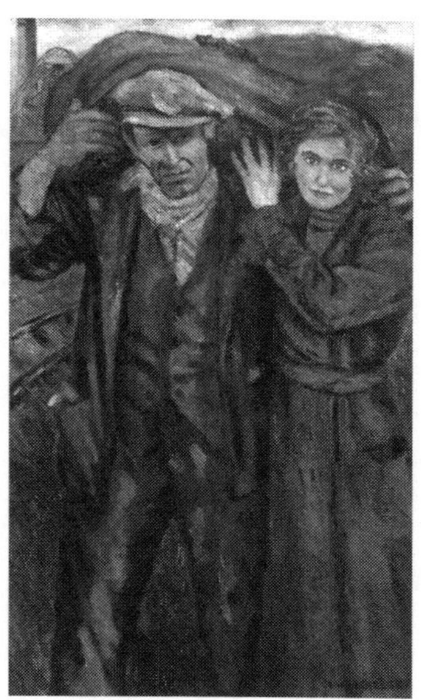

The pictures keep coming.

In 2003 I received an enquiry from a person living in the south east of England about some paintings that she had acquired. The subjects were colliers and their families living at the village of Talywain near Pontypool. They had been painted in 1937 by an artist called Maurice Sochachewsky, but I knew nothing of him and could find no reference to his work. I apologised for being unable to help, labelled a file with the artist's name, inserted a copy of her email, and the matter went to the back of my mind.

Maurice Sochachewsky, *Welsh Miners, Talywain*, 1937
National Museum Wales

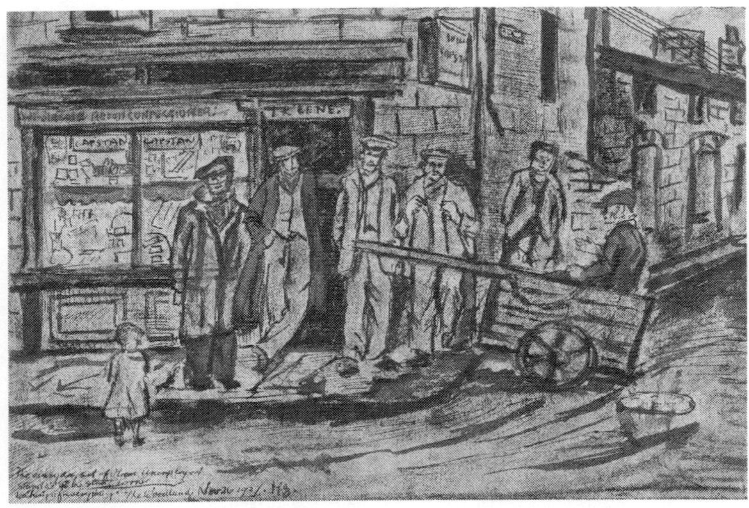

A couple of years later, while reviewing my research on Archie Griffiths for the television programme I was about to make, I took down my copy of Rhys Davies's *The Story of Wales* – the only book to include an illustration of a picture by Griffiths that had been published during his lifetime. I was wondering how Davies had come across the watercolour, called *Standing a Post*. Although the picture was in the collection of the National Museum, it had hardly been considered by them as a prized acquisition, to which they might have drawn the author's attention. Davies had moved between Wales, England and continental Europe in the early 1930s, but it seemed possible that he had been in London at the time of Griffiths's exhibition at the Young Wales Centre in 1932. Perhaps he had seen the exhibition and met Griffiths there? Through the Blitz both men were certainly in London, where *The Story of Wales* was published in 1943, but neither did I have documentary evidence to suggest that they knew each other at that time.

Looking again through *The Story of Wales* I noticed another of its illustrations – a drawing of a group of unemployed miners standing on a street corner. I remembered noting the picture when I had first come across the book, some years earlier, but the name of the painter had meant nothing to me at the time, and had not stuck in my mind. To my surprise, I saw now that it was Maurice Sochachewsky. His picture was very different from that painted by Griffiths, with its biblical allusion to Jesus carrying the cross to Calvary. Sochachewsky's picture was direct, with an inscription that reinforced its documentary rather than metaphysical significance – 'the everyday set of Men Unemployed, stand at the street corner, talking of everything. The Woodlands Nov 26 1937.' Griffiths's generic collier had been the focus for a meditation on the human condition, whereas Sochachewsky's work engaged with the living conditions of the individuals it depicted. The context for his picture, painted a decade after Griffiths's work, seemed clear. It was made at a time when social conditions in the Valleys – 'the distressed areas' was the official aphorism – were becoming well known outside Wales. It was the period of Rhys Davies's novels set in the Rhondda, that pioneered fiction writing about the Welsh industrial proletariat. The ambiguities of that writer's sense of identity with the people of whom he wrote, which seem so apparent in retrospect, were rendered invisible to most contemporary readers by the dominant wider discourse concerning national characterisation, class, social crisis and political response. The body of fiction dealing with these issues expanded as the decade proceeded, and 1937, the year of Sochachewsky's picture, was the most productive. Perhaps he read Lewis Jones's *Cwmardy*, and it was hard to imagine that he was unaware of Orwell's *The Road to Wigan Pier*, with its distressing, matter-of-fact documentation of mining life in northern England. Late in the year, James Hanley's *Grey Children* was published, dealing with conditions in the south Wales coalfield in a way inspired, in part, by Orwell's book.[154] Sochachewsky's documentation seemed entirely consistent with the developing literary context, though how Rhys Davies had come across his work in particular, along with that of Griffiths, and chosen it to illustrate *The Story of Wales*, remained a mystery. I made no progress in trying to link the three men.

Then, in 2011, the catalogue for an auction at a saleroom in Colwyn Bay included two pictures that immediately caught my attention. The first was an etching by Archie Griffiths, untitled in the catalogue, but that I recognised as *Miners Descending* of 1925. The second was an oil painting, also untitled, by Maurice Sochachewsky. The painters were together again. Works by Griffiths rarely appear in the art market, and I had never come across a picture by Sochachewsky for sale. I decided to go to the auction in person. The Griffiths etching was easy to find among the hundreds of pictures in the auction rooms – it was framed and a clean copy, and I knew that I would try to buy it, though I suspected that it would fetch a price well beyond its estimate, following the television programme and the publication of my essay about him in *The Meaning of Pictures*. Locating the Sochachewsky painting was more difficult, as it was nowhere to be seen hanging. A sale-room assistant led me to it, downstairs, on the floor, leaning against the wall like a forgotten reject from a previous auction. Its size surprised me – it was nearly four feet high – and it was in a dire state, dirty, unframed, the stretcher broken and part of the canvas rotted by damp at the bottom. It depicted a collier and his wife returning from picking waste coal on a tip. The young man was looking slightly across the painter, though the woman stared straight out, with a passive but intense expression, more accusation than despair. I felt immediately that it was a powerful and important document. Then I turned the painting around. The back of the canvas was taken up entirely with a long inscription, painted urgently in roughly formed capital letters. The damp had obliterated some of the words in the last two lines:

... THIS PAINTING PORTRAYS THE YOUNG COUPLE BOTH WEARY AND DIRTY COMING FROM THE PIT. THE PIT HEAD GEAR SEEN IN THE DISTANCE IS SEEN IDLE ... 10 YEARS ... UNEMPLOYMENT ... MANY ... THIS DAY ...

I tried not to linger over the picture. It doesn't do to show too much interest before an auction. I had arrived early at the sale-rooms, but the small group of enthusiasts who buy Welsh pictures had already begun to gather. I felt sure that someone would sense, as I did, how significant the picture was, and there was a practical problem because it was due to be sold late in the day, and I could not stay. I felt sure that I would lose the picture if I didn't bid in person. The auction began. I bought the Griffiths etching against a telephone bidder at a price well over estimate, as I had suspected I would have to do. I didn't mind – I feel strongly about his work, and it's become a mission, I suppose – but it reinforced my apprehension that there would be similar competition for the Sochachewsky, in my absence. However, I had to leave and so, reluctantly, I placed a bid for all I could afford with the secretary and drove home, trying to put out of my mind what I felt certain would be the loss of the picture.

In the middle of the following week, an invoice arrived from the auctioneer. My bid had been successful and I was delighted, but it puzzled me that, apparently, nobody else had felt the power of the picture. It was arranged that a friend would retrieve it from Colwyn Bay, and I returned to the search for information about Maurice Sochachewsky and his Welsh paintings. I found that the situation had changed since my previous efforts. A local historian in Monmouthshire, Ruth Edwards, had interviewed the son of a collier with whose family, it appeared, Sochachewsky had lodged when making his pictures in 1937, and had published the material.[155] Although he was too young to remember the painter himself, her informant, Mr Ken Clark, was familiar with the story of Sochachewsky from his mother's accounts. The painter had stayed four months at Talywain. The Clark's house in the village, on Bluett's Road, had been dilapidated:

> It had one living room downstairs, the door of which opened straight onto the street, and a small pantry to the one side. There was no electricity and the water was obtained from a communal pipe lower down the row. The communal toilets were at the bottom of the row of four houses. There was a stone spiral stairway to the two bedrooms, only one of which was usable … Maurice slept downstairs on an old sofa …[156]

For over sixty years the story of Sochachewsky's stay at Talywain had remained strongly present in the memory of Mr Clark because of the painter's association with a family tragedy. This is what had happened, described by Sochachewsky himself:

> [Ivor Clark] and his family gave me everything, though he was unemployed …

> One day Ivor got a job. He came from his first shift in the mine and I painted a picture of him standing there with his baby boy in his arms. Next day Ivor was killed by a fall of

stone. When they brought him home I locked everyone out and painted him as he lay.[157]

The painting, 'the dead man's blackened face lying starkly above the white sheet',[158] was one of twenty five that Sochachewsky would exhibit at the Bloomsbury Gallery in London in May 1938. Among the others would be the portrait of Ivor Clark with his young son – Ken – painted the day before the tragedy.

Ruth Edwards's essay also revealed, to my embarrassment, that at the time of his London exhibition a group of six of Sochachewsky's drawings had been bought by the National Museum. I believed that I had trawled the Museum collection thoroughly in the 1990s when writing *Industrial Society*, and I had no idea why they had escaped me. Furthermore, it transpired that a few years after that book was published, Maurice's younger brother, Ephraim, had visited the Museum to look at them. He was trying to trace the pictures that had been shown at the 1938 exhibition. Ephraim had given the Museum copies of press cuttings about his brother's stay at Talywain, and soon after I visited the Museum and read these, I found also an interview with the painter that had been published in the photo journal *Today*, published in 1950. I began to put together the events leading up to Sochachewsky's visit to the village.

Maurice Sochachewsky was born in 1918 in Hackney. His father, Ben A. Sochachewsky, had arrived in London before the war, from Poland. He was Yiddish-speaking, a writer and a poet. He set out to earn a living as a journalist. He married a Russian actress who had toured all over eastern Europe. Maurice was their second child. He showed talent in drawing and at the age of 14 he entered St Martin's School of Art on a scholarship.[159] It was shortly after leaving the art school that he decided to travel to Wales to paint. According to *Today*, 'His imagination and pity were inflamed by newspaper accounts of the nightmarish distress then grieving the mining areas of Wales, and he was determined to go down there and portray what he saw on the spot.'[160] Why he had chosen Talywain remained unclear to me, but he had certainly established contacts early on with influential people in the area, in particular Arthur Jenkins, the MP for Pontypool. Jenkins was an intellectual who had studied at the Sorbonne and at Oxford, before becoming Vice-President of the South Wales Miners' Federation. His son, who must have been about seventeen at the time of Sochachewsky's visit, was Roy Jenkins, who would become deputy leader of the Labour Party, Chancellor of the Exchequer and Home Secretary. Two other Labour politicians, Rhys Davies, MP for Westhoughton, who had worked as a collier in the Rhondda for ten years, and J.H. Hall, member for the Whitechapel district of Stepney, also appeared to have been involved with Sochachewsky's work, since they would open the Bloomsbury Gallery exhibition in 1938.

The Bloomsbury Gallery was noted for giving opportunities to young painters, several of whom subsequently became well-known – Edward Ardizzone and Roger Hilton among them. The prominence of the venue resulted in a high press profile and the exhibition was reviewed thoroughly. Indeed, it appeared that the left-wing *Daily Herald* had been forewarned, since it carried a photo feature of the work and an interview with the painter conducted before he left Talywain, in December 1937:

How true it is that half the world does not know how the other half lives. It is equally true that half the world cares little how the other half lives so long as its own bread is buttered. Not long

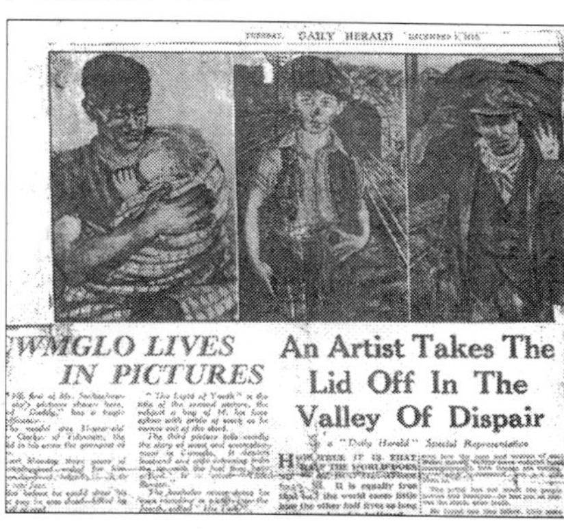

ago a young London Jew was reading about distressed areas, or half-starved people in a civilised country, of people living in houses which were gradually crumbling, of the flower of young manhood bordering on despair in an atmosphere of hopelessness. He found it hard to believe. Who could blame him? – he was living in the midst of plenty. But he wanted to know how his fellow men lived, he wanted the truth about these 'distressed' areas. Today he knows – and the knowledge has inspired him to paint a series of pictures which may shortly open the eyes of London's complacent, often unbelieving people …

I found this young man in a dimly lit room in Talywain, a little mining township set high up on the mountainside in the Eastern Valley of Monmouthshire. Four months ago he left London in search of a great truth. He went among humble folk, into a widow's home, where much of the tragedy of the mine and the problem of unemployment has already been experienced. He took me to his little bedroom,

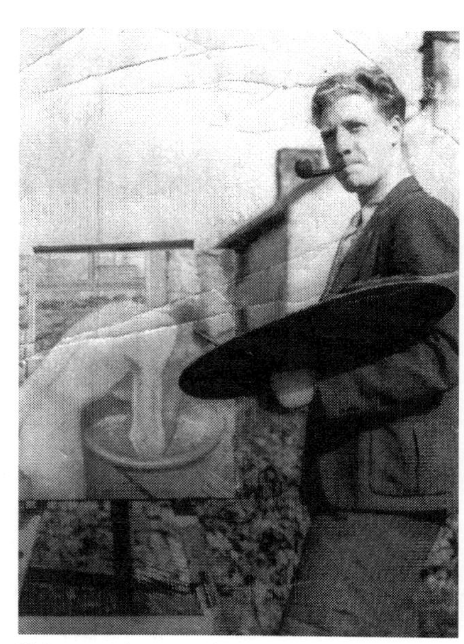

Unknown photographer,
Maurice Sochachewsky
at Talywain, 1937
Private collection

leading the way up darkened stairs, carrying an oil lamp in his hand. And, one after the other, from a corner of his bedroom-cum-studio, he showed me canvasses which live.

Among them was the picture that nobody noticed, seventy-four years later, on the floor of the sale-room in Colwyn Bay. It was one of the paintings photographed for inclusion with the article:

> The third picture tells vividly the story of want and
> unemployment in Cwmglo. It depicts husband and wife
> returning from the tip with the fuel they have picked.
> It is called 'Their Burden'.[161]

From the moment I saw *Their Burden* I had felt that the picture had the quality to become an icon of its period, though the facility with which that term sprang to my mind worried me. The business of scavenging for waste coal on the tips was a humiliating and disgraceful necessity of life for unemployed colliers and their families in the 1930s. Though suggesting also humanity and love in the sharing of their burden, the painter had presented the scene in all its ugliness and degradation. The picture was surely a condemnation of the practice and of the failure of capitalism that it represented, yet, carelessly, I had begun the process of transforming it into currency by thinking about it in iconic terms, and buying it in that frame of mind. I paid little enough for it, but it was more money than the man and woman who are its subject could have expected ever to see. Nevertheless, of all the images of industrial Wales, collecting waste coal is the one that consistently attracted the attention of painters and photographers from the middle of the nineteenth century, and if one is to think and write about the picture at all, it seems important to note the fact as a part of the process of understanding what Sochachewsky's picture was saying in 1937. For at least the previous sixty years, the image had expressed variously the voyeurism, humane sympathy, social conscience or political indignation of those who witnessed such scenes, whether they were outsiders or, occasionally, artists whose roots grew within the community they depicted. To those in the past who witnessed it as a present reality – as life before art – that image of degradation had proved compelling.

Working for the London illustrated magazine, *The Graphic*, in 1875 Herbert Johnson produced what were, at the time, revelatory drawings of the hardship endured by colliers and their families. The intensity of some of his drawings might easily be interpreted as suggesting that he was born into a community such as that he depicted.[162] T.H. Thomas, who also worked for *The Graphic*, certainly was born into such a community, though only in a geographical sense since he belonged to the middle-class. He grew up in Pontypool, where Sochachewsky would arrive to begin work nearly a century later. As Johnson had done in several drawings, in his picture *Sackcloth and Ashes* Thomas concentrated on the situation of women, presenting what seemed to contemporary liberal conscience to be the afront to femininity represented by their hard and dirty manual labour. In the 1920s, Archie Griffiths's picture, *On the Coal Tips,* also presented women as the main subject, but did so in a more complex and allusive way. As an insider in the fullest sense, perhaps it is significant that he, of all these image makers, did not take a documentary approach in his most considered work, which is simultaneously both deeply engaged and detached. Griffiths did not have to choose to live with colliers, because he was born among them. In fact, his choice was to leave.

Cedric Morris was an insider of a different kind. Briefly, during 1935, he returned from his artist's life in Paris and London to live with collier families, just as Sochachewsky would do, soon afterwards. His letters reveal an ambiguity of feeling of which he was himself deeply conscious:

> Am staying here in an out of work miner's cottage – all extremely uncomfortable and filthy food, but nice people and clean and it is the landscape I want – 30/- per week – I shall stay a week or so – have finished one picture and there are 3 or 4 more – I am getting on to something. I am edging towards Swansea and getting used to living with these people. It is really heartbreaking the way they have to live – I am not enjoying it ...[163]

Morris was as conflicted in his attitudes to proletarian Wales as was Rhys Davies, and for two of the same reasons – sexuality and class. As a homosexual, like Davies, and as upper class, he was an insider who felt himself on the outside. The money that paid for young Cedric – later Sir Cedric – to undertake his art training in Paris was the inheritance of the eighteenth-century entrepreneurship of his ancestor, John Morris, founder of Morriston. No picture of the unemployed was forthcoming from Cedric, for all the offence (if it was not guilt) that he felt at the sight of the trials of the common people. The darkened industrial landscape that was the background to their lives was as near as he would approach.[164]

Morris's return to Wales reflected as much a wider awakening of interest among left-wing visual artists in the condition of working-class people as it did the personal circumstances that drew him to the Swansea Valley in particular. Photographers, including Bill Brandt and Edith Tudor Hart, had already visited and produced powerful documentary work. As a Communist, Edith Tudor Hart embraced the image of the people 'not for posterity but for the day'.[165] She was clear that her art served her political agenda. It was an attitude shared by visiting film makers. Alberto Cavalcanti had shot part of *Coalface* in Wales in 1935. W.H. Auden, Benjamin Britten and Humphrey Jennings were also involved with the film. Two years later Jennings would help to found Mass Observation, a project that, in the long term, contributed in great measure to the refocusing of history on the experience and perception of the common people. For the moment, mining communities, and in particular the mining communities of south Wales, provided the most intense experience which the left could deploy in its attempts to change public perceptions and the political order. A year after *Coalface*, Ralph Bond filmed the dark industrial sections of *Today We Live* in the Rhondda. He incorporated footage shot earlier by Douglas Alexander – a sequence of men scrambling for waste coal on the precipitous side of a tip, enveloped by gusting swirls of choking dust, which is perhaps the most shocking of all the renditions of that persistent image. Bond observed that 'The only contacts miners have with coal are the slag-heaps where sometimes they are permitted at ever present risk to life and limb to scramble for enough to keep the fires burning in their own homes.'[166] *We Live* and Douglas Alexander's own film, *Eastern Valley*, were both released in 1937, the year that Maurice Sochachewsky also decided to confront the issues they raised. His pictures, too, were made for the present. Surely he must have seen those films? *Eastern Valley* was shot at Cwmavon, just a couple of miles north of Talywain.

Given the wider background and what little I knew of Maurice's own circumstances, the empathy he felt for those people he came to know in Wales seemed unsurprising, though the observation made in the *Daily Herald* interview of 1937, that he had been living 'in the midst of plenty' struck me as somewhat misleading. Certainly, it appeared that Maurice's father had succeeded in providing well enough for the family, but in a wider context the painter's personality and convictions must surely have been formed by his proximity to one of the most deprived areas of urban England. He was part of a huge Jewish community, many members of which were, like his own parents, first or second generation immigrants. They became intensely politicised as he grew up. Many supported the Communist Party. A year before Maurice left for Wales, in October 1936, they had expressed themselves in the most explicit manner, at the Battle of Cable Street. Despite police protection, Oswald Mosley's Black Shirts were driven out of the East End by the direct action of hundreds of thousands of protesters, led on the day by the Communist Phil Piratin. Certainly, Maurice Sochachewsky's association the following year with Labour Members of Parliament suggested that he was not a member of the Communist Party.[167] Indeed, in Poland his father had been active in the Jewish Labour Bund, a Socialist movement that would be suppressed after the Communist revolution. But the Cable Street protesters were a broad coalition of anti-Fascists. Perhaps Maurice was among them? After all, as Graham Greene observed, 'It was impossible in those days not to be committed ...'[168]

Maurice Sochachewsky died in 1969, and it was clear from the material I had that his career as a painter after the war had not been successful. There was little written information and his only work in a public collection, apart from the National Museum, appeared to be a single painting in the Jewish Museum in London. There was no trace of the Welsh paintings, apart from those in the possession of the collector who had initially contacted me, many years earlier. Now she refused me access to them. However, the National Museum was able to put me in touch with Maurice Sochachewsky's son, David,

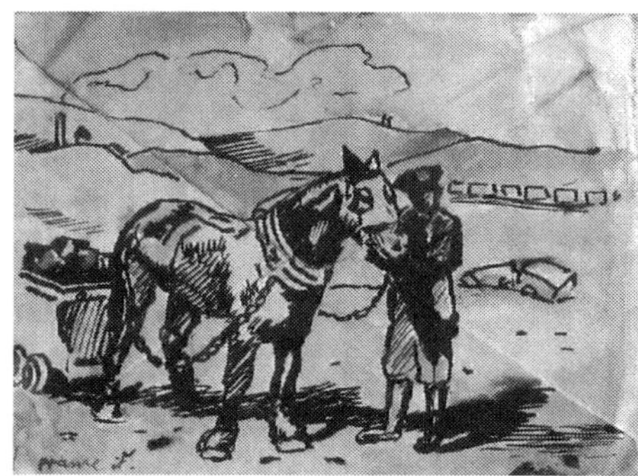

Back of an envelope
enclosing a letter from
Maurice Sochachewsky
to his parents, 1937
Private collection

who told me that the painter's younger brother, Ephraim, was alive, well and always keen to talk. Maurice, big brother, had been his hero. With David, I met Ephraim at his home in London – a flat in the Jewish community building at North Chingford. Generations of extended family bustled about, everyone chipping in to the conversation, East End accents, warm and welcoming. I recorded Ephraim's memories, and in the course of the conversation it emerged that although the family had no knowledge of the whereabouts of the pictures from the 1938 exhibition, David had some letters written by his father from Talywain.

Another six months have passed, and now I am able to read the letters. They are remarkable:

Thursday 12 August 1937.
Dear Pap, Mum and Eph,

Today at 2 o'clock I went with Arthur, the son of the landlady – description of him: a giant of a fellow, 6' 4", a real he-man – down to the colliery …

We started down the slope at 2.30. I was clean except for my helmet, just a minor detail, but without wearing it my head would have been a mask of muck. The walk down the slope was a stretch of over two miles. It meant walking in mud, water and filth at a height of about two feet in places. The fumes and gases were simply reeking. All around is pitch black except the weak flicker of our lamps.

Throughout the journey I had to walk doubled up. After a time my stomach and back became a refuge for pain. The road, if one may call it so, is up and down all the time, one minute I am walking slightly bent in another my head is on the same level as my knees. By walking in this way for over an hour you are inclined to feel a strain on your neck … There are falls in the ground with quite a depth of the most hellish slimes you could come across in the worst African swamp. If you are unaware of this you find yourself sprawling in this evil smelling slimy inferno.

We walked in this horrible manner for the whole two miles – the time it took exceeded one hour. After exploring about and around and being shown different surroundings and implements we got to the face, that is, where they get the coal. I thought we passed through the worst part of it but no, there was yet worse to come. We got to [the] face just when they were blowing it by means of inserting sticks of dynamite into the holes drilled in [the] wall (you will understand this better when you see the painting).

I was crouched down there and every few minutes the damp dripping walls, in fact the whole damned place, shook as if it was struck by the Almighty's wrath. The men, black as soot, were sweating beads of what looked like black worm[s that] slowly trickled from their foreheads. The after-effects of these explosives were terrible. You could not see at all with the lamp as the pit was so thick with hot choking smoke …

We walked thus until we came to the garrows. This is the worst part in the world … The garrows is actually a trench 21 inches high, 7 inches of which is this horrible muck. This travels for a stretch of 150 yards. The men work in this dirt by lying on their sides and picking at the face of the coal. Even in this fashion they have no space with which to breathe in. When they have to move on further they crawl flat on their stomachs …

What I have written is nothing compared to what it really is. Hell I think must be a more heavenly place than this. And so these miners live their life, hour after hour, day after day, year after year …

Maurice writes to his parents every few days for four months, and returns to Wales to work again in 1938. There are sixty letters in all. He knows a Jewish family in the area, the Robinsons, whose portraits he paints. Mr Robinson comes to visit, and 'another chap came with him. His name is Forester. He saw the work and criticized. I had arguments with him, and sometimes told him he was speaking from an ignorant point of view …' But this must be Lord Forester, who part-funded *Eastern Valley*, and who was deeply involved with the settlement at Cwmavon, which was its subject. Clearly, Maurice is unaware of the film and of the settlement. The letters are idealistic and naïve. They remind me that he is very young – still only nineteen – and that the tidy links that history constructs between things in retrospect are so often hidden in the uncertainty of the present. Maurice visits the settlement, in the company of a German artist – 'Futurist and Surrealist' – who he finds is teaching there. 'He has his own car and [from] what I could make of it a regular income. He is about as old as you are, Pap, and his family is in Deutschland'.

Last night I went to the settlement with the German, and [we] took with us a couple of paintings. It is a wonderful place, and I think I am getting somewhere … The pupils are grown up, and many faces I knew. For instance, one chap (a very nice fellow) is a bus conductor and [many] a time he has taken my money as fare, yet we never exchanged a word of greeting. Well last night I was surprised to see that he is interested in the fine art, such as painting. The German, Mr Mach, teaches a class of 5 students including the bus conductor – three girls and two chaps.

They were very interested in the work, and we spoke the whole evening on the miners paintings. Then Mr Mach introduced me to the staff who reside in this building – ultra modern! The chief head of the settlement lives there with his wife – a very young couple, communists. And they all went mad over the work, and they want to arrange an exhibition there for me …

These people are cultured in every way and haven't just the skeleton idea of painting, like Robinson or even Jenkins, but know the root of it, from the inspiration to the completed canvas. They are all a fine crowd and will do any thing for me I think. I shall be going there more often. Mr Mach is arranging to bring the five students and maybe all of them round to my digs to see the work. I think this is where I have struck lucky in finding people that don't look upon artists as a bankroll. Things might happen now …

In my painting I am doing what no other artist has done before, and the canvases are bound to vibrate with life because I paint straight from the subject whenever I can, not by a preliminary sketch. Right now (this morning) I am going to take my easel, large canvas and paint etc. round the corner and paint the old dissipated houses in the row and a couple of out of work colliers pushing their coal trolley up the row [with] coal they have acquired from the tips. I think this will be extraordinary …

The letters are revealing in detail the progress of Maurice's work at Talywain – the frustrations of his relationship with potential patrons, his lack of money to buy materials, as well as his moments of exhilaration and success, and then this:

I would like to get a reporter down with his camera as I am painting a sensational picture which I will complete today. It is of an out of work miner and his wife trudging with a sack of coal upon their weary backs. The scene is at the coal tips whence they [go] to collect fuel for their wintry ice cold evenings. The canvas is 5ft. x 3ft. and when I finish it I think I will have something …

It is *Their Burden*. As I write, the picture hangs on the wall beside me and Maurice's letter, dated 28 September 1937, lies on the table in front of me. They were last together seventy-five years ago, when Maurice wrote to his parents from his sparse bedroom in Mrs James's terraced house at Talywain, the paint still wet on the canvas.[169]

I wonder how my cousin Gertrude would have interpreted the picture, the social trauma that lay behind it, and the politics that emerged from it in the 1930s? She would have had plenty to tell me, because Gertrude was a Communist Party activist in east London at the time. She had trained as a pianist at the London College of Music. Later, she formed a piano quartet to give concerts in aid of party funds. She sold the *Daily Worker* on the street. Was she there on that day in 1936 when, led by Phil Piratin, they drove Mosley and his followers out of Jewish east London? After the war, Piratin took the Mile End parliamentary seat for the Communist Party. Received family wisdom has it that Gertrude became party secretary in the Stepney constituency that replaced it in 1950. I have not checked the facts and she is no longer here to ask. Perhaps it doesn't matter. Only belief is real, in the end. In the 1950s and 60s, when occasionally I met her, she would return from trips to Moscow with gifts stamped 'CCCP' for her uncle, my grandfather – a bulky black and cream plastic wireless, I remember in particular. My last memory of her is on a visit to the yellow and red brick semi of my repressed adolescence, my *Daily Express*-reading father restraining himself, scrupulously avoiding politics. He swopped war experiences with John Jones, Gertrude's husband – they could talk safely about that. She talked music to me. 'So Shostakovich does it for you?', she asked. He certainly did, though at the time I didn't know why, and it hadn't occurred to me to ponder the matter.[170] Wisely, Gertrude didn't suggest either the question or the answer – she just looked at me, very straight and into my eyes. I thought she was beautiful. I remember the look and now I know a few fragments of what lay behind it – of her life's experience and, flowing from it, perhaps, a sense of the hopelessness of communication across the gulf that divided her pre-war world of purpose and my post-war world of complacency. In best 1930s radical fashion, Gertrude continued to wear her hair bobbed.

Cousin Gertrude, Sochachewsky, Shostakovich, Rhys Davies, Archie Griffiths, through the picture all their burdens – communists, musicians, writers, painters, my life, their lives – swirl around, sometimes excitingly touch, more often frustratingly elide. In pictures, the past lives.

The Canopy of Honour

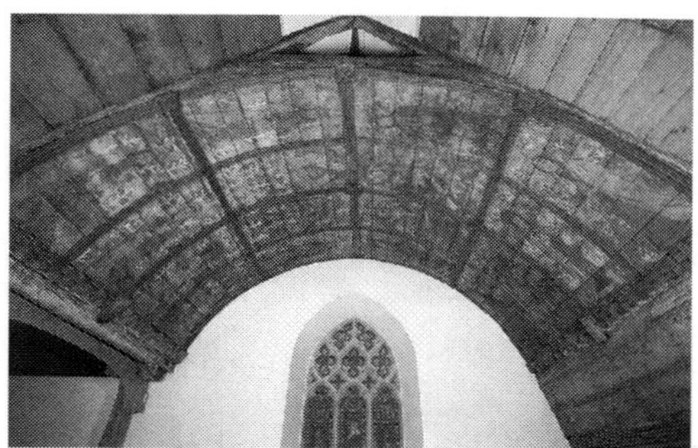

i.

In his letter to the Hebrew Christians, St Paul described the relationship between the future and the past in terms of life lived in the presence of 'a cloud of witnesses'.[171] Paul created this image in the course of an exposition of the nature of Christian faith. For him, faith was 'the substance of things hoped for, the evidence of things not seen.' It seems that he perceived the existence of faith in a person almost as a material phenomenon – as substantial evidence, like a fingerprint on a glass or a footprint on a flower bed in a detective story. Faith is tangible evidence of the authenticity of belief – and, without it, 'it is impossible to please him: for he that cometh to God must believe that he is, and that he is a rewarder of them that diligently seek him.'

From a barrel vault above the altar in the Church of St Benedict at Gyffin, near Conwy, sixteen saints look down. Each is identified by his or her conventional token or symbol. The arrangement is known to church historians as a 'canopy of honour'. It is difficult to gauge to what extent, through story-telling, the narratives of these saints would have been familiar to the largely illiterate common people of the 15th century, and how their privileged location as prime witnesses to the sacraments was understood.[172] They were exemplars of faith, perhaps – benign fellow communicants who existed in a duality of time that seems not to have been problematic to the congregations of the middle ages – figures from a thousand years past who were yet somehow present.

Only through this visualisation of the saints and martyrs painted on the ceiling of their church, and through the interpretation of priests, can the common people of late medieval Gyffin have understood the words of St Paul on the subject of faith. Four hundred years later, at the beginning of the nineteenth century, the words of St Paul, as well as the pictures, had become accessible directly to the people. It was the achievement of Welsh Protestantism and the subsequent drive to literacy, led by Nonconformists. Among those common people who might well have both seen and heard was a child of the parish of Gyffin called John Gibson. He would grow up to become the greatest sculptor in the world, in the estimation of many patriotic Victorians. In Rome, looking back from those heights, Gibson himself would recall the early influence upon him of simple artisan paintings – those in the church, perhaps, and certainly the signs above the taverns in the streets of Conwy at which he 'gazed in admiration'.[173] As an adolescent he attended the Sunday School of the Calvinistic Methodist chapel at Pall Mall in Liverpool, where the word was dominant. There, surely, he would have been made familiar with the teaching of St Paul. It certainly exercised the mind of his contemporary pupil at Pall Mall, the painter Hugh Hughes. Like Gibson, he had been born in 1790, but just the other side of the River Conwy, in a farmhouse on the sea shore of what would become the resort of Llandudno. From the poverty-stricken circumstances of their homes, both families joined the flood of Welsh people emigrating to Liverpool at the turn of the century. By that time – indeed, according to his own testimony, since the age of eight or nine – Hughes had 'known, believed and loved the gospel'.[174] He kept faith in that belief, alongside the woman he married, though both would be tried by theological disputes and by personal tragedy. All three of their children would pre-decease them. After the death of their first-born at the age of 13, Sarah Hughes would write an angst-ridden memoir of the child, a daughter, in which evidences of her faith were retrospectively sought. 'The question as to whether my children should become heirs of God and of heaven, or whether they should be found in the day of judgement of the unredeemed multitude, lay, with a weight inadequate only to its awful importance, always rested upon my heart …' Only faith would be rewarded with resurrection and eternal life, but to the Calvinist, faith was the gift of God, either present in the individual or not, according to his whim, like a pre-installed computer programme that might only be revealed by its sudden and unpredicted functioning. If it had not been installed – if the individual was not among God's elect – then damnation awaited. As Calvin himself acknowledged, it was an inexplicable and therefore a terrifying notion.[175]

In the 1980s, when I was writing a biography of Hugh Hughes, this concept of faith as material evidence of a reality of eternal consequence caused me great difficulty. It was (and remains) a concept that I cannot grasp. To my way of thinking, salvation (like damnation) beyond the grave is among those 'things that don't make any sense', to which Ken Ames referred when we spoke about folk art religionists a few years ago.[176] Nevertheless, it must be acknowledged that an explanation is required for a concept whose influence over the minds of generations of thoughtful and perceptive human beings has been so profound. I sense that it may be approached through consideration of Paul's concept of the cloud of witnesses. The idea that the past surrounds us, embodied in the witness of the saved, expresses a need for individual location that is, I suspect, universally felt – a need for location within a community, among a people. 'They seek a country', as Paul himself put it.[177] I cannot understand the witnesses as a quasi-material reality of living souls as, apparently, the Christian is required to do. Nevertheless, Paul's image represents a powerful psychological reality.

ii.

The paintings on the canopy of honour and, perhaps, a few other such pictures in church, were probably the only visual images of fellow human beings available to the common people of Gyffin, like others of their condition throughout Europe. The modern European sees more pictures in a morning than the medieval European saw in a lifetime. In this house alone, there are over a hundred paintings on the walls, the majority of them portraits of individuals who, like the saints and martyrs of a canopy of honour, each have their own narrative. As a cloud of witnesses, I imagine their meaning is, in a broad sense, the same for me as was the canopy of honour for the people of medieval Gyffin – though unlike the saints, these are pictures that I have chosen for myself. The distinction is important. At one level, the pictures simply witness the history of a particular place, as in a museum. But for myself, underpinning the particular instance, the pictures witness also a framework of principle about the very idea of place – the idea that living within an identifying matrix of history, topography and language is of fundamental importance to the human psyche. The principle which flows from the idea is that, recognising its fundamental importance, doing what one can to maintain the coherence of the matrix is a responsibility for us all. However, between the general principle and the particular expression of it – manifested in the pictures by which I am surrounded – are located a number of difficulties.

In my case, the application of the principle involved a transfer of allegiance. All but a few of the pictures in this house were made by or for Welsh people, or about Welsh people, places and issues. It is perhaps inevitable that such a transfer leaves a residue of unease and of doubt. Notwithstanding the commitment I made in the 1970s, there have been times when I would like to have pointed out that I was not simply a cause of disintegration in the matrix of identity in this place, but a displaced consequence of it in another. In the 1960s I observed the destruction of the architectural and linguistic particularity of the place of my birth and, through that, experienced the disruption of my sense of its historical continuity. When I came to live in Wales in 1974, I found myself among people who, unlike the people of my birth place, seemed to understand what was happening to them and to possess the will to contest it. It was exciting. The issues were clarified by the existence of a language which, I discovered, was not simply a marker of mild cultural eccentricity within the

British political frame, but a medium of thought through which the world was perceived in a different way, whether considering the past or the future. To a previously monolingual person, this discovery was both difficult and liberating. It was difficult because it undermined my assumptions about the relationship between language and thought, and opened a fracture of incomprehension between me and the incomer community around me.[178] On the other hand, it was liberating because it cleared a pathway towards a relocation of ideas that had not sat well within the cultural framework in which I had previously operated. The people I met were creating a body of thought around issues that were important to me also, and in particular a political philosophy that had the potential to change a power structure which seemed to have been as damaging to my own sense of place as it had to theirs. The situation was clear. As my colleague Clifford McLucas memorably conceived it, as an incomer, one could choose either to be a part of the problem or to offer one's services as a part of the solution.[179]

St Paul's image of the cloud of witnesses was designed to comfort the oppressed and to strengthen the powerless. He identified many of his witnesses in terms of their suffering. Indeed, he set about creating a fellowship of suffering, to be endured in the certainty of ultimate salvation. But obligation as well as comfort was implied in his exhortation to faith. Knowledge of the suffering of the ancestors is compelling to their descendents, because it creates within them the sense of moral obligation. In practice, I suspect that, at Gyffin, the understanding of the saints and martyrs of the canopy of honour as fellow communicants or as benign exemplars came hand in hand with a sense of them as figures of authority, their judgements expressed in the here and now through the priest below them. To conceive of the cloud of witnesses as a living jury, keeping account of daily actions in the knowledge that, in another world, condemnation and punishment must follow failure to live up to their example, would be to go beyond the biblical text. Paul himself cannot have understood the witnesses also as judges, since only his god could judge. Nevertheless, I think that it is implicit in his idea that the witnesses require the individual at least to judge him or her self. The cloud of witnesses is a manifestation of conscience. I return to the image of Dai Tŷ'n Ddraenen, standing above me on top of the bank at the edge of his field, his back bent over his work, mending the fence between us in the soaking drizzle of October 1974.[180] At that moment I was deeply disturbed by a sense of trespass and intrusion that has never left me. Perhaps it acted so powerfully upon me because of an underlying sense of personal guilt that I felt, which was the bequest of my childhood. But certainly, the collection of pictures in this house – this personal cloud of witnesses – manifests a response to the dictates of conscience.

On the whole, the portraits in this house do not represent individuals suffering in a cause, in the manner of the saints and martyrs of a canopy of honour. Dic Aberdaron, painted by William Roos at Caernarfon in 1838, was troubled by mental disorder that led to poverty and homelessness, and Maurice Sochachewsky's young collier and his wife suffered the degradation and demoralisation of unemployment during the Depression, but most of the sitters probably were content enough. Indeed, many of the portraits of the middle-class patrons of artisan painters – the likes of the Pwllheli surgeon apothecary – and the few gentry sitters represented here, are expressions of self-satisfaction. The tensions of cultural displacement are more immediately evident in the lives of the painters. Issues of nationality and language, as well as transcendental matters, certainly troubled Hugh Hughes. Fifty years after his death, for the artists of the national revival – T.H. Thomas, Kelt Edwards, Goscombe John – cultural identity and its political expression were both personal issues and issues that formed an important part of a Europe-wide intellectual context which affected their ideas. The drawings in front of me, made by Christopher Williams in 1911 for his painting *Wales Awakening*, stand at the centre of the artistic response to the expression of Welsh identities in this crucial period. Tensions arising in the changed intellectual context after the Great War strongly marked the work of the subsequent generation – Archie Griffiths and Evan Walters, in particular. Nevertheless, it is collectively, rather than

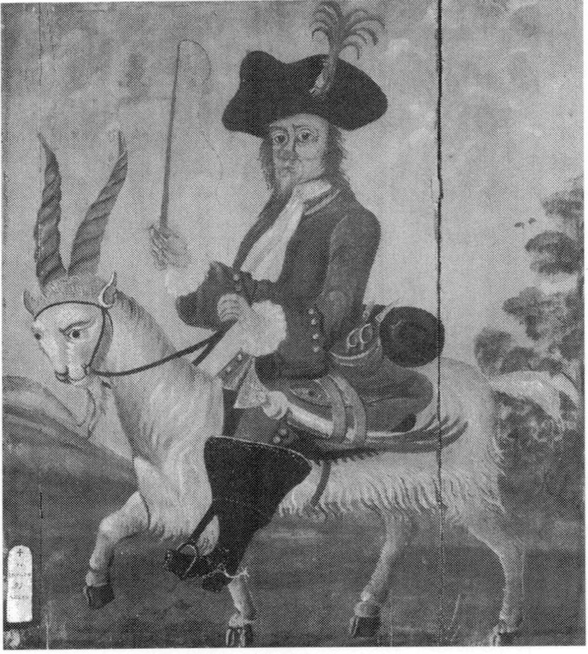

Unknown painter, *Poor Taf*, c.1790–1820

individually, that these works stand as representatives of a cultural crisis – as an image of a threatened framework of identity, a nation exploited and despised, but confused and conflicted in its response. It found visual expression as early as the mid-eighteenth century in the figure of Poor Taf, who rides to London to seek his fortune on the back of a goat, a leek in his hat – the threadbare Welsh gentleman of absurd pretentions, whose image, drawn first as satire in the London popular prints, appears to have become grotesquely adopted as a token of self-identification.

iii.

In about 1975 I borrowed a recording of a meditation on a passage from the Book of Job, given by the philosopher J.R. Jones. The recording had been made not long before his death, five years earlier. The intensity of its feeling made a great impact upon me, and led me to study his work.[181] In his essay 'Y Syniad o Genedl' (The Idea of Nation), Jones reflected on St Paul's image of the cloud of witnesses, though he took as his point of reference not the biblical source but the celebrated couplets from Waldo's poem 'Pa beth yw dyn?' (What is man?):

> Beth yw bod yn genedl? Dawn
> Yn nwfn y galon.
> Beth yw gwladgarwch?
> Cadw tŷ mewn cwmwl tystion.'[182]

> What is being a nation? A gift
> In the depth of the heart.
> What is love of country? Keeping house
> Within a cloud of witnesses.

Jones described two ways in which identity – the sense of psycho-logical location – is formed. He called them explicit and implicit (or sometimes direct and mediated), and associated them with different kinds of people. He proposed that the identity of the intelligentsia was informed in an explicit way. They had direct knowledge through their 'literary, religious, antiquarian or purely historical' interests. On the other hand, the 'mass of the ordinary people' acquired their identity unconsciously, mediated through 'national symbols, and especially institutions that are politically and culturally symbolic' and that form 'a consistent background to life'.[183] Jones's polemical polarisation of the two mechanisms was made in order to explain what he regarded as the conflicted nature of the national identity of the Welsh people. It was an identity mediated through institutional symbolism which, at that time, almost unrelievedly reflected the English construction of Britishness. For him, it was a conflict that could be resolved only by political change.

Clearly, in my own case and, I imagine, in that of most incomers who choose, as adults, to identify with a new place, a sense of relocation is primarily an explicit acquisition – a learned identification that gradually becomes deeply felt as a consequence of its resonance with a reservoir of experience which is the legacy of another place. Undergoing that process in Wales in the 1970s, and especially having come from England, my awareness of the weakness of the mechanisms that facilitated the other means of identification – implicit identification – was particularly acute. That is why the Art Department of the National Museum and the Arts Council became foci for my own polemical activities. But, in practice, Jones's two mechanisms are more a matter of varying proportion within the individual than of one or the other, since we are all affected by both ways of absorbing identities. Similarly, the pictures in this house collectively operate as identifiers both implicitly and explicitly. Notwithstanding the establishment of the National Assembly and the consequent changes in self-presentation made by many institutions since Jones's death in 1970, the overwhelming dominance of the London broadcast and print media continues to require that individuals self-consciously construct the cultural ambience that facilitates here what in other places is the natural absorption of a coherent sense of place. The pictures are an evolving framework within which I have chosen to function – a 'consistent background to life' which implicitly reinforces that choice.

There was much in J.R. Jones's writing with which I identified closely. In particular, he understood the 'golden image' of material prosperity as a false promise cynically made by governments to detach peoples from their past, and thereby, in the Welsh instance, absorb them in the British state – what he starkly described as 'genocide by assimilation'.[184] In response, like St Paul, he deployed the emotionally compelling idea of suffering – though in the twentieth-century context, specifically economic deprivation, projecting it into a Welsh future almost as if it would be the means for a ritual purification of the nation: 'That is, if the only way out of Egypt – as in the ancient history of Israel – is through the desert, then it will be necessary to face the desert'.[185] J.R. Jones was a political puritan, and in this sense he was heir to many of the protestant and nonconformist thinkers who had been identified as the founders of national tradition in a hundred and fifty years of Welsh historiography. Emotionally, he stood in the mainstream, though intellectually – in terms of dogma – he rejected some of the orthodoxies of his Christian tradition. He followed Simone Weil in taking a mystical view of a god totally absent in this world – indeed, of a god whose absence, paradoxically, provided the clearest evidence of its reality. Coincidentally, perhaps, Jones's puritanism would resonate with that of the back to the land movement of the decade following his death. It would be manifested in the attraction to Plaid Cymru of radical incomers, such as myself, that resulted in the election of a nationalist member of parliament for the Ceredigion constituency in 1992. Yet although J.R. Jones was an intellectual stimulus and an emotional inspiration when I read him in the 1970s, I could not follow him in the connection he made between a political philosophy and his answer to the fundamental question of the crisis of meaning – the issue that directed all his thought – in the person of Jesus. Jones prefaced his collected essays with a psychiatrist's observation on the emergence of an 'existential vacuum' – of 'a sense of total meaninglessness', that lay at the root of the increasing manifestation of mental illness in western society. He came to link that existential crisis with the crisis of his contemporary Wales – as if the problem of cultural continuity was a metaphor for the problem of individual human continuity at the most funda-mental level, simply at the level of being. He was right to do so, but mistaken, I feel, in fusing Welsh nationalism and Christian belief in his attempt to formulate an answer. It was a problematic position even in his own time, if nationalist politics was ever to be influential and persuasive. It resonated with the depressing dogmatism of Lewis Valentine, whose rejection of a free but 'pagan' Wales left too many people excluded.

The decline of Christian influence and the subsequent evolution of nationalist thought, especially in terms of the notion of civic identity, has largely removed this difficulty from the agenda, but a second aspect of Jones's polemics has emerged to prove equally troublesome. Having built a new road around one obstacle, the traffic has coagulated further down, in a place that previously seemed trouble free. The conundrum of meaning has moved from god to history. Though rooted in a different place, like J.R. Jones I inherited, largely unquestioned, the concept of historical projection – the idea that the past defines and justifies a direction of political travel. Embedded in the concept is an implication that somewhere, leading through the morass of past events and ideas, lies a path which (when expressed in messianic terms) reveals a destiny – a class destiny perhaps, a religious destiny, or a national destiny. The role of history is to disclose the path – the true path, deriving from the true past – and that of politics is to direct the traveller onto it.

This assumption about history was incorrect and, therefore, my inferences about the politics that flowed from it were false. I continue to visualise cultural evolution as a two-directional process, divided at the moment of the present. Looking back is still called history and looking forward is still called politics, but it is clear to me now that history is determined by politics, and not politics by history. But if history is a political tool, does this not imply that all histories are potentially valid – that, perhaps, there are no wrong histories? This suspicion would appear to undermine the notion that a matrix of identity of which history is one component (along with language and topography) can provide a secure psychological framework within which meaningful actions can be performed in life. However, even if there may be no wrong histories, in an absolute sense, there are certainly *immoral* histories, and since they are the expression of immoral politics, the importance of history as a foundation of identity is not necessarily diminished by acknowledging its mutability. Its authority becomes moral, rather than quasi-legalistic.[186]

iv.

In the explicit sense, as defined by J.R. Jones, the pictures in this house are an exposition of a construct of art historical tradition that was at odds with the received wisdom both about art and about the social and political forces that sustained that wisdom into the late twentieth century. As a collection, made by someone who perceived himself to be part of a disintegrating force, personally the pictures are a justification to conscience. More widely, they are the development in material form of the arguments that I made in the 1980s, which were directed towards reinforcing the matrix of identity in this place. As a tangible manifestation of an idea of history, I hope that they make a contribution towards restoration. Mending things has been an instinct with me since the 1960s – the reconstruction of the past into something more than a chaotic wasteland of discarded material and intellectual fragments, dysfunctional, concluded and, as a consequence, potentially lost. Making and ordering a collection contributes to the evolution of the matrix of identity – to finding St Paul's country, in the form of a collective particularity, of a sense of distinctness that invests with meaning the actions of the everyday life of individuals. In this, the materiality of the past is crucial. Certainly, the pictures in this house are a symbolic guide to what I hope is a morally coherent construct of history – but in a much simpler and tangible way they witness the ability of human beings to find meaning through making. Often, it is the humanity of the artefact that fascinates or moves us most – simply the realisation that it *was* made, and outlives its maker. From his or her hands it comes for a time to our hands, and we experience its feel, its smell, its sound, as well as the sight of it. Perhaps alone, perhaps in company, we experience it in every dimension and aspect, not imagined or reproduced in a book, or conjured in the virtual spaces that presently threaten our understanding of the fundamentals of our own materiality and that of the world that sustains us. History is the after-image of that materiality. In an artefact, the after-image of a vanishing moment of human existence is captured – the lost maker and the maker's lost world seem within reach. It is as close as we can get.

For me, it has become necessary to abandon the notion of the construction of history as a contest between belief and reality, uncertainty and truth, and to recognise that, in the end, the only meaningful reality is, indeed, belief. This is difficult enough, but the next step is even more so. It is to find within myself the faith that, two thousand years ago, St Paul perceived to be psychologically crucial, but to do so now, in a time in which beliefs can be sustained by nothing more concrete, absolute or certain than honest endeavour of mind, guided by a moral sensibility grounded in Humanism. The beliefs are difficult enough – intellectual honesty and a coherent morality are terribly vulnerable to self-deceit – but faith is even more difficult, and loss of faith is frightening to contemplate.

The folklorist (and Communist) Bert Lloyd invested a lifetime's creativity in his pursuit, especially through music, of the roots of English and Australian identities. On his deathbed he experienced only frustration that his contribution to the process of cultural evolution could not continue: 'It's a bugger, isn't it', he said to a friend. 'There's so much to do.' With faith, apparently, it can be as simple as that.

Endnotes

1 Collection of Cyfarthfa Castle, Merthyr Tydfil.

2 G. Blacker Morgan, *Historical and Genealogical Memoirs of the Morgan Family as represented in the Peerage of England by the Right Hon. The Baron Tredegar* (London, n.d.), p. 39.

3 The false identification of the sitter was reinforced when he was first exhibited and then published as Jenkyn Williams in Eric Rowan (ed.) *Art in Wales 2000BC–AD1850* (Cardiff, 1978), p. 102.

4 Jan Stewer (Albert J. Coles), *A Parcel of Ol' Crams* (1930, new edition Gloucester, 1970), pp. 213–4.

5 In 1841 the quarry at Foggintor was described by George Giles, the agent of the landowner, Sir Masseh Lopes, descendent of a Spanish-Jewish family, which had prospered in Jamaica.

6 See 'The Bells of Lübeck' in Peter Lord, *Gwenllian: Essays on Visual Culture* (Llandysul, 1994), pp. 186–191.

7 Larry McMurtry, *The Last Picture Show* (New York, 1966).

8 Ian Mikardo regarded Reading, which had been his first parliamentary constituency, as a 'political desert' in the same period.

9 Robert Motherwell, given in *David Smith by David Smith*, ed. Clive Gray (London, 1968), p. 8.

10 *David Smith by David Smith*, p. 172.

11 Ibid., p. 166.

12 Though Eve Balfour was of a Scottish family and developed her pioneering environmentalism – and her system for keeping chickens – while farming in Wales.

13 The evolution of Healy's affiliations and his leadership of various factions and groups on the left in this period is difficult to follow. I associated him at this time with the SWP, but soon afterwards he lead the group known as the Workers' Revolutionary Party.

14 Robert Graves, *Goodbye to All That* (London, 1929), Penguin edition, 1960, p. 237.

15 Ibid., p. 225. Graves continues … 'that perhaps one of our children might revert to coal-black.'

16 Jeremy Hooker, *Englishman's Road* (Carcanet, 1980).

17 For Williams's perception of his relationship with the people of Mynydd Bach, see Gwyn Williams, *Summer Journal 1951* (Aberystwyth, 2004).

18 We were committee members of the Arts Council together during the angry debate that surrounded my paper 'Cultural Policy', for which see 'The State of the Art' in Peter Lord, *The Meaning of Pictures. Images of Personal, Social and Political Identity* (Cardiff, 2009).

19 Myrddin Fardd, 'John Roberts, Llanystumdwy', *Cymru* VIII (1895), 64, translated from the Welsh.

20 'He walked lightly, but in an unhurried manner, noting objects to left and right in an attentive and inquisitive manner, and he would pass the occasional fellow traveller without even seeing him. But if you were fortunate enough to attract his attention, you would be greeted with a "good morning" or "good afternoon" such as none but John Roberts himself could deliver.' Ibid., 65.

21 Ibid., 63.

22 NMW accession file, letter from R.E. Hughes to Iorwerth Peate, 2 March 1965, translated from the Welsh. Unfortunately, R.E. Hughes seems to have muddled the later family history. He notes that Roberts moved to Llandudno, that he was married to a French woman, and that he died between 1895 and 1900. This must surely be the son, who Myrddin Fardd records was also a painter. John Roberts senior had died in 1884, and was buried at Llanystumdwy, 'between two melancholy yews'.

23 The only battlefield portrait showing the Marquess on a white horse, which also has him in a very similar pose to the John Roberts version, is that painted by Peter Edward Stroehling for either King George III or the Prince Regent, engraved in 1818 by Meyer. A large coloured engraving published by Jenkins in London in 1816 is similar in conception, but depicts the Marquess from the other side. This engraving seems to have no specific antecedent in the form of an academic painting, though it resembles the picture by Jan Willem Pieneman in many respects.

24 John Michael Vlach, *Plain Painters. Making Sense of American Folk Art* (Smithsonian Institution, 1988), p. 31.

25 Eric Rowan, *Art in Wales: An Illustrated History 1850–1980* (Cardiff, 1985), p. 86.

26 Nochlin's seminal essay, 'Why Have There Been No Great Women Artists?' had been published in ARTnews (January 1971), 22–39, 67–71.

27 *Welsh in Education and Life* (HMSO, London, 1927). I am grateful to Prof. Geraint H. Jenkins for drawing my attention to this opinion. Further authoritative statements in a similar vein are given in Peter Lord, *The Aesthetics of Relevance* (Llandysul, 1992).

28 For the reception of these documents by the art establishment see 'The State of the Art' in Lord, *The Meaning of Pictures*, pp. 168–186.

29 O.M. Edwards reported amusingly on the air of pomposity surrounding the commission of Barrett's portrait, for which see Lord, *Gwenllian*, p. 69.

30 This turned out not to be the case. At about the same time, Paul Joyner, subsequently of the National Library of Wales, was writing his doctorate at Cambridge on the subject of Welsh painters, and he too had noticed the work of Hugh Hughes. Paul would publish his research as *Artists in Wales, c.1740–c.1851* (Aberystwyth, 1991).

31 NLW Ms.6358B.

32 For the group portrait and its meaning, see 'Quality, Value, Validation' in Lord, *The Meaning of Pictures*, pp. 55–67.

33 Roos had attracted the interest of the literary historian and critic Bedwyr Lewis Jones, also a familiar and popular figure on radio and television. Bedwyr had published a short piece about him in *Y Casglwr*, based largely on his local knowledge of Anglesey.

34 For the portrait and the evolution of the image, see Lord, *Gwenllian*, pp. 46–9.

35 Jonathan Richardson, *An Essay on the Theory of Painting* (London, 2nd edition, 1725), p. 22.

36 Clive Bell, *Art* (London, 1914), 1920 edition, pp. 80–1.

37 William Heward Bell is recorded living at Cowbridge in 1861 and at Drymma House, Neath, in 1875. Clive Bell was born in 1881. He grew up at Cleeve House in Wiltshire. His mother was a Cory, though not of the Welsh branch of the family.

38 John Berger, *Permanent Red* (London, 1960), p. 153 (my italics).

39 John Berger, *Ways of Seeing* (London, 1972), p. 33.

40 Mary Black, *Ammi Phillips: Portrait Painter 1788–1865* (New York, 1968), p. 48, implies that the sitter is Dr Elmore Everitt, known to be the subject of a closely similar portrait.

41 The picture was shown at the exhibition 'Arlunwyr Gwlad/ Artisan Painters' at Oriel Plas Glyn-y-Weddw, Llanbedrog, in 2011, and illustrated in the exhibition catalogue.

42 *Girl in Red with Cat and Dog* first became well known to the public when it was shown in the exhibition 'The Flowering of American Folk Art' in 1974. The market value for portraits by Phillips is unusually erratic, and some pictures have sold in the last decade for under $100,000. However, *Girl in Red* belongs to

a group of similar portraits that all fetch the highest prices at auction. The top price to a private buyer is $1,248,000, and another was sold in 1985 for $682,000. It had been purchased in the 1930s for $60. A double portrait by Phillips was sold for $1.3 million in 2007.

43 The Museum had borrowed some $32 million to fund the building, which proved to be a disastrous risk. In 2011 the Museum was forced to sell to its neighbour, the Museum of Modern Art, and move to much smaller premises.

44 Interview with Peter Lord for *The Big Picture*, a television series by Ceri Sherlock (Element for BBC Wales, 1999).

45 For the debate, see Lord, *The Meaning of Pictures*, pp.168–179.

46 Richardson, *An Essay on the Theory of Painting*, p. 4.

47 Bell, *Art*, pp. 266–7.

48 Ibid., p. 36.

49 See 'Improvement: the Visualisation of "Y Werin", the Welsh Folk', in Lord, *The Meaning of Pictures*, pp. 78–121.

50 In the 1970s I had been excited to find exhibited in Bath the Andras Kalman collection of what was described as 'English Naïve Art', but which included a substantial body of artisan portraits. On the basis of that collection and, significantly, that of the American collector Dallas Pratt, the English art historian James Ayres had also made the American connection, though in his publications he did not choose to engage with the methodological problems that arose. See in particular James Ayres, *The Art of the People in America and Britain 1750–1950* (Manchester, 1985) and his earlier *English Naïve Painting 1750–1900* (London, 1980), based largely on works in the Kalman and Judkyn/ Pratt collections. At about the same time, another body of artisan portraiture, strikingly similar to that of Wales and the United States, that had been the product of the French- and Valdôtain-speaking community in the north Italian Vallée d'Aoste, was brought to my attention by Ned Thomas.

51 Subsequently, Field would commission a mural from Picasso.

52 For instance, Winifred Coombe Tennant visited the Cazin atelier in Normandy in August 1904, and noted in her diary: 'A little way off was a huddled collection of what I took to be peasants' cottages … Architecturally they were practically untouched – but they had been turned into pictures – exquisite interiors – beautiful Cheminées – old china, pewter – ancient beds draped with ancient hangings … matted floors, old painted plates …' Peter Lord, ed., *Winifred Coombe Tennant: The Journal, 1897–1910* (privately published, 2011), p. 151.

53   As the painter William Merritt Chase famously had expressed it in 1899.

54   The connoisseurial origins of the American folk art construct are examined in Eugene W. Metcalf, Jr. and Claudine Weatherford, 'Modernism, Edith Halpert, Holger Cahill, and the Fine Art Meaning of American Folk Art', in Jane S. Becker and Barbara Franco, eds., *Folk Roots, New Roots. Folklore in American Life* (Lexington, Massachusetts, 1988), pp. 141–166. In part this essay was informed by Beatrix T. Rumford, 'Uncommon Art of the Common People: A Review of Trends in the Collecting and Exhibiting of American Folk Art' in Ian M.G. Quimby and Scott T. Swank, eds., *Perspectives on American Folk Art* (Winterthur/New York, 1980), pp. 13–53.

55   Lewis Corey, *The Decline of American Capitalism* (New York, 1934), given in Elizabeth B. Crist, *Music for the Common Man. Aaron Copland during the Depression and War* (Oxford, 2005), p. 116.

56   Stuart Davis in the *New York Post*, given in Jonathan Harris, *Federal Art and National Culture: The politics of Identity in New Deal America* (Cambridge, 1995), p. 146.

57   See Anthony W. Lee, *Painting on the Left. Diego Rivera, Radical Politics and San Francisco's Public Murals* (Berkeley, 1999), and for contemporary opinion, *Art for the Millions. Essays from the 1930s by Artists and Administrators of the WPA Federal Arts Project*, ed. Francis V. O'Connor (New York, 1973).

58   Virginia Tuttle Clayton, Elizabeth Stillinger and Erica Doss, *Drawing on America's Past: Folk Art, Modernism, and the Index of American Design* (Washington, 2002).

59   She was not the first to deal commercially in the material. Isabel Carlton Wilde was advertising the sale of 'American Primitives' through her antiques business in Cambridge Massachusetts by 1926. Halpert opened her folk art gallery three years later, for which see Lindsay Pollock, *The Girl with the Gallery. Edith Gregor Halpert and the Making of the Modern Art Market* (New York, 2006).

60   Jean Lipman, 'American Primitive Portraiture: a Revaluation', *The Magazine Antiques*, 1941.

61   One contemporary American art historian did note the limitations of elitist English art history in making comparisons between the two countries. In 1947, James Thomas Flexner reported C.H. Collins Baker's patronising assessment of Joseph Blackburn, that since he 'was a more primitive artist than the leading London practitioners, it is logical to regard him as an indigenous American product'. Flexner

suggested an alternative interpretation: 'Mr Baker seems to have fallen into the age-old pitfall of English art scholarship, the assumption that there was no place in England but London, and no place in London but the court. He has not considered the possibility that Blackburn was a provincial English workman.' James Thomas Flexner, *History of American Painting*, Vol.I, *First Flowers of our Wilderness (The Colonial Period)* (Boston, 1947), Dover edition, 1969, pp. 316–7. Flexner was correct, though Blackburn also worked in Wales for the Morgan family of Tredegar House and Ruperra. C.H. Collins Baker had been formerly Keeper at the National Gallery in London, but at the time of Flexner's comments was working in California.

62 Copland is believed to have written the piece partly in response to a speech made by Vice-President Henry A. Wallace, in which he used the phrase 'century of the common man'. Wallace was on the left of the Democratic Party and sympathetic to the Soviet Union. His political ascendency was brief. He was replaced as Vice-Presidential candidate in 1944 by Harry Truman and found himself increasingly isolated in mainstream politics.

63 By Ralph M. Easley.

64 Jean Lipman in Lipman and Alice Winchester, *The Flowering of Amercan Folk Art (1776–1876)* (Whitney Museum of American Art, 1974), p. 7.

65 Jean Lipman, Elizabeth V. Warren and Robert Bishop, *Young America. A Folk Art History* (New York, 1986), p. 8.

66 For instance: 'The colonial portrait painters of the Hudson River Valley ... influenced each other and the following generation of painters in New York ... Delanoy and Durand provide a direct connection between the Upper Hudson River Valley painters and the late eighteenth-century Connecticut folk artists who, beginning with Winthrop Chandler, became the leading producers of folk portraits in the new republic. In turn, the Connecticut painters directly influenced artists like John Brewster, Jr., J.Brown, Ammi Phillips, and Erastus Salisbury Field.' Mary Black in *American Folk Portraits of Three Centuries* (NY Whitney Museum of American Art, 1980), p. 45. In the same vein, Beatrix Rumford wrote of the portraits of Ammi Phillips, 'Women often lean forward in fashionable languid posture, while men frequently appear in Border Period poses, that is, with one hand draped over the crest rail of a stencilled chair in easy self-assurance. Form here is described in shorthand by dropping the subtle

graduation of middle tones to create a high-contrast likeness of great impact.' Beatrix T. Rumford (ed.) *American Folk Portraits. Paintings and Drawings from the Abby Aldrich Rockefeller Folk Art Center* (Boston, 1981), p. 149.

67   For a thorough discussion of this matter and its relationship to cultural expression see Susan Hegeman, *Patterns for America: Modernism and the Concept of Culture* (Princeton 1999).

68   John Gordon in the catalogue *Masterpieces of American Folk Art* (Monmouth Museum, New Jersey, 1975), unpaginated. Gordon, who died in 2003, had been a force in the expansion of the folk art market after the Second World War. His collection fetched $2.8 million when sold at Christie's in 1999.

69   Kenneth L. Ames, *Beyond Necessity. Art in the Folk Tradition* (Winterthur Museum, 1977), p. 64. Prominent among the 'perceptive writers' to whom Ames referred was Henry Glassie, whose work was highly influential on his generation of folk life specialists.

70   Scott T. Swank, Introduction to Ian M. G. Quimby and Scott T. Swank, eds., *Perspectives on American Folk Art* (New York, 1980), pp. 2–3.

71   Kenneth L. Ames, 'Folk Art: The Challenge and the Promise', in Quimby and Swank, *Perspectives on American Folk Art*, p. 294.

72   John Michael Vlach, '"Properly Speaking": The Need for Plain Talk about Folk Art', in John Michael Vlach and Simon J. Bronner, eds., *Folk Art and Art Worlds* (Michigan, 1983), p. 22.

73   Nancy Druckman, Director of the American Folk Art Department, Sotheby NY, in Laura Stewart, 'Naïve Paintings Maybe?', *Masterpiece*, Autumn 1999.

74   This and following quotations are taken from my interview with John Vlach, recorded in Washington on 23 March 2010.

75   Nina Fletcher Little, a major collector of American folk art and writer of numerous essays on various aspects of the subject, took a different view of interactions between enthusiasts in her autobiography, *Little by Little: Six Decades of Collecting American Decorative Arts* (New York, 1984), pp. 25–6. She described the emergence in the Boston area in the early 1930s of collecting clubs to which members brought their latest discoveries and research as 'the most stimulating development of the decade.'

76   This and following quotations are taken from my interview with Ken Ames, recorded in New York on 24 March 2010.

77   Stacey C. Hollander, *The Seduction of Light. Ammi Phillips/Mark Rothko. Compositions in Pink, Green, and Red* (New York, 2008),

pp. 11; 10. In 1995 I commented on an exhibition of Welsh quilts at Llanidloes, where the captions attempted to elevate the status of the objects by associating them with high art, in the manner of Stacey Hollander. Quilts were described as 'A Family-Sized Paul Klee' and 'A Practical Mark Rothko'. Peter Lord, 'Resonant Objects', in *Planet* 113 (October/November 1995), 19–20. For a critique of Jean Lipman's facile use of similar visual parallels, see John Michael Vlach, 'The wrong stuff', in *New Art Examiner* (September 1991), 22.

78 Metcalf and Weatherford, 'Modernism, Edith Halpert, Holger Cahill, and the Fine Art Meaning of American Folk Art', p. 162. Cahill had described the work of the American common man as 'primitive in the sense that it is the simple, unaffected and childlike expression of men and women ... who did not even know that they were producing art.'

79 Lipman, Warren and Bishop, *Young America. A Folk Art History*, p. 9.

80 Ames, *Beyond Necessity*, p. 99.

81 John Michael Vlach, *Charleston Blacksmith: The Work of Philip Simmons* (Athens, University of Georgia Press, 1981).

82 Vlach, 'The wrong stuff', 24.

83 Ibid.

84 See 'Quality, Value, Validation' in Lord, *The Meaning of Pictures*, pp. 52–75.

85 If not otherwise attributed, Levy is quoted from my memory or from my interview with him recorded in 1995, National Screen and Sound Archive of Wales, Visual Culture of Wales Research Project Deposit.

86 Mervyn Levy, *The Paintings of L.S. Lowry* (London, 1975), p. 12.

87 John Petts in Meic Stephens (ed.), *Artists in Wales 3* (Llandysul, 1977), p. 177.

88 Mervyn Levy, 'No Time Like the Present (I take my stand)', in *Wales*, ed. Keidrych Rhys, 4 (December, 1958), 70.

89 Given on the title page of Mervyn Levy, *Reflections in a Broken Mirror. Fragments of an Autobiography* (Richmond, 1982). Levy gives as the source '*Senses of Occasion*, a British Broadcasting Corporation programme, 2nd December 1981'.

90 Levy, 'No Time Like the Present', 72.

91 Levy, *Reflections in a Broken Mirror*, p. 14.

92 NLW MS23417E, f.100. Edwards was a prominent figure in the Welsh establishment of the day. He was a curator at the V&A. See Lord, *The Meaning of Pictures*, p. 73.

93 Levy, 'No Time Like the Present', 72.

94   David Alston, *Lowry in Wales* (Swansea, 2002), no pagination.

95   Levy, *The Paintings of L.S. Lowry*, p. 22.

96   Ibid., p. 15.

97   Ibid., p. 18.

98   Ibid., p. 25.

99   Ibid., p. 23.

100   Ibid.

101   Kyffin Williams, *Portraits* (Llandysul, 1996), p. 66.

102   NLW Jack Raymond Jones Papers, item 43. Recorded for Wales TV in London 15 March 1966, as part of 'Horizons hung in air', a programme about Kyffin Williams made by John Ormond and broadcast 20 April 1966.

103   Ibid., item 14, letter from Kyffin Williams dated 9 August 1974. The context of Kyffin's remark was a joint exhibition in Swansea of the work of Jack Jones and Will Roberts.

104   Ibid., letter from Kyffin Williams dated 23 September 1974.

105   Some art historians, working in the tradition of Folk Art studies in the United States, have created the category of 'Memory Painter', to locate practitioners such as Jack Jones. In Wales, the nineteenth-century painter Robert Hughes of Uwchlaw'r Ffynnon, might well be categorised by them in the same way.

106   NLW Jack Raymond Jones Papers, item 14, review of Kyffin Williams exhibition at the Leicester Galleries, September – October 1966. Prominent among the depreciators of Kyffin Williams was Eric Newton, much despised by Jack Jones.

107   Ibid., letter from Kyffin Williams, dated 21 August 1970. Dorothy Thomas provided Jones with his most important outlet for pictures, at the Attic Gallery in Swansea.

108   Jack Jones makes a point in several essays of referring to Kyffin as a Welsh speaker. Certainly, Kyffin's ability to quote the Welsh of others in his often hilarious anecdotes makes it clear that he understood the language well, and those who knew him intimately are clear that he spoke it in conversation when he chose. Nevertheless, his choice in public speaking and in conversation about the arts was almost always to use English.

109   Williams, *Portraits*, p. 66.

110   Before the Second World War, Kyffin had been an officer in the Royal Welch Fusiliers until it was discovered that he suffered from epilepsy.

111   Subsequent visits to the attic revealed more pictures, including three tiny Gwen John drawings, hidden inside a dusty and insignificant folder. The catalogue raisonné of Winifred's remarkable collection is published

in Peter Lord, *Winifred Coombe Tennant: A Life through Art* (Aberystwyth, 2007).

112 *The Journal 1897–1910*, 28 May 1898, p. 19.

113 *The Journal*, 3 May 1904, p. 138.

114 The work and life of G.F. Watts were an inspiration to Winifred. *Whence, Whither?* was among her favourite paintings. 'I am reading the *Life of Watts*. It is a gospel to me. I read it not without tears. I read it *through* my tears, with such an aching heart and such a longing for God knows what – all that is beautiful and high in life, and for the companionship of those who could help me.'

115 *The Journal*, 3 May 1904, p. 139.

116 *Between Two Worlds: The Diary of Winifred Coombe Tennant 1909–1924*, ed. Peter Lord (Aberystwyth: 2011) p. 61. The words are those of Sir Oliver Lodge.

117 *The Journal*, 16 March 1898, p. 15.

118 Augustus after the Emperor, who brought peace to Rome, and Henry after Henry Sidgwick, another prominent deceased figure in the SPR from whom Winifred believed that she received messages.

119 Isaac Williams quoted in Winifred's diary for 20 November 1924. See Lord, *A Life through Art*, p. 84.

120 *Between Two Worlds:* The Diary, entry for 23 June 1920.

121 For an analysis of the picture, see Peter Lord, 'Biblical and Marxist rhetoric in the literature and painting of the Depression', in *Moment of Earth. Poems and Essays in Honour of Jeremy Hooker*, ed. Christopher Meredith (Aberystwyth 2007), pp. 206–8.

122 Bell, *Art*, p. 27.

123 Bell, *Art*, pp. 68, 70.

124 Winifred was particularly fond of Browning's poetry. He had been a member of the circle of her mother-in-law, and her sister-in-law, Eveleen, had photographed him.

125 *Between Two Worlds:* The Diary, entry for 9 November 1927.

126 Ibid., 16 and 17 November 1927. The Latin is 'Magna est veritas et praevalebit'. Winifred quotes from the Book of Edras (Ezra) in the Vulgate Bible. 'CCT' was Charles Coombe Tennant, husband of Winifred.

127 Ibid., 7 December 1927.

128 For the Caradoc Evans incident, see Lord, *A Life through Art*, p. 182.

129 Ibid., p. 140.

130 *Between Two Worlds:* The Diary, entry for 18–19 July 1947.

131 Tate Gallery, Cedric Morris Papers, 8317.3.1, item 2, script of the broadcast.

132 'Mr. Steegman … went over pictures in Picture Room & asked for a gift to N Museum of 'Courting' by Evan Walters …' *Between Two Worlds:* The Diary, entry for 14 November 1947.

133 Ibid., 8 September 1928.

134 Winifred's relationship with Griffiths is explored in 'The Construction and Destruction of Archie Rees Griffiths', in Lord, *The Meaning of Pictures*, pp. 122–165.

135 Archie Griffiths to Winifred Coombe Tennant, 8 December 1928. NLW Winifred Coombe Tennant Papers.

136 'Oh, you mean Uncle Archie?' The informant was not related to Archie Griffiths. She called him 'Uncle' because she had been a close friend of his niece. *Tro yn yr Yrfa: Archie Rhys Griffiths*, a film by Geraint Ellis (Cwmni Da for S4C, 2007).

137 I now consider the picture to have been painted *c.*1930.

138 Rhys Adrian Griffiths (1928–90) wrote 32 plays for radio, the first of them broadcast in 1956. He also wrote for television. See Paul Singer *'All the time I sit here. Not responding.' A Critical Study of Rhys Adrian's Radio and Television Drama*, unpublished PhD thesis, Roehampton University.

139 The absence of any documentation in the College archives suggests that the mural may not have been carried out, and that the surviving photograph is of a cartoon.

140 In my account of Diana meeting her father on the Bayswater Road given in *The Meaning of Pictures*, p. 164, I stated that she had been in the company of her brother, Rhys. I was reporting the story as I remembered it told during the intense television interview. In her subsequent letter, Diana says that she was with her husband, not her brother.

141 *South Wales Evening Post*, 10 October 1935. Williams died the following year.

142 Colwyn E. Vulliamy, *Calico Pie* (London, 1940), pp. 101, 103.

143 Winifred Coombe Tennant is quoted from her diary.

144 Augustus John to Mitchell Kennerley, 22 November 1926, given in Michael Holroyd, *Augustus John. The New Biography* (London, 1996), p. 483.

145 Gwladys Williams to Winifred Coombe Tennant, NLW Winifred Coombe Tennant Papers.

146 Nevertheless, Williams appears to have painted a portrait of Evan Walters. The sitter is not identified on the canvas, among those discovered by Mike Jones at Clydach, but the figure bears a striking resemblance to the painter in portly maturity, with flamboyant hat and cane.

147 Helen Ramage was the first to publish extracts from the letters in *Portraits of an Island. Eighteenth Century Anglesey* (Anglesey Antiquarian Society and Field Club) in 1987. My essay 'Life before Wilson', which included reference to the archive, was published in *Planet* 95 (October/ November 1992).

148 Morgan accumulated a large library, which after his time found its way first of all to Bodewryd, Ann Owen's family home, and then to Penrhos. It was dispersed at the 1939 sale. The schoolmaster at Ross was John Tudor, whose family hailed from Trawsfynydd.

149 The Edward Owen letters are chiefly in the archive of Bangor University, Penrhos Papers. Other material is in NLW Bodewryd Papers.

150 Kneller died in 1723, but the discrepancy in the date may be accounted for by the recent arrival of Owen, straight from school and ignorant of professional affairs in London. No candidate of the status indicated by Owen's comments died in 1724.

151 As yet no record of the picture has been found. The church was heavily restored during the nineteenth century, when the picture, if ever completed, may have been lost.

152 'Felly mae'r byd yn myned hebiaw.' The letter, dated 27 September 1741, states clearly that Owen had died six months previously. Isaac Williams, who gave 1748 as the date of death, appears to have misread the inscription on the rear of the self-portrait when he found it in 1926. Ramage mistakenly gave Owen's date of death as 16 March 1740. Owen did indeed die in March 1741.

153 Little, *Little by Little*, p. 128.

154 James Hanley, *Grey Children. A Study in Humbug and Misery* (London, 1937). Hanley chose to quote the words of one of the many miners he interviewed in 1937 to open his text: 'We're about fed up with people coming down here looking us over as though we were animals in a zoo. Put that in the headlines for a change.'

155 Ruth Edwards, *The Aristocrat, the Artist, and Talywain* (Abersychan and Garndiffaith Local History Group, n.d.).

156 Mr Ken Clark, reported by Edwards, *The Aristocrat, the Artist, and Talywain*.

157 *Sunday Referee*, May 1938.

158 Ibid.

159 He had first studied at Southend School of Art, at the age of 13.

160 John Carruthers, 'Pilgrim with a Pencil', in *Picturing To-day (Photo World)*, Vol.II, No.6 (London, December 1950) p. 27.

161 *Daily Herald*, 7 December 1937.

162 For examples of the engravings after Johnson's drawings, see Peter Lord, *The Visual Culture of Wales: Industrial Society*, (Cardiff, 1988) pp. 145, 149.

163 Tate Gallery, Cedric Morris Papers, 8317.1.4, item 92.

164 For Morris's continuing engagement with the issue, and his role in art education in Wales, see Lord, *Industrial Society*, pp. 203–209.

165 Wolf Suschitzky, *Edith Tudor Hart, The Eye of Conscience* (London, 1987), p. 10.

166 Ralph Bond, 'Making *Today We Live*', *World Film News*, vol.2, no.6 (September 1937). The quotation is given in David Berry, *Wales and Cinema. The First Hundred Years* (Cardiff, 1994), p.134, in which the work of Bond and other left-wing film makers is discussed fully. The image of collecting waste coal from the tips eventually reached popular cinema, albeit clumsily presented, in Pen Tennyson's *Proud Valley*, starring Paul Robeson (1940).

167 Indeed, J.H. Hall, who opened Sochachewsky's exhibition, had lost his Stepney seat in 1931 as a result of the heavy support for the Communist Party candidate that split the left vote. He regained it only because the party did not stand in 1935.

168 Graham Greene, *Ways of Escape* (London, 1980), 1999 edition, p. 34. Greene speaks of the years 1933–7.

169 Other letters are given, and Maurice's career is examined from a different point of view in *Planet*, 210 (Summer 2013), pp. 17–29.

170 This is why: 'Both [the music critic, Zhdanov] and the aesthetes are equally against music reminding people about life, about tragedies, about the victims, the dead. Let music be beautiful and graceful and let composers think about only purely musical problems. It'll be quieter that way. I've always protested harshly against this point of view and I strove for the reverse. I always wanted music to be an active force. This is the Russian tradition.' *Testimony. The Memoirs of Dmitri Shostakovich*, ed. Solomon Volkov (London, 1979), p. 121.

171 'Wherefore seeing we are compassed about with so great a cloud of witnesses, let us lay aside every weight, and the sin which doth so easily beset us, and let us run with patience the race that is set before us, looking unto Jesus the author and finisher of our faith …' Hebrews 12:1–2.

172 There are a few references to church paintings in the Welsh language poetry of the late middle ages, but these represent the perceptions of an intellectual elite. See for instance Peter Lord, *The Visual Culture of Wales. Medieval Vision* (Cardiff, 2003), p. 118. No medieval reference to the Gyffin paintings is known.

173 Thomas Matthews, *The Biography of John Gibson RA Sculptor, Rome* (London, 1911), p. 3.

174 Cristion (that is, Hugh Hughes), *Y Drefn Ddwyfol* (1849), p.16.

175 François Wendel, *Calvin, the origins and development of his religious thought* (1963), pp. 273, 280. For the death of Sarah Phillips Hughes, and her mother's understanding of its meaning, see Peter Lord, *Hugh Hughes, Arlunydd Gwlad, 1790–1863* (Llandysul, 1995), pp. 235–240.

176 See above, p. 159.

177 'These all died in faith, not having received the promises, but having seen them afar off, and were persuaded of them, and embraced them, and confessed that they were strangers and pilgrims on the earth. For they that say such things declare plainly that they seek a country.' Hebrews 11:13–14.

178 This change from a universalist to a relativist understanding of linguistics was not stimulated by a reading of theory, of which I was largely unaware at the time, but by observation and experience.

179 For McLucas, see Peter Lord, 'Homogeneity or Individuation. A Long View of the Critical Paradox of Contemporary Art in a Stateless Nation', in Jonathan Harris, ed., *Globalization and Contemporary Art* (Chichester, 2011), pp. 56, 66–8.

180 See above, p. 78–9.

181 Many of his most important writings are collected in J.R. Jones, *Ac onide* (Llandybie, 1970).

182 Waldo Williams, *Dail Pren* (Aberystwyth, 1957), p. 67.

183 Jones, *Ac onide*, p. 140.

184 Ibid., p. 169.

185 'Hynny yw, os yr unig ffordd allan o'r Aifft – fel yn hanes Israel gynt – yw drwy'r anialwch, yna mae'n rhaid wynebu'r anialwch.' Jones, *Ac Onide*, p. 177.

186 Some months after writing this chapter, I took down from the shelf George Orwell's novel *1984*, which I had not read for many years. I found that the expression 'the mutability of the past' was his. (Penguin Modern Classics edition, 1970, p. 170.)

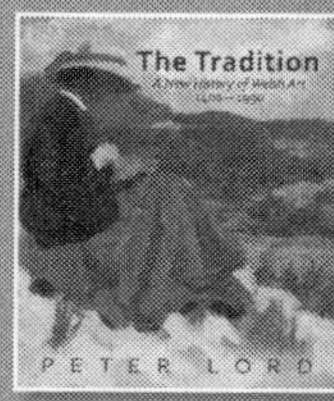

VISUAL WALES

PARTHIAN

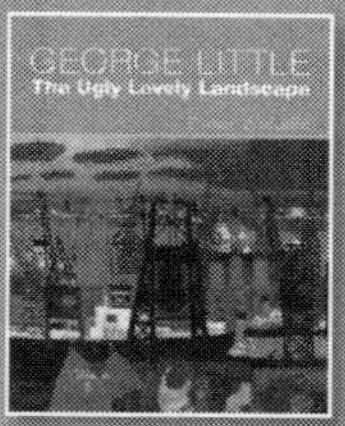

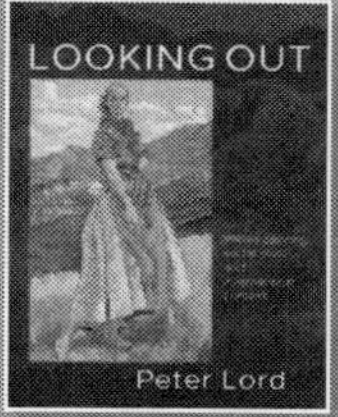

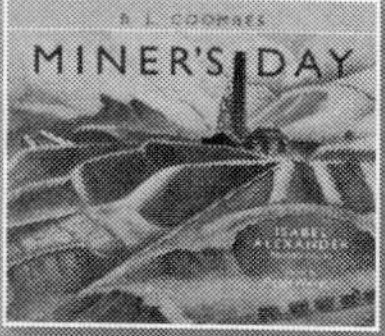

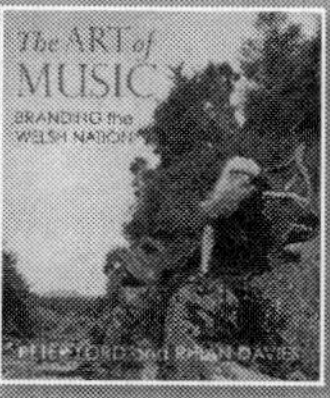

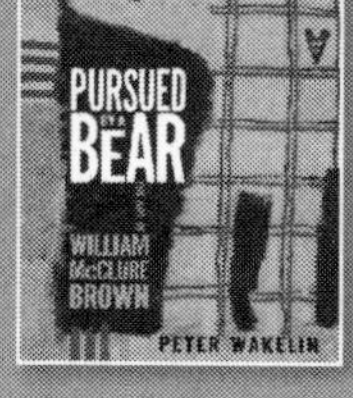

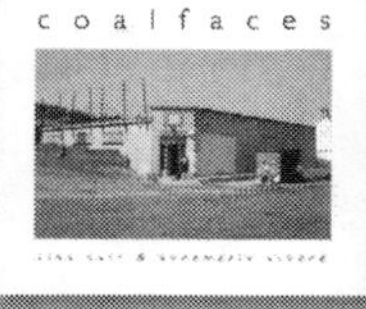

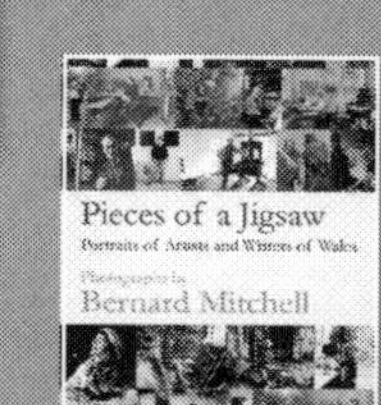

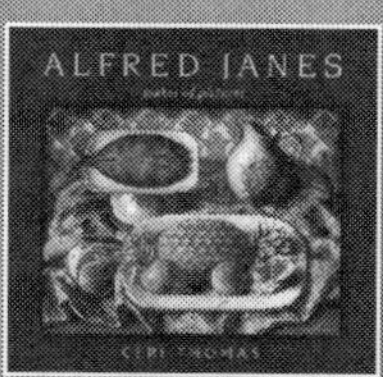

THE TRADITION

Peter Lord

978-1-917140-38-6 / £50

'A remarkable and
important book'
Murdo Macdonald, *Planet*

Winner of Wales Book of the
Year Creative Non-Fiction

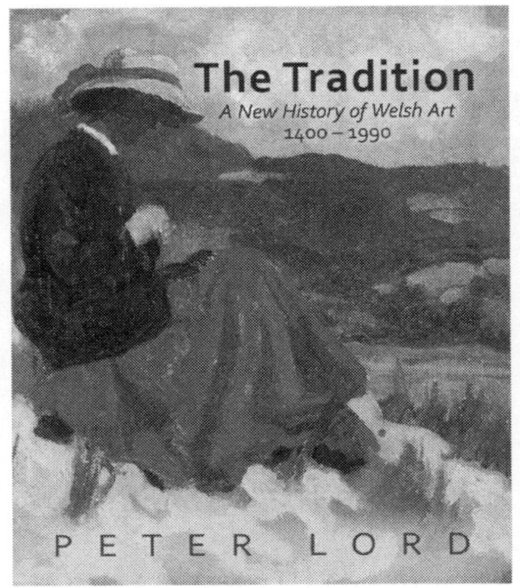

Peter Lord surveys the evolution of the visual culture of Wales from
the Renaissance to the end of the twentieth century in this new, single-
volume history. The author describes both how the work emerged from
its Welsh historical context and was related to the art of other cultures.
Revealing the many discoveries made since the first publication of *The
Visual Culture of Wales* series in 1998, *The Tradition* is the only study now
in print that encompasses the whole field of Welsh visual art. Written for
everyone with an interest in the art and history of Wales, the volume
illustrates some 400 landscapes and portrait paintings, prints and
sculptures.

GEORGE LITTLE THE UGLY LOVELY LANDSCAPE

Peter Wakelin

978-1-914595-66-0 / £40

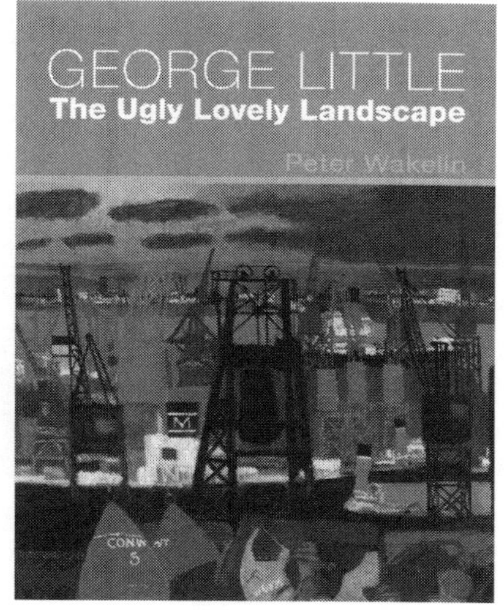

'A well-written and meticulously researched study which is a splendid synthesis of art history and industrial archaeology.'

Dr Barrie Trinder

'No artist has been more committed to interpreting industrial and ex-industrial environments than George Little. Born in the east end of Swansea in the lead-up to the Great Depression, he spent his long life exploring the nearby docks, bomb sites, abandoned copper smelters and left-behind streets. The 'ugly, lovely' oxymoron coined by Dylan Thomas captured simultaneously the warmth of his and George Little's hometown on its glistening bay and the sadness of its industrial decline and scruffy irregularity. George found a visual language to restate the contradiction. He did something extraordinary in his expression of the place.

As his friend, the historian Prys Morgan, wrote in 2017, he transformed its ugliness into 'memorably lovely paintings'.

Peter Wakelin

MINER'S DAY

B. L. Coombes

978-1-913640-38-5 / £20

Originally published in
1945, *Miner's Day* tells of
the coal-mining life of the
thirties in south Wales.
With images by Isabel
Alexander. Edited with
an introduction by
Peter Wakelin

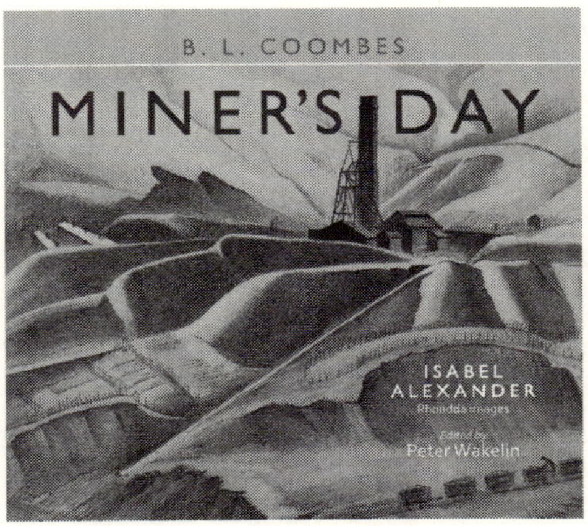

'Coombes and Alexander each had a passion to show the real life of
coalmining communities to a wide public, Coombes through words
and Alexander through pictures. Coalmining was veiled more opaquely
than almost any other sector from the view of educated people and
metropolitan elites. Many of its particularities, literally hidden below
ground, were unimaginable to outsiders who had never contemplated
what it might be like to spend the day in darkness, to labour in a space no
higher than a dining chair, to bear the daily crush of fear that a husband
or father might not come home from work, or to suffer injustices of wage
cuts, industrial disease and injury.'

From the introduction by Peter Wakelin

The images of Isabel Alexander have the overriding and lasting virtue
of individual vision. The republication of *Miner's Day* in the wider context
of her presentation to the world of individuals scarred by hardship and
deprivation is an important and beautifully presented venture.

Peter Lord, *Wales Arts Review*

THE ART
OF MUSIC

Peter Lord

978-1-914595-25-7 / £40

Tracing the evolution of the mythology of Welsh musicality. With 280 full-colour illustrations

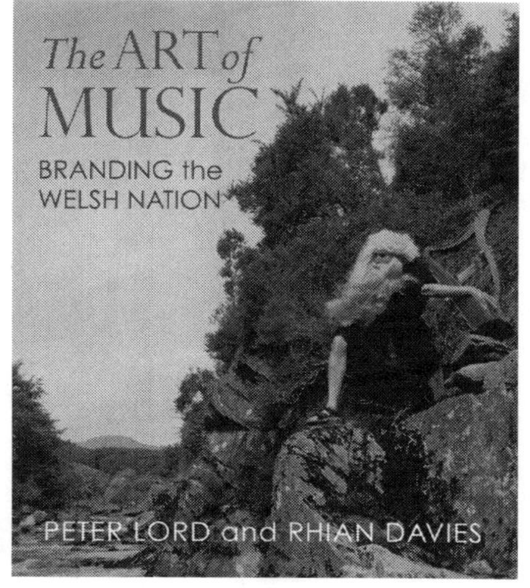

Writing the history of any branch of art is a challenge, but to examine two such branches and their interaction over a span of several hundred years demands rare skill and judgement. Fortunately, this volume displays both. It brings together two experienced authors who are established authorities in their fields: Peter Lord, who has done so much to enlighten us about the artistic tradition in Wales, and Rhian Davies, whose research on Welsh music has likewise added considerably to our knowledge and understanding. Together they set out to trace the evolution of the concept of Wales as a musical nation as reflected in its art. The result is a very satisfying and thought-provoking survey.

Robert Burns once famously asked for the gift 'to see ourselves as others see us'. What this remarkable study shows is that how we portray ourselves in a complex and ever-changing world is just as important. Meticulously researched, beautifully illustrated and sumptuously produced, this is a book which will instruct and delight in equal measure.

Rhidian Griffiths, *Gwales*

LOOKING OUT

Peter Lord

978-1-912681-97-6 / £40

'Over the last twenty-five
years, almost single-handedly,
Peter Lord has transformed a
collection of poorly understood
evidence of art created in
Wales, and lazy theoretical
assumptions about it, into
a discipline in its own right,
equipped with analytical
frameworks and supported
by an accumulating body of
knowledge.'

Andrew Green, *Wales Arts Review*

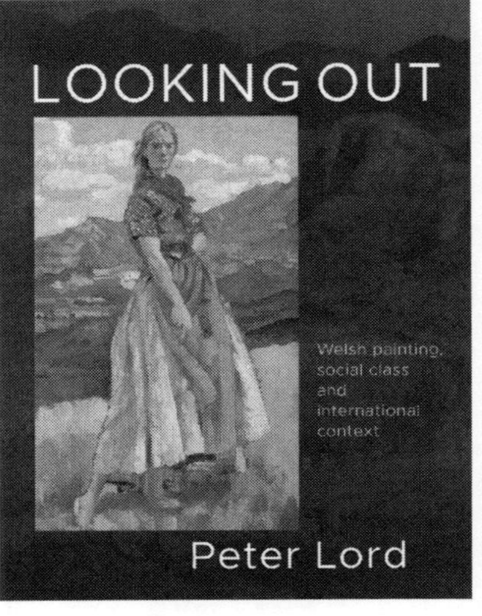

'Peter Lord has long been recognized as our foremost and indeed
most prolific historian of Welsh art. His perceptive and eminently
readable analyses in his substantial publications have transformed
our understanding of the development of art in modern Wales.

Looking Out comprises six scholarly essays focussing on the evolution of
Welsh art, predominantly painting, from about 1870 onwards. The author's
primary aim throughout is to move away from the traditional interpretation
of Welsh art history as something inherently marginal and peripheral,
largely isolated from contemporary trends in other European countries.'

J. Graham Jones

PURSUED BY A BEAR THE ART OF WILLIAM MCCLURE BROWN

Peter Wakelin

978-1-914595-99-8 / £20

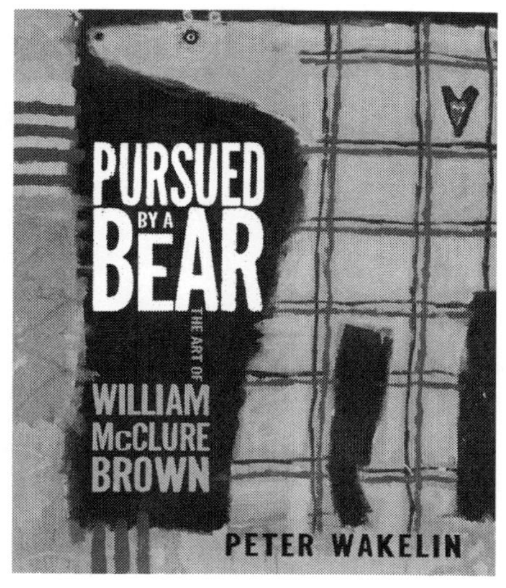

'A defining trait of human nature is, I believe, the imagination – at once the alleviation of tedium, the bringing of a sense of fun and maybe, just maybe, illumination.'

William Brown

Polar bears and Arctic explorers, the lore of the loup-garou, the mischief of the Mari Lwyd, fighter-jets in desert skies: William McClure Brown's mind travelled many paths to celebrate story-making and the power of the unexpected in vivid imagery. Born to Scottish parents in Canada in 1953, as a teenager he knew painters in the Toronto scene and began to evolve his own creative language. From 1977 he was based in London and south-west England before settling in Wales in 1990. While he exhibited internationally he was admired most in his close community of fellow artists. He found inspiration in Devon, northern France, Galicia, North Africa, the South Wales valleys and the Inuit communities of Hudson Bay. He collaborated with painters and poets, learned Welsh, made public art, held residencies in schools, and created images for Gorky's Zygotic Mynci. William Brown died in 2008, age 54. This is the first book to explore the full range of his startling, audacious work.

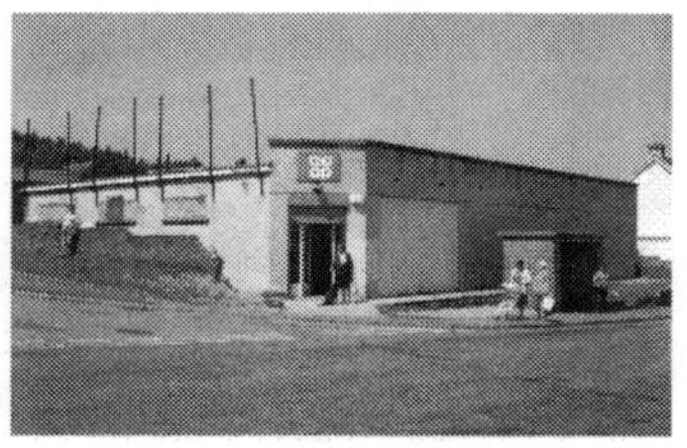

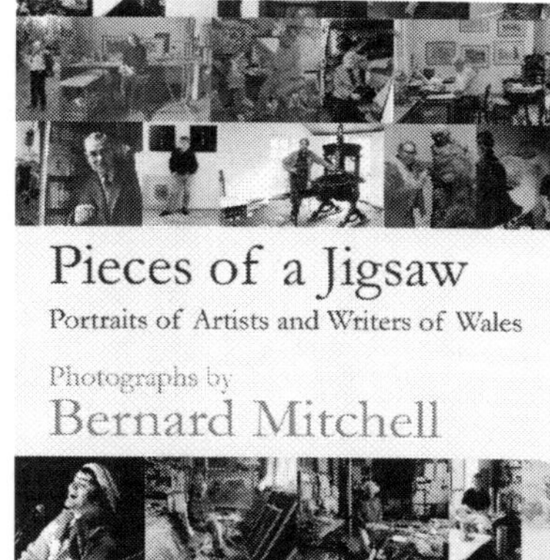

COALFACES

**Tina Carr and
Annemarie Schöne**
978-1-917140-64-5 / £25

With a new foreword
by Dr Bronwen Colquhoun
'These photographs, gritty,
beautiful, empathetic, sad and
humorous… provide us with
a much-needed reminder of
communities all too easily
forgotten about.'

John Green, *Morning Star*

PIECES OF A JIGSAW

Bernard Mitchell
978-1-910901-97-7 / £30

An unprecedented collection
of photographic portraits of
notable characters within the arts
community in Wales. Featuring
many leading artists and writers
who have significantly contributed
to Welsh culture in the late
twentieth century.

CEFNOGWCH EICH SIOP LYFRAU LEOL

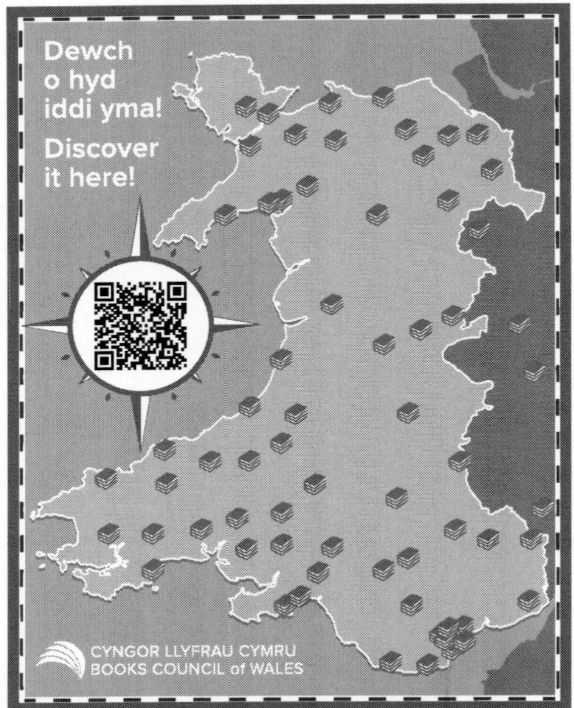

SUPPORT YOUR LOCAL BOOKSHOP

There are many excellent bookshops to be enjoyed across Wales and just over the border. This map will lead to a world of books. Just scan the QR code.